sunny's
kitchen

EASY FOOD
FOR REAL LIFE

sunny's kitchen

SUNNY ANDERSON

PHOTOGRAPHS BY **JOHN LEE**

CLARKSON POTTER/PUBLISHERS
NEW YORK

Published in the United States by Clarkson Potter/Publishers, an imprint of
the Crown Publishing Group, a division of Random House, Inc., New York.
www.crownpublishing.com
www.clarksonpotter.com

CLARKSON POTTER is a trademark and POTTER with colophon
is a registered trademark of Random House, Inc.

Library of Congress Cataloging-in-Publication Data
Anderson, Sunny.
Sunny's kitchen : easy food for real life / Sunny Anderson;
photographs by John Lee. — First edition.
pages cm
Includes index.
1. Cooking, American.   2. International cooking.
3. Anderson, Sunny—Anecdotes.   4. Cooking—Anecdotes.   I. Title.
TX715.A56666   2013
641.5973—dc23   2013007784

ISBN 978-0-7704-3678-0
eISBN 978-0-7704-3679-7

Printed in the United States

All photos are by John Lee with the exception of photos on pages 8, 13, 65, 95,
113, 130, 185, 231, 283, 297 courtesy of the Anderson family archives.

Book and cover design by Ashley Tucker
Book and cover photography by John Lee

1 3 5 7 9 10 8 6 4 2

First Edition

to daddy
& mommy

With no manual, you somehow raised a
dreamer willing to do the work. I continue
to dream and work. Thank you, Mutt-Mutt.

A view of Manhattan from Sunset Park, Brooklyn

CONTENTS

FOREWORD

My grandma Williams is the archetype of all grandmas. There is always a cake on the counter, and big hugs and words of wisdom for a grandchild in need. We are able to talk like girlfriends, and I love her so much. I asked her to share some words with you, and although they aren't all related to cooking, they have everything to do with me and my first book.

from my grandma williams

Sunny has a type of cooking that reaches back from her childhood and her family roots in North and South Carolina, all the way to Brooklyn, where she lives now. And there is a lot of variety in these recipes—they aren't all the same type of food. There are even some fancy things for Sunday dinner. Sunny is truly country to town in one bite. Good ol' basic old-time country meals—that's what Sunny has here.

She may be young, but she's seen many things in her lifetime that she brings back and revives in her home kitchen. She shares all of the spices and national foods from her travels, without being all fussy about it. And now I'm using them too. These are the things that make a difference to me in a cook. You have to grow. You have to keep learning. And you have to be inviting, to welcome people into your kitchen. It's what I do and I guess in some way she got that from me. We love her here in Fayetteville, North Carolina. It makes us feel good that Sunny's cooking. It's a career like working in a beauty shop—just like someone is always gonna be getting their hair done, someone is always gonna need to eat.

Cooking remains new for a lot of people, even people like me who have been cooking for a long time. I never knew how she fixed her collards so quick, so Sunny showed me and I watched. And I said, "Well, that's between you and them, Sunny; all I do is cut the stems and put them in a pot with some ham hock and seasonings. But seeing you do it without pork, I know people are learning something new."

A romantic, Granddaddy gave Grandma a rose on a family trip to France when they visited us while we were living in Germany. **(1987)**

She's easy to learn from. I'm just so proud—what a trip her life has been.

I always looked forward to seeing Sunny and her brother in the summer for the one week we had together. It meant a lot to me. I got to feed them and hug them, and I call that making memories. I'd take Sunny to the country and her uncle Buddy would kill a hog for us to roast on the spit. Her brother would pour all the feed into the pig pen when he was supposed to put in only a handful, and the adults would laugh. The kids would turn my tomatoes from the garden into bowling pins and ruin them making strikes in my backyard. To me, at the age I am now, those memories mean more than anyone will know. I hope that you create memories like that with your families around food and maybe even travel like we did.

Because Sunny and her bother were military kids, I didn't get to see them so often, so their granddaddy and I decided to visit everywhere the military sent their parents. When Sunny was born on the Fort Sill Army Base in 1975, I took my first plane trip to Oklahoma. Then, in the following years, her parents took us places we would never ever have gone, like Paris and Germany. I can see her granddaddy now, sitting in a castle's window ledge in Germany, taking pictures and smiling. That's priceless. I thank God it turned out as good as it did for our family. We've had food and family memories in so many places all our lives, and it makes me feel good. Sunny's life has taken me far, and now it's taking her far too.

Everywhere she's ever been, her granddaddy and I wanted to be there, and I'm here with her now for both of us. Anyone reading *Sunny's Kitchen* is getting a piece of life, a piece of our family history, and a piece of our heart. I hope you enjoy this book as much as I love Sunny.

GRANDMA'S
words to live by

- When I get ready to cook I use the same equipment over and over. I still mix biscuits out of the same bowl because in some way, I feel the bowl was meant for them.

- If grocery stores can keep food in their freezers, why can't we do the same at home? Buy vegetables and fruits in season and freeze them. You can have a craving for soup and go right to your freezer for out-of-season ingredients. That's how you save money. I've been putting collards in my freezer for years.

- Don't shortchange your cooking and expect it to turn out good. My half sister gets on me for putting four sticks of butter in a cake, but to me that's a cake. The batter is the basis of the cake no matter what you put between the layers, and I think there should be four sticks of butter.

INTRODUCTION

HOME IS WHERE THE KITCHEN IS

I hope you enjoy every page of this book—not only the recipes, but the stories and photos too. Creating this for you has truly been a dream of mine since I was sixteen years old.

I worked as a journalist in San Antonio on the James Madison High School yearbook staff during the day, then after school would head to KSAT-12, the local ABC station. I actually produced video and wrote the words the anchors would read for the evening news. I remember calling home and reading my script to my parents before the news came on so they would know which words were mine. As a high school intern, it was a powerful and rewarding feeling to know that adults deemed my work on par with my older coworkers. I worked hard at fitting the right words into the right amount of script time and loved every single learning moment; it didn't even feel like a job. I knew then that I loved words, documenting life, and sharing it. I told myself that not only did I want to pursue journalism as a career, but that somehow I also wanted to make my words permanent and be published one day.

So, I joined the United States Air Force right out of high school as a journalist and was stationed in Seoul, South Korea, as a radio disc jockey. Although I loved music and even spun records at a few clubs while in high school, being a radio host wasn't quite my plan. But the military trains its journalists to do a host of communicating jobs, and it was just the luck of the draw that I landed in radio. My success in Seoul landed me a job in San Antonio as a radio journalist at the world news headquarters for all the branches of the military (the Armed Forces News Agency) and I was overjoyed with my

assignment. Finally, for the first time in my life I was moving to a city I knew. I still thought about being published, though. At the time I had no idea how to get closer to my dream, so I continued to work hard as I'd watched my dad do in the United States Army, hoping one day the opportunity would arrive.

My dad built a career in medicine while serving in the U.S. Army, and he always told me to do what I love. I have vivid memories of him coming home from work every day smiling and happy. This set such a good example for me in every city and country our family moved to, because no matter the location, he loved his job, and it wasn't just about work.

Food and travel are also things my parents taught me to love early on. My first memory of this was when we were stationed in Columbus, Georgia, at Fort Benning. My dad came home one day with a box full of German language tapes and

above: It was the summer of 1993. I was 18 and the United States Air Force's newest recruit. What a journey ahead. **opposite:** Mommy and me suited up for some kitchen fun. **(Columbus, GA, 1982)**

books and announced to the family that after a quick move to Virginia, we would be on our way to live in Germany. I was in second grade and for the next few months, as a family, we practiced the German language after dinner and read about local customs. Most important to them were table manners and how to order food.

My parents' excitement about eating new things and seeing new places was infectious even that early in life. My mom was already a culinary sponge, picking up recipes pretty much everywhere we went. Being a military wife made that easy because our neighbors in every military community were as diverse as New York City, which is probably why I love living in Brooklyn so much now as an adult. It feels like home, with people from all over the world right in my backyard. I can knock on my neighbor's door and ask them for a recipe from their native land and surprisingly get a warm welcome from someone happy to share their heritage. I saw my mom do this in every state or country we moved to, and it shaped the mind of a young culinarian.

Each move brought new recipes and ingredients. In Fort Benning it was bushels of oysters from the bayou; Texas brought Vietnamese dumplings from the Tran family across the street, not to mention chorizo, chiles, and all things Tex-Mex. In Bad Kreuznach we gathered a long list of recipes that started at Rosie's Restaurant, just steps from our off-base housing. As Americans, we did our best to fit in, speaking German to Rosie, sharing our stories and family recipes, and then she did the same. As an honor she gave us a permanent table (called a *stammtisch*) and she'd always sit with us for a minute to catch up, lovingly making a plate for our family dog, Ginger.

Our neighbors in every military community were as diverse as New York City, which is probably why I love living in Brooklyn so much.

Germany was in perfect proximity to much more travel and food, so almost every weekend our family would pile in a car and attend *volksmarches,* which were walking marathons, mapped through the hills and streets of villages. There were checkpoints along the way where you were expected to stop, have a local bite, and for my parents, drink some beer. When we reached the finish line there was a big tent of people doing the same, eating, drinking, and getting to know strangers. We'd get a plate or a beer stein for our participation, and our wall at home filled with these trinkets over the three years we lived in Germany.

We went skiing on the border between Austria and Germany and had the best waffles and hot chocolate at the peak of the tallest mountain in Europe, the Zugspitze. (I vividly remember being called chocolate by some giggling kids on one trip up the Rhine River on a tourist boat. It wasn't mean or malicious; in fact, the kids smiled. I was quite possibly the first black person they'd ever seen, and they touched my skin to see if it rubbed off. I still giggle at the memory; being called chocolate was, well, pretty sweet.) There were visits to France, the Netherlands,

Denmark, and everyplace in between. Each visit was about history, sightseeing, and food. My parents would sit and talk for hours about flavors, spices, and neat new ingredients found along the way.

I knew food was the glue that held us together as we moved from place to place. My mom made breakfast and dinner every single day. In fact, as many times as we moved, the most important boxes to open first were the ones labeled "kitchen." I remember one time being very upset with my brother because he labeled a box that contained my mom's various types of flour, "flower." I thought, how are we going to have pancakes when we get to our next house if we can't find the flour? That may sound silly now, but having our kitchen in order is what made us feel at home.

When we moved from Europe to Pennsylvania, my mom put up a new decoration in the kitchen, and I still think about it. By then, I was in middle school and very aware of how difficult it must be for my parents to pick up the family every year for a new town or city. I myself was growing tired of losing friends. These were the days of letters with stamps; there was no e-mail, cheap long-distance calls, or Skype. I knew that each friend I gained would soon be lost. The only thing that stayed the same was the nucleus of our family and the things we saw inside our home. The new decoration my mom hung on the wall was a wooden house with banners strung by chains beneath it. Each banner listed a different city we'd lived in thus far, and the first banner read "Home Is Where the Heart Is." I thought it powerful that she hung it in the kitchen, because we all knew that the kitchen was the beating heart of our family.

When I got to Yongsan army base at age eighteen for my first assignment, I did what my parents taught me and my brother as kids—I learned the local customs, picked up some of the language, and enjoyed all the authentic Korean food I could. And continuing our tradition, the first thing I unpacked was a recipe book my mom had given me and a small box of dishes for the kitchen. It was 1993 and there I was, an ocean away from family, and I was lonely. But I knew that if I wanted to feel at home, all I had to do

> I knew food was the glue that held us together as we moved from place to place. As many times as we moved, the most important boxes to open first were the ones labeled "kitchen."

the red plate

Forget cookies and ice cream or a trip to ShowBiz Pizza Place.
After a good report card all I wanted was to eat on the red plate.
Since I can remember, if our schoolwork was stellar, or if we
achieved in another area of life, my parents rewarded me and
my brother with the distinct honor of eating on our family's one
red plate. Each time I got to use it I felt like a princess. When I
started filming my TV show *Cooking for Real*, I called my parents
to ask if I could use the red plate for the studio set. After all,
they were done rewarding kids, right? My mom actually said no,
and that's when I realized my parents were still rewarding each
other with red-plate meals. Cute. So I bought my own and now
continue the tradition anytime I feel I need a priceless reward
and great memories of past red-plate meals.

was cook. So, I got in the kitchen and the first thing I made was something familiar, pancakes.

Years later I have shared that pancake recipe with countless others and opened my life of travel and food to anyone willing to listen. I feel truly fortunate to be able to do what I love and to share what I love with you. I don't take this opportunity lightly; the sixteen-year-old in me is very happy and fulfilled. All I had to do was live my life to its fullest.

After I left the military, I continued broadcasting and I ate my way through the New Orleans seafood scene, barbecue in Montgomery, Alabama, then had every rivaling bowl of chili in the competitive market of Detroit. When I landed in New York as a radio host for HOT 97, I cooked for friends and recording artists, and that led to starting a catering company. Soon, I got one of those calls you hear about, but this time it was happening to me—on the other end it was the Food Network asking me to share my stories and recipes from my kitchen on an episode of *Emeril Live*. That was the day this all started for me. Two years later, at thirty-two, I landed a job where people asked me, "When are you coming out with a cookbook?" Unbelievable.

Thanks to a life of travel and exploring new flavors, my book was there all along. That said, no one should have to move for good food or wait for it to come to them, because it's as close as your own kitchen. I can't always get to Germany, Korea, or anywhere else I've visited physically, but when the smells fill my kitchen and my plate, just a bite is all I need to feel transported. That's what comfort food is, more than flavors—it's the feeling that goes along with it, the memories, friends, and celebrations. In my kitchen I usually find myself trying to hit that emotional mark, so it's my hope this book helps you reach yours and inspires you to experience more life through food. Thank you for letting me into your kitchen. These are my stories; these are my recipes and I'm honored to share them with you.

With sunshine in my heart,

HOW TO COOK, FOR REAL

TOOLS My first show, *Gotta Get It* (on Food Network in 2007), was about gadgets. I cohosted with Marc Istook, and we shared the 411 on egg separators, electric peelers, and spinning ice cream cones. I love gadgets, but when I mean business, all I need is a rasp and a sharp knife, my favorite kitchen tools. A properly stocked kitchen takes time; I suggest adding a few items once a month or a season to treat yourself to something nice. Many kitchen tools and gadgets have very practical substitutes, so don't stress if you don't have them. It's your kitchen, you can make it work!

SHOP WITH YOUR EYES WIDE OPEN Many times we shop on autopilot, like we drive home the same way every day without thinking about the specific turns we make. One day, walk into your local grocer and dedicate yourself to walking up and down every aisle, looking top to bottom. You'll find not only flavor differences among brands, but new products to play with like liquid smoke (see German Baked Potatoes with Sweet Bacon and Scallion Dressing, page 238, and Caprese Steak, page 136) and fun frozen vegetable packs that can inspire a new recipe (see Southwestern Chicken Pot Pie on page 204).

BE YOUR OWN SOUS CHEF When you're done shopping, give yourself some kitchen preparation time right away, to rinse herbs, chop vegetables, break down meat, and freeze seasonal fruits or excess food from value packs. This simple step will help you get food on the table much faster. Plus, it's great to have frozen cranberries in the spring when they are hard to find (see Chicken and Wild Rice Casserole, page 184).

THINK OF A MASTER PLAN You hear it all the time and that's because it's great advice: read the recipe first. Many times there are steps you can flip, do a day before, or you may find answers to questions you have along the way.

MEASURE, THEN FREESTYLE A pinch is a pinch and a grind is a grind. They are subjective and should be done with personal preference in mind. However, how you measure is important for some ingredients. The rule of thumb I use for seasoning with salt is a teaspoon of salt per pound of meat. This usually puts me right in the flavor zone I'm looking for, so I measure salt for meat dishes. When measuring brown sugar, always pack it tight, and measure liquids in a liquid measure and dry ingredients in a measuring cup, leveling off with a straight edge. Use a dry measure for chopped herbs and pack them only if mentioned in the ingredient list. I give exact and rounded measurements to help you get to the finish line. Just remember no two "bunches" are alike, so use judgment. When you get comfortable using exact amounts, go rogue and leave the measuring tools alone.

ROOM TEMPERATURE IS IMPORTANT One tip that can really improve your chicken, beef, pork, lamb, or turkey—actually most anything you cook, unless directed otherwise—is to make sure it is room temperature before you cook it; this ensures that your food will cook evenly. For meats, the government regulators say it is safe to leave them out at room temperature for up to two hours. Don't be scared; rest the meat on the counter away from warm ovens or other large appliances.

internal temperatures

In each of my handwritten kitchen journals, I write a table of temperatures on the back page for quick reference. I should have these things memorized, but I save that brain power for song lyrics and obscure information. Feel free to photocopy this and put it on your fridge

beef
RARE 130°F
MEDIUM RARE 135°F
MEDIUM 145°F
MEDIUM WELL 160°F
WELL DONE 170°F

veal chops
MEDIUM RARE 135°F
MEDIUM 145°F
MEDIUM WELL 160°F

lamb chops
MEDIUM RARE 135°F
MEDIUM 145°F
MEDIUM WELL 160°F

pork chops & roasts
MEDIUM 145°F
MEDIUM WELL 160°F

poultry 165°F

fish & shellfish 145°F

MAKE MISTAKES What I love about every move I've made is getting lost on unfamiliar streets. You never know what you'll find. I use this same philosophy in my kitchen—mistakes are okay. Sometimes they end up as masterpieces.

Strawberry-Blueberry-Banana-Nut Muffins
with Cinnamon-Raisin Butter (PAGE 50)

BREAK FAST

Jeff's Cheesy Vacation Potatoes
   with Sweet & Spicy Sausage Patties

Rosemary T-Bone Steak and Cheese Eggs

San Antonio Migas

Fried Oysters and Catfish Nuggets
   with Creamy Grits

Huevos Rancheros with Salsa Verde

Chicken and Chorizo Hash with OJ Gravy

Lemon-Maple Chicken and Waffles
   Casserole

PB&J Pancakes with Blackberry Syrup

Loaded Puff Pastry Sticky Buns

Sweet and Corny Hoecakes

Quick Bacon, Cheddar, and Scallion Biscuits

Strawberry-Blueberry-Banana-Nut Muffins
   with Cinnamon-Raisin Butter

Pumpkin Pecan Pie French Toast
   with Butterscotch Syrup

Most mornings when I was a child, a loud grinding, slumber-shattering noise would echo through our house. It was the coffee grinder. Long ago there was an army ad campaign that said, "We do more before 9 a.m. than most people do all day." That was totally true of my dad; he woke up early and needed his coffee, so the whole house woke up with him. My parents were so serious about their coffee that they found a company that would deliver select coffee beans to us wherever we lived. I never miss breakfast and, yes, it often includes a stiff cup of what I call alarm-clock coffee (no recipe for that, just make it really strong).

Breakfast can be pretty simple for me, but sometimes this first meal of the day doesn't happen until lunchtime, so it's really brunch. I also love breakfast for dinner. I have so many personal favorite recipes that I hate to choose; it's like having children. If I say I like my PB&J Pancakes with Blackberry Syrup (page 42) the most, then my Huevos Rancheros (page 35) may get green with envy. These are the recipes that always put a smile on my face at the start of the day, whether that's in the morning, somewhere around noon, or late that night.

Jeff's Cheesy Vacation Potatoes
(PAGE 24)

this is for my best buddy, Jeff. He's the kind of friend I'd do anything for, and when we're together, there's no break in the laughter. I've known him since my radio days in New Orleans, but only recently began cooking for him, and these are *his* potatoes. One time I made them on vacation and ever since, they're his number one request from me in the kitchen. Think of a potato gratin that is tender throughout, but also has a bit of crunch from pan-frying the potato slices first. Add melting cheese and pico de gallo, and it's kind of like a potato pizza born in Texas (though it was first made for Jeff on Eleuthera in the Bahamas). Make it for your best friend and continue the chain. **SERVES 4 TO 6**

jeff's cheesy vacation potatoes WITH SWEET & SPICY SAUSAGE PATTIES

FOR THE POTATOES

- 3 russet potatoes, unpeeled, sliced ⅛ inch thick (poker-chip thick)
- Peanut or vegetable oil
- Kosher salt

FOR THE PICO DE GALLO

- 2 Roma tomatoes, seeded and chopped
- 2 scallions, finely minced (white and green parts)
- 1 teaspoon hot sauce (I like Frank's Red Hot)
- 1 teaspoon fresh lime juice
- ⅛ teaspoon ground cumin
- ⅛ teaspoon cayenne pepper
- Kosher salt and freshly ground black pepper

1 **Prepare the potatoes.** Put the potato slices in a large bowl with ice water to cover and soak for 30 minutes, stirring a bit. Transfer the potatoes to a colander and rinse until the water runs clear. Pour the potato slices onto a clean kitchen towel or several layers of paper towels and pat dry as much as possible. Preheat the oven to 375°F.

2 **Fry the potatoes.** In a large straight-sided pan or a stockpot over medium-high heat, pour oil 1 inch deep. Fry the potato slices in batches, flipping halfway through until golden and crisp, about 3 minutes on each side. They should be stiff and crispy on the outside, but remain fleshy inside. Taste one, cook's treat! Transfer each batch to a paper towel–lined plate and immediately season with a sprinkle of salt.

3 **Prepare the pico de gallo.** In a small bowl, toss the tomatoes with the scallions, hot sauce, lime juice, cumin, cayenne pepper, and a pinch of salt and pepper. Set aside.

4 **Bake the potatoes.** Butter the bottom of a pie pan or an 8 × 8-inch baking pan. Using half the potatoes, layer the slices in a circular pattern, beginning at the outside of the pan and moving toward the center, with the slices slightly overlapping. Cover the entire bottom this way. Then evenly sprinkle half the Cheddar/Jack blend over the potato layer. On top of that sprinkle half the pico de gallo, then half the mozzarella. Repeat the layers, ending with the mozzarella cheese. Bake until the cheese is melted and golden on the edges, about 18 minutes. Cut into slices and serve warm with a dollop of Mexican crema.

FOR THE CASSEROLE

1 tablespoon unsalted butter

½ cup shredded Cheddar/ Monterey Jack blend

½ cup shredded mozzarella cheese

Mexican crema, for garnish

sweet & spicy sausage patties MAKES 8

1 **Mix the sausage seasonings.** In a small bowl, combine the onion powder, garlic powder, red pepper flakes, fennel seed, paprika, salt, pepper, and brown sugar.

2 **Add the seasonings to the beef.** Break the beef into chunks and put in a large bowl. Sprinkle the seasoning mixture evenly over the top, then with your hands, gently mix the beef until the seasoning is evenly distributed.

3 **Prepare the patties.** Portion the beef into 8 servings and roll gently into balls. Place each ball between 2 sheets of parchment paper. Using a rolling pin, flatten the balls into ⅛-inch patties. Refrigerate between the sheets of parchment for at least 2 hours.

4 **Cook the patties.** Heat the olive oil in a large skillet over medium-high heat. Peel the parchment away from the sausage (you may need to use a dull knife) and cook the patties in batches. Sear on one side until caramelized and golden on the bottom, about 2 minutes, then flip to cook just 1 minute more.

1 teaspoon onion powder

1 teaspoon garlic powder

1 teaspoon crushed red pepper flakes

½ teaspoon fennel seed, crushed with a knife or mortar and pestle

¼ teaspoon Hungarian or hot paprika

1 teaspoon kosher salt

¼ teaspoon freshly ground black pepper

1 tablespoon plus 1 teaspoon tightly packed light brown sugar

1 pound ground beef chuck (80% meat, 20% fat)

1 teaspoon olive oil

tip! Like with a good meatloaf, you can use a blend of ground meat for these patties; just make sure the total weight is still a pound.

It's neat to hear food pop up in the lyrics from some of my favorite recording artists. The pairing here is based on a line by the rapper Notorious B.I.G. After a night of partying he craved to fill his belly with "a T-bone steak, cheese eggs, and Welch's grape." I can't tell you how many times I played that song as a hip-hop radio DJ in Montgomery, Detroit, and New York City. Instead of just throwing the steak in a pan with salt and pepper, in my kitchen I baste it in a garlic-scented rosemary butter and serve it alongside perfect, fluffy scrambled eggs with cheese whisked in and sprinkled on top. Ask anyone in the South how they like their cheese eggs, and you'll start a huge debate—is the cheese in or on the eggs? I solve all debates by doing both. **SERVES 4**

rosemary t-bone steak and cheese eggs

FOR THE STEAKS

4 T-bone steaks, 1½ inches thick

Kosher salt and freshly ground black pepper

1 tablespoon liquid smoke (hickory or mesquite)

3 tablespoons vegetable oil

2 sprigs fresh rosemary, cut in half

FOR THE ROSEMARY BUTTER

6 tablespoons unsalted butter

1 teaspoon kosher salt

2 garlic cloves, smashed

3 sprigs fresh rosemary

1 Season the steaks. Arrange the steaks in a dish, sprinkle with a pinch of salt and a few grinds of pepper on each side, sprinkle evenly with liquid smoke, and drizzle with the oil. Nestle the rosemary beneath the steaks and let them rest on the counter at room temperature for 2 hours, turning them halfway through to infuse both sides with the rosemary.

2 Make the rosemary butter. In a medium saucepan over medium-low heat, combine the butter and salt. Stir to dissolve the salt, then add the garlic and rosemary. Continue cooking over low heat until the butter is fragrant, 10 to 12 minutes. Remove from the heat and discard the garlic and rosemary.

3 Grill the steaks. Preheat a grill or grill pan to high heat. Remove the steaks from the dish, discard the rosemary, and place the steaks on the grill. Cook for about 5 minutes on both sides for medium rare. Remove from the grill, and allow to rest under loosely fitted aluminum foil for 10 minutes before serving.

4 **Make the eggs.** In a large bowl, vigorously whisk the eggs and add a splash of water, nothing more than a tablespoon. Melt the butter in a large nonstick pan over low heat but do not let it brown. Add the eggs, cook, using a whisk the entire time to release cooked egg from the bottom and sides of the pan while incorporating the uncooked egg. When the eggs are still wet but almost done, 5 to 6 minutes, remove from the heat. Add half the cheese, a pinch of salt, and a few grinds of pepper and continue to whisk until done. Sprinkle the remaining cheese on top.

FOR THE EGGS

8 eggs

2 tablespoons unsalted butter

1 cup shredded Cheddar cheese

Kosher salt and freshly ground black pepper

migas are scrambled eggs with personality and texture. I also think they're what a good Tex-Mex breakfast taco encompasses: eggs, chiles, bell peppers, onions, and tomatoes all jammed into a golden fried tortilla and topped with cheese. Imagine eating that with a fork and no juices running down your wrist, and you have migas. Sure, some like a soft taco, and I occasionally do, but the crunch of freshly fried corn tortillas scrambled with eggs and vegetables does the trick for me. **SERVES 4**

san antonio migas

8 eggs

3 tablespoons unsalted butter

3 tablespoons vegetable oil

4 corn tortillas, sliced into ½-inch strips, then cut into 2-inch rectangles

½ cup chopped red bell pepper

1 4-ounce can green chiles, drained

½ cup chopped Vidalia or sweet onion

Kosher salt and freshly ground black pepper

2 Roma tomatoes, seeded and chopped

½ cup shredded pepper Jack cheese

1 **Whisk the eggs.** In a large bowl, whisk the eggs and 2 tablespoons water vigorously. Set aside.

2 **Cook the tortilla strips.** Heat the butter and oil in a large skillet over medium-high heat. Once the butter melts and the oil begins to swirl, add the tortilla strips and cook, stirring and tossing, until they are all golden and crispy.

3 **Add the vegetables.** When the tortillas are crisp, add the bell pepper, chiles, and onion. Season with a pinch of salt and a few grinds of black pepper. Cook until the peppers and onion are tender, about 5 minutes.

4 **Add the eggs and serve.** Add the eggs to the pan and reduce the heat to medium-low. Cook, stirring to scramble and combine, until most of the moisture is cooked out, then remove from the heat and add the tomatoes for a final stir. Serve topped with cheese.

tips! Add a cup of shredded rotisserie chicken or cooked sausage right after the tortilla strips crisp to give the migas another hit of protein. ■ Turn these into "egg rolls" by piling the migas into double-ply Bibb lettuce leaves and rolling like a burrito, tucking in the ends.

When I was in grade school we lived in Columbus, Georgia, while my dad worked at Fort Benning. My parents would often buy a bushel of raw oysters. They'd roll the big bin out to the back porch and, along with my older brother, they'd shuck and eat them on the porch in the hot sun. I didn't like fish or any other seafood, but I loved oysters with a squeeze of lemon, a bit of horse-radish, some hot sauce, and a cracker. I pretended I didn't know how to shuck, so I ate while they did the hard work. I finally admitted I faked stupidity back then to my parents, just before I revealed it on an episode of *Cooking for Real*. They told me they knew all along! Oysters are still my favorite shellfish—whether they're raw, baked, or fried. They're even better with creamy grits alongside what I call "the Official Fish of the South," catfish. **SERVES 4 TO 6**

fried oysters and catfish nuggets WITH CREAMY GRITS

FOR THE OYSTERS AND FISH

2 eggs

1 tablespoon whole milk

¼ teaspoon cayenne pepper

Kosher salt and freshly ground black pepper

16 oysters, shucked

1 (6- to 8-ounce) catfish fillet, cut into 1-inch chunks

1 cup all-purpose flour

½ cup fine-milled cornmeal (I like Indian Head)

Peanut or vegetable oil

1 Soak the catfish and oysters. In a medium bowl, whisk together the eggs, milk, 1 tablespoon water, cayenne pepper, a pinch of salt, and a few grinds of black pepper. Add the oysters and catfish and soak at room temperature for 30 minutes.

2 Prepare the coating. In a large paper bag, combine the flour, cornmeal, a hefty pinch of salt, and a few grinds of black pepper. Close the bag and shake to mix.

3 Make the grits. In a medium pot over medium-high heat, combine 3 cups water, a pinch of salt, and a few grinds of black pepper. Bring the water to a boil, then stir in the grits and milk. Bring to a boil again, then reduce to a simmer and cook for about 4 minutes. When the grits begin to thicken but there is still plenty of moisture left, add the mozzarella, Cheddar, and scallions. Stir to melt the cheese, taste, and season with more salt if needed. Turn off the heat and cover to keep the grits warm. If they thicken, you can loosen them with water or milk.

4 **Dredge and fry the oysters and fish.** In a large heavy-bottomed pot or fryer, pour enough oil to fill the pan halfway. Heat until a deep-frying thermometer reaches 360°F. Using a slotted spoon and working in batches, remove the oysters and fish from the egg mixture and drop into the paper bag. Close and shake. Transfer each floured batch to a plate and repeat with the rest of the oysters and fish. Then fry the oysters and fish in batches so they are not overcrowded. Cook, turning once, until golden and cooked through, about 3 minutes. Transfer to a paper towel–lined plate and season lightly with salt. Serve on top of a bowl of the creamy grits and add a shake or two of hot sauce on top.

FOR THE GRITS

Kosher salt and freshly ground black pepper

¾ cup quick-cooking grits

1 cup whole milk

½ cup shredded mozzarella cheese

½ cup shredded Cheddar cheese

2 scallions, finely chopped (white and green parts)

Hot sauce, for serving

tips! You can soak the oysters and fish in milk for up to 1 hour for a less fishy flavor. ■ Clams work great in this recipe, too. ■ If you have leftover cold grits, just add a splash of chicken stock, milk, or water and use a potato masher to vigorously break up the grits as you reheat them.

I wasn't born in Texas, but I got there as quick as I could. That's a paraphrase of a bumper sticker I saw as my family drove into the state for the first time in 1989. It was the summer before my freshman year in high school and I had no idea what to expect from the state where reportedly "everything is bigger." Breakfast sure is bigger in Texas. Inspired by ranch hands who needed to start the day with plenty of fuel, huevos rancheros are hearty. The oozing yolk of the sunny-side up egg, the velvety black beans, the crispy tortillas, the tang from the fresh lime juice, and the heat of the salsa—the combination just works. When you've cleaned your plate, you should be ready to herd cattle, children, or piles of work.

SERVES 4

huevos rancheros WITH SALSA VERDE

FOR THE BLACK BEAN SAUCE

- 1 tablespoon vegetable or olive oil
- ½ cup roughly chopped Vidalia or sweet onion
- Kosher salt and freshly ground black pepper
- 2 Roma tomatoes, seeded and chopped
- 1 teaspoon ground cumin
- 2 garlic cloves, thinly sliced
- ½ teaspoon hot sauce (I like Frank's Red Hot)
- 1 15-ounce can black bean soup

FOR THE TORTILLAS

- Vegetable, canola, or peanut oil
- 8 6-inch white or yellow corn tortillas

1 Make the black bean sauce. In a saucepan over medium heat, combine the oil, onion, a pinch of salt, and several hefty grinds of black pepper. Cook, stirring, until the onion is tender, about 5 minutes. Add the tomatoes, cumin, garlic, and hot sauce. Stir and cook until the skins begin to peel off the tomatoes and the garlic becomes tender, about 8 more minutes. Add the black bean soup and bring to a boil, then reduce to a simmer for 10 minutes. Stir the pot a bit to make sure the beans don't stick, then keep them warm over low heat.

2 Fry the corn tortillas. In a straight-sided skillet, heat about 1 inch of oil over medium heat until it begins to swirl. Cook the tortillas 1 or 2 at a time, flipping halfway through, until the centers begin to bubble and the edges become golden, about 2 minutes. Transfer to a paper towel–lined plate.

continues

¼ cup (½ stick) unsalted
   butter

8 eggs, room temperature

   Kosher salt

½ bunch cilantro, leaves only

½ small red onion, sliced
   paper thin on a
   mandoline

2 ripe avocados, halved,
   pitted, and sliced

2 limes, cut into wedges

   Salsa Verde (recipe
   follows)

3 **Make the eggs.** Melt the butter in a large non-stick pan over low heat. If the butter browns, the heat is too high, so wipe out the pan and start over. Once the butter is melted, crack each egg into the pan, making sure they don't run into each other. You may have to divide the butter and do this in batches or separate pans. I prefer to make mine in a small pan, one at a time, and often do what I call "Frankenyolking." Raise the heat to medium-low and cook until the whites are completely cooked and the yolks are still runny, 8 to 10 minutes. At no time should the whites begin to bubble on the edges; keep the heat low enough that the edges don't brown or become crisp.

4 **Prepare the plate.** Place two overlapping tortillas on a plate and pour a scoop of the black bean sauce over them. Top each tortilla with a sunny-side up egg, or one Frankenyolked egg for the entire plate. Sprinkle a pinch of salt on each yolk. Top with a sprinkle of cilantro leaves and red onion slices. Place a few slices of avocado on the side along with a few lime wedges for spritzing. Drizzle a spoonful of the salsa on top.

salsa verde MAKES 2½ CUPS

Make the salsa verde. Place the tomatillos, onion, jalapeño, and garlic in a large pot, cover with 1 inch of water, and bring to a boil. Reduce to a simmer and cook for 5 to 8 minutes, or until the tomatillos are mushy. With a slotted spoon, transfer solids to a blender or food processor. Add the cilantro and lime juice and blitz until as smooth as possible. If needed, spoon in a bit of the poaching water to help it along. Taste and season with a pinch of salt and sugar to balance.

1 pound tomatillos, husked, cleaned, and quartered

½ large Vidalia or sweet onion, cut into chunks

1 jalapeño pepper, halved

2 garlic cloves

½ cup tightly packed fresh cilantro leaves

2 teaspoons fresh lime juice

Kosher salt

Sugar

tips! Scrambled eggs or whites also work great here. ■ "Frankenyolking" is simply using one whole egg then adding the separated yolk of another to make a two-yolk egg.

hash is the home of "kitchen sink" cooking. On the weekend I make hash as a pantry and refrigerator cleanout, to great success. I might find the chicken breast left over from dinner, a few sausage links in the meat drawer, some vegetables on their last days, a potato or two from the pantry, and then I chop away. On one occasion I had no potatoes, but I did have a green plantain, so I threw it into the mix and discovered a fabulous starchy addition to hash. Truly a great personal moment in pantry cleaning history! **SERVES 4**

chicken and chorizo hash
WITH OJ GRAVY

FOR THE HASH

- 8 ounces Mexican chorizo
- 1 small green plantain, peeled and diced
- Kosher salt and freshly ground black pepper
- 4 to 6 sprigs fresh thyme, leaves stripped and chopped
- 2 garlic cloves, thinly sliced
- 1 scallion, chopped (white and green parts)
- 1 tablespoon chopped pickled jalapeños
- ½ rotisserie chicken, skin removed, meat shredded or chopped

FOR THE GRAVY

- 1 tablespoon all-purpose flour
- 1 tablespoon Worcestershire sauce
- 1½ cups orange juice
- 2 tablespoons sour cream

- Chopped fresh flat-leaf or curly parsley, for garnish

1 Start the hash. Remove the casing from the chorizo and put in a large pan over medium heat. Vigorously break up the sausage into little bits with a potato masher or wooden spoon as it cooks. Once it resembles ground meat, add the plantain. Sprinkle with a tiny pinch of salt and a few grinds of black pepper. Toss to coat everything in the fat and allow to cook without stirring for a few minutes to develop color on the plantains, then toss and wait again. Cook this way until the plantains are caramelized on most sides and tender, and the chorizo is browned, about 15 minutes.

2 Finish the hash. Add the thyme, garlic, scallion, and jalapeños. Toss to coat and cook, stirring, until the garlic is tender and fragrant, about 5 minutes. Add the chicken and stir to coat.

3 Make the gravy and garnish. For this step use a wooden spoon. Sprinkle the flour over the top of the hash and stir in until it disappears, then cook for a few more minutes to remove the flour taste. Add the Worcestershire sauce and orange juice. Continue to stir, allowing the juices to thicken. Remove from the heat and stir in the sour cream. Garnish with parsley.

I love crunchy chicken and sweet waffles separately, but the magical combination reminds me of my six-month stint as a Californian. I lived outside of Los Angeles, but every time I had a meeting in the city, I was more excited about going to Roscoe's House of Chicken and Waffles on Pico and La Brea, then on the way home stopping at Lucy's Drive In at the same intersection. Even though this was a stressful time in my life, the promise of bookending my meetings with good food made it way better. This casserole's lemony crust is one of my favorite casserole toppings developed in my kitchen. **SERVES 6**

lemon-maple chicken and waffles casserole

FOR THE WAFFLES

2 cups all-purpose flour

1½ teaspoons baking powder

2 tablespoons granulated sugar

½ teaspoon kosher salt

3 eggs, separated

2 tablespoons packed light brown sugar

1¾ cups whole milk

¼ cup vegetable oil

½ teaspoon lemon extract

Grated zest of 1 lemon

Cooking spray

FOR THE CUSTARD

1 cup heavy cream

1 cup grade A maple syrup

½ cup buttermilk

2 scallions, finely chopped (white and green parts)

½ teaspoon Hungarian or hot paprika

1 **Mix the dry ingredients.** Sift the flour, baking powder, 1 tablespoon of the granulated sugar, and the salt into a large bowl.

2 **Mix the wet ingredients.** In a small bowl, vigorously whisk the egg yolks until smooth, then add the brown sugar, milk, vegetable oil, lemon extract, and lemon zest. Whisk until the brown sugar is dissolved.

3 **Mix the batter.** Make a well in the center of the dry ingredients. Pour in the wet mixture and gently stir the batter with a wooden spoon until just combined. Be careful not to overmix the batter. You can also use a hand beater or a stand mixer on low speed just pulsing. In another small bowl, whisk the egg whites until foamy. Add the remaining 1 tablespoon granulated sugar and beat until soft peaks form. Gently fold the whites into the batter.

4 Cook the waffles. Preheat the oven to 150°F. Heat the waffle iron and coat both the top and bottom surfaces with cooking spray. Pour ¼ to ½ cup batter, depending on the size of the waffle iron, and close. Cook until crisp and golden brown, 5 to 6 minutes, or according to the iron settings. Place the waffles directly on the middle oven rack and toast them until a tap feels more hard than soft, as if they were stale. Once toasted, use the squares as a guide and cut each waffle into its individual squares. Raise the oven temperature to 350°F.

5 Mix the custard. In a large bowl, whisk together the heavy cream, maple syrup, buttermilk, scallions, paprika, thyme, garlic, and a few grinds of black pepper. Taste and season with 1 or 2 pinches of salt, then add the 5 beaten eggs and whisk to combine.

6 Assemble the casserole. Add the chicken and waffle squares to the custard and stir. Allow to rest for 10 minutes, stirring here and there, to soak the waffles with the custard. Grease an 8 × 8-inch baking dish with cooking spray. Pour the chicken and waffle mixture into the dish and pat down gently. In a medium bowl whisk to combine the maple syrup, lemon zest, and lemon juice. Add the French-fried onions. Stir to coat, then sprinkle evenly on top of the casserole.

7 Bake the casserole. Bake until the crust is golden and crispy in parts and the custard is set, 25 to 30 minutes. Allow to cool 10 minutes before slicing and serving with a drizzle of maple syrup.

½ teaspoon ground thyme

1 garlic clove, grated on a rasp

Kosher salt and freshly ground black pepper

5 eggs, beaten

1 rotisserie chicken, skin removed and meat chopped

FOR THE CASSEROLE TOPPING

2 tablespoons grade A maple syrup, plus more for garnish

Grated zest of 1 lemon

2 teaspoons fresh lemon juice

2 cups French-fried onions, crushed in a plastic bag or with bare hands

ancakes were the first breakfast I cooked when I was stationed in Seoul, South Korea. This was the first time in months I had a kitchen. It was shared within my apartment complex, or barracks. I had only a small repertoire of recipes in my head, and pancakes was one of them. Growing up, our family cookbook had sticky pages where there was a recipe for pancakes on one side and waffles on the other. These pancakes were created for a guy I wanted to please; he loved peanut butter and I loved him. This blackberry syrup is very easy to make, and you can swirl it in oatmeal, drizzle it over vanilla ice cream, or put a spoonful in a glass and top it off with champagne.

MAKES TWELVE 5-INCH OR 24 SILVER-DOLLAR PANCAKES

pb&j pancakes WITH BLACKBERRY SYRUP

FOR THE PANCAKES
- 1 cup all-purpose flour
- 1 tablespoon baking powder
- ½ teaspoon kosher salt
- 2 tablespoons sugar
- 1 egg, beaten
- 1 cup plus 2 tablespoons whole milk, plus extra if needed to thin
- 2 tablespoons vegetable oil
- ½ cup peanut butter (creamy or crunchy), gently heated to loosen
- 1 to 4 tablespoons unsalted butter

FOR THE SYRUP
- 2 pints (24 ounces) fresh blackberries
- ¾ cup sugar
- Grated zest of 1 lemon
- 1 tablespoon fresh lemon juice

1 **Prepare the batter.** In a large bowl, whisk together the flour, baking powder, salt, and sugar. In another bowl whisk the egg, milk, and oil until combined. Add the peanut butter and vigorously whisk to combine. Make a well in the center of the dry ingredients and pour in the wet mixture. Gently whisk, starting in the center and moving out to combine. The batter should be slightly thicker than grade-school glue. Add a little extra milk if the batter feels too thick. Let the batter rest for 10 minutes; it will thicken as it rests.

2 **Make the syrup.** In a saucepan over medium heat, combine the blackberries, sugar, 1 cup water, the lemon zest, and lemon juice. Bring to a boil, stirring until the sugar dissolves. Reduce the heat to a simmer and cook, using a wooden spoon or potato masher to break down most of the blackberries. Simmer until the liquid is reduced to a syrupy consistency, about 10 minutes. Keep warm.

3 **Make the pancakes.** Preheat the oven to 125°F. Preheat a nonstick griddle pan. Add 1 tablespoon butter and tilt the pan around to coat. Pour about ¼ cup of batter on the griddle for each 5-inch pancake. Look for three things before you flip: air pockets start to pop up on the edges, the center is uncooked but not wet on the top, and a quick peek of the underside reveals a golden pancake. Repeat with the remaining butter and batter. Keep the finished pancakes warm in the oven while making the rest.

4 **Serve.** Serve the pancakes with blackberry syrup. Refrigerate any remaining syrup in an airtight container for up to 1 month.

tips! Other berries, or even a mixture of a few, work great for the syrup. ■ Add a sprinkle of chocolate or peanut butter chips to each pancake after it sets up a bit, but before it starts to bubble, then flip.

these sticky buns are an outright guilty pleasure in every sense of the term. For me, the best guilty pleasures are the shortcuts on things I don't want to do, like make puff pastry. I can devour this whole pan of buns in no time flat, so to spend hours making the pastry just doesn't seem right. No matter where I go outside of my kitchen for a sticky bun, there's never enough glaze to satisfy me, so making these at home allows me to pour on the fun and stuff them with all my favorite flavors. **MAKES 12 BUNS**

loaded puff pastry sticky buns

FOR THE PAN AND PASTRY

5 tablespoons unsalted butter

Kosher salt

2 frozen puff pastry sheets, thawed

FOR THE FILLING

¾ cup packed light brown sugar

¾ cup chopped pecans

1 Honey Crisp or Fuji apple, peeled, cored, and chopped

½ cup raisins

Grated zest of 1 lemon

Grated zest of 1 orange

1 tablespoon pumpkin pie spice

¼ teaspoon ground cardamom

Kosher salt

1 Prepare the pan. Use 1 tablespoon of the butter to grease the sides and bottom of a round 9-inch cake pan. Line with parchment paper cut to fit the bottom and set aside. Preheat the oven to 400°F.

2 Prepare the puff pastry. In a small pot, melt the remaining 4 tablespoons butter with a pinch of salt. Flatten the puff pastry and roll over it with a rolling pin or glass jar to even it out and seal any perforated seams. Brush the butter on all but a 1-inch wide strip along one of the long edges. Repeat for the second puff pastry sheet.

3 Prepare the filling. Put the brown sugar, pecans, apple, raisins, lemon zest, orange zest, pumpkin pie spice, cardamom, and a pinch of salt in a large bowl. Stir until combined. Sprinkle this mixture evenly over the pastry sheets, being careful to leave the unbuttered edge of each sheet free of the filling.

4 Roll the pastry. Starting from the long end opposite the clean edge, begin to tightly roll the pastry. Tuck and press as you go, keeping the log as even as

continues

3 tablespoons unsalted butter

¼ teaspoon vanilla extract

3 tablespoons fresh lemon juice

3 tablespoons orange juice

1½ to 2¼ cups confectioners' sugar

Kosher salt

possible. When the edge is reached, roll the pastry onto itself and pinch to seal. Repeat with the second pastry sheet. Using a serrated knife, trim the edges and gently cut 6 equal slices from each log.

5 **Bake the pastry.** Place the slices spiral side up in the prepared cake pan. Start around the edges and fill in the center last. It's okay if the edges touch. Bake until the pastry is cooked through and golden brown, 35 to 40 minutes.

6 **Make the glaze.** In a small pot, melt the butter over low heat. Add the vanilla, lemon juice, and orange juice and begin whisking in the confectioners' sugar in ¼-cup increments. Continue to add the sugar, whisking between additions, until the glaze thickens. Taste and season with a tiny pinch of salt, then remove from the heat. When the buns are done, remove them from the oven and drizzle the glaze over the top.

tip! Flip the recipe—instead of filling the puff pastry with the nuts, apples, and raisins, layer them on the bottom of the prepared cake pan and place the buns on top. After baking, invert them onto a plate so the fillings are on the top. Drizzle glaze over the top.

oecakes are pancakes' corny Southern cousin. I went forever not thinking about them; then one trip to Savannah brought all my memories flooding back. I was there to tape an episode of *Paula's Best Dishes* with Paula Deen and had dinner planned at her restaurant, The Lady & Sons. Instead of first bringing bread and butter or chips and salsa to the table, a waiter plunked down a hefty plate of biscuits and hoecakes with softened butter and syrup. With one bite I was back in my grandma's kitchen. So now I make hoecakes regularly. I know we are hanging out in the breakfast and brunch section, but if you feel like getting your Savannah on, next time you have people over for dinner, serve these as an appetizer and watch your guests turn into kids. **MAKES 14**

sweet and corny hoecakes

1 cup all-purpose flour

1 cup fine-milled cornmeal (such as Indian Head)

1½ teaspoons baking powder

1 teaspoon kosher salt

¼ cup sugar

1 egg, beaten

1½ cups whole milk, plus more to thin the batter

2 teaspoons vegetable oil, plus more for frying

½ cup corn kernels

¼ cup chopped pickled jalapeños

Grade A maple syrup, for serving

tip! For a fun appetizer, make sand-dollar-size hoecakes and top them with bacon, or a bit of fresh corn tossed in maple syrup with a tiny pinch of salt.

1 **Mix and rest the batter.** In a large bowl, combine the flour, cornmeal, baking powder, salt, and sugar. In a medium bowl, whisk the egg, milk, 2 teaspoons vegetable oil, corn, and pickled jalapeños. Pour the corn mixture into the bowl with the flour mixture and stir to combine. Allow to rest for 5 minutes. If it thickens to where it cannot easily pour, add an extra tablespoon of milk at a time until the consistency is right.

2 **Cook the hoecakes.** Preheat the oven to 125°F. Heat about ½ inch of vegetable oil in a cast-iron pan over medium-high heat. When the oil begins to swirl, add batter in batches, using a small ice cream scoop or ¼-cup measure. Gently spread each hoecake into a circle, if needed. Flip the hoecakes when air pockets begin to pop on the surface of the batter and a peek beneath reveals golden edges, about 2 minutes. Once the second side is golden brown, transfer to a baking sheet in the warm oven and continue making the rest of the hoecakes. Serve with maple syrup.

Okay, let's talk biscuits. In my family we fight for the "center biscuit," steaming hot from the oven. My cousin Monique often wins the battle because she is smart to call it as it goes in the oven. It's soft like a pillow, with no rough edges, but really, if Grandma is making them, there are no losers because I'll take her edges any day. Her recipe is "a big scoop of flour" and "a handful of lard" with "some buttermilk." It stumped me for years, my attempts never tasting quite right. I then discovered her specially milled flour with butter flakes, which made all the difference. It's hard to find; in a pinch I make these. They're perfect with dinner, but a smear of jelly makes for a great brunch. And there's no fighting over these, because they're all the same! **MAKES 10 TO 12**

quick bacon, cheddar, and scallion biscuits

2 cups all-purpose flour

1 tablespoon plus 1 teaspoon baking powder

2 teaspoons kosher salt

1 teaspoon Hungarian or hot paprika

1 teaspoon onion powder

1 cup whole milk

½ cup (1 stick) unsalted butter, melted

8 strips bacon, cooked until crisp, cooled and crumbled

1 cup shredded Cheddar cheese

2 scallions, finely chopped (white and green parts)

1 egg

1 **Mix the dry ingredients.** Preheat the oven to 425°F. In a large bowl, combine the flour, baking powder, salt, paprika, and onion powder. Mix to blend, then make a well in the center of the bowl.

2 **Prepare the biscuits.** In the center of the dry ingredients, add the milk, butter, bacon, cheese, and scallions. Mix gently with a wooden spoon, or channel my grandma and use one hand in a squeezing motion. The dough will be wet and sticky, so scrape off your fingers or the wooden spoon. Use a ¼-cup measure or ice cream scoop to portion the batter onto a baking sheet, spacing the biscuits an inch or so apart.

3 **Bake the biscuits.** In a small bowl, beat the egg and 2 tablespoons water. Brush this mixture on top of each biscuit, then bake until golden brown and a toothpick inserted in the center of a biscuit in the middle of the pan comes out clean, 20 to 22 minutes. If you notice uneven browning, rotate the pan halfway through baking.

When I make these muffins, they take me back to my childhood. My daddy would get a pint of strawberries, hull and chop them, sprinkle generously with sugar, and put them in the refrigerator. The next day, a thick syrup would appear! We'd pour these strawberries over cereal, ice cream, pancakes, anything really. No matter where we lived, this sight in the fridge always made me feel at home. When I moved to Rancho Cucamonga, California, I wanted to get a little bit of home in my kitchen. I'd just left my radio career and moved for a love that ended up not working out. So, finding comfort in my daddy's strawberries in syrup it was. I had surplus, so I came up with these most delightful, moist muffins. This is one of the first recipes I pitched to the Food Network when I moved back to New York, chasing a dream. Now no matter where or when I make these, it's bittersweet, but they feel like home. **MAKES 12 MUFFINS**

strawberry-blueberry-banana-nut muffins WITH CINNAMON-RAISIN BUTTER

FOR THE STRAWBERRIES

1 cup chopped fresh
  strawberries

2 tablespoons sugar

FOR THE BATTER

Cooking spray

1½ cups all-purpose flour

¼ teaspoon cinnamon

½ teaspoon baking soda

¼ teaspoon grated nutmeg

1 teaspoon kosher salt

1 ripe banana, mashed

2 eggs

¼ cup vegetable oil

1 cup sugar

Grated zest of 1 lemon

6 to 8 ounces blueberries

1 cup chopped walnuts

1 **Macerate the strawberries.** In a large bowl, mix the strawberries and sugar. Toss and stir a bit, until the strawberries give off their juices, about 15 minutes. Preheat the oven to 350°F. Spray a muffin tin with cooking spray.

2 **Make the batter.** In a small bowl, mix together the flour, cinnamon, baking soda, nutmeg, and salt. To the bowl of strawberries and juices, add the banana, eggs, oil, sugar, and lemon zest. With a wooden spoon, gently mix the dry ingredients into the strawberry mixture until combined. Fold in the blueberries and walnuts. Allow to rest while you make the topping.

3 **Make the topping.** Put the sugar, flour, lemon zest, butter, and walnuts in a food processor and pulse until combined, but not pulverized.

4 **Bake the muffins.** Scoop the batter evenly into the prepared muffin cups, then top each with an even sprinkle of topping. Bake until a toothpick inserted in the center of a muffin comes out with a few crumbs but not wet, about 30 minutes.

5 **Make the compound butter.** While the muffins are baking, combine the butter, cinnamon, raisins, brown sugar, and a pinch of salt in a small bowl. Blend with a rubber spatula or the back of a spoon until the sugar becomes less granular. Refrigerate at least 30 minutes. Serve softened.

FOR THE TOPPING

1 cup sugar

¼ cup plus 2 tablespoons all-purpose flour

Grated zest of 1 lemon

¼ cup (½ stick) unsalted butter, ice cold

½ cup walnuts

FOR THE COMPOUND BUTTER

¾ cup (1½ sticks) unsalted butter, room temperature

½ teaspoon cinnamon

¼ cup raisins, chopped

2 tablespoons packed dark brown sugar

Kosher salt

tip! I play with compound butter all the time. Try a savory twist on these muffins by substituting plenty of fresh thyme and lemon zest for the cinnamon and raisins, then leave out the sugar and add a pinch of salt instead. Also try almonds and a drop of vanilla with sugar, or hazelnuts and sugar.

bread is baaad. To quote the great poet LL Cool J, it's "not bad meaning bad, but bad meaning good." The English often have something called "fried bread" for breakfast and that's it, no frills, just bread fried to a crisp in fat! When I lived in New Orleans while attending Loyola University, my sophomore twenty could easily be attributed to the Creole answer to fried bread for breakfast, pain perdu. I make my own kind of fried bread, known by most as French toast. This is one of the recipes I never have to measure, and I find plenty of ways to play with the flavors. The dash of pumpkin pie spice really warms up the flavors.

MAKES 8 SLICES

pumpkin pecan pie french toast WITH BUTTERSCOTCH SYRUP

FOR THE BATTER

4 eggs

½ cup whole milk

2 teaspoons pumpkin pie spice

½ cup pumpkin puree

1 tablespoon granulated sugar

1 tablespoon packed light brown sugar

FOR THE COATING

3 cups cornflakes, crushed

1½ cups finely chopped pecans

Kosher salt

FOR THE FRENCH TOAST

8 slices stale Texas toast, 1½ inches thick

2 tablespoons unsalted butter, plus more for frying

2 tablespoons vegetable oil, plus more for frying

1 **Make the batter.** In a shallow dish, whisk together the eggs, milk, pumpkin pie spice, pumpkin puree, and sugars.

2 **Mix the coating.** In another shallow dish, combine the cereal, pecans, and a pinch of salt.

3 **Dredge the bread.** Place the bread slices in the egg dish and soak on each side until well coated and soaked through, but not soggy. Immediately place the bread in the coating and press down on both sides and the edges to coat. Repeat with the remaining slices, place on a parchment-lined plate, and refrigerate for 20 minutes.

4 **Make the syrup.** In a small pot, melt the butter over low heat. Add the butterscotch and pecan liqueurs and bring to a simmer, then add the maple syrup and stir. Taste the syrup and season with a tiny pinch of salt. Keep warm over low heat.

5 Fry the bread. In a large skillet or griddle over medium heat, melt 2 tablespoons butter and 2 tablespoons oil. Remove the bread slices from the refrigerator and cook until golden, turning once, 5 to 7 minutes per batch. Add 1 more tablespoon of butter and oil for each batch, if needed.

6 Serve. Serve warm with the butterscotch syrup. Refrigerate any remaining syrup in an airtight container for up to 1 month.

FOR THE SYRUP

2 tablespoons unsalted butter

¼ cup butterscotch liqueur

¼ cup pecan liqueur

1 cup grade A maple syrup

Kosher salt

tip! If you want to make your own pumpkin pie spice blend, start with cinnamon, then add a little ground allspice, ginger, and nutmeg until you like your personal blend.

APPS
& SANDWICHES

Blackened Catfish Sandwiches
with Spicy Tartar Sauce

Smokey Crab-a-Mole

Maple Bacon and Chicken Quesadillas

Curry Pork Burgers with Spicy Ketchup

Chopped Chops and Goat Cheese
Sandwiches

Korean Fried Dumplings

Mini Scallion and Parmesan Meatballs

Brooklyn Beef Patties

Southwestern Carne Asada Wraps

Ground Lamb Kabobs
with Cucumber Mint Sauce

Gouda-Stuffed Burgers with Roasted Garlic
and Onions

Pepper Jack Grilled Cheese

Tomato and Pesto Tarts

Spinach and Artichoke–Stuffed
Baguette Slices

Vine-on Roasted Tomatoes and Goat Cheese

In my early days of cooking I had a problem with making appetizers because all I really wanted to eat was the main event. I loved to order a meal of appetizers in restaurants, but I felt like they just didn't matter at home. Who makes themselves appetizers? Then friends started coming over for informal hangouts and I had to build a lineup of recipes that worked for these occasions. I had breakfast and dinner down, but what about small bites?

In the beginning I'd just make smaller versions of entrées or reinvent leftovers. Truly anything on a crostini feels like an appetizer, if you ask me. I'm talking meatloaf crumbled on crostini with a scoop of tomato sauce, or even vegetable sides puréed and smeared on crusty bread with a drizzle of olive oil. Same with a sandwich—I'd put heavenly leftovers between two pieces of bread and call it a day. There's nothing wrong with that, but I began to really embrace the idea of creating dishes specifically to start the meal, pass around for a dinner party, or feed lunchtime guests. These are just some of my small bites; make a few and you have a meal.

Tomato and Pesto Tart (PAGE 82)

I had been hosting my TV show *Cooking for Real* for three years, feeling pretty good about my career, when I went to Elloree, South Carolina, for a family reunion on my dad's side. Well, family always keeps you grounded and I was there for only five minutes when a distant relative came right up to me and said, "Where's the catfish?" He wanted to know why I hadn't cooked catfish on my show yet. He thought maybe I didn't know how to make it. I had to explain that I did know and I promised to put it on the show for the next season. So, for my family and you, here is the ultimate blackened catfish sandwich. This reminds me of my Detroit radio buddy, Bushman. We had one of these a couple of times a week together after workouts. **MAKES 4**

blackened catfish sandwiches
WITH SPICY TARTAR SAUCE

FOR THE CATFISH

- 1 teaspoon Hungarian or hot paprika
- 1 teaspoon garlic powder
- 1 teaspoon onion powder
- ½ teaspoon dried oregano
- ½ teaspoon dried thyme
- Grated zest of 1 lemon
- Kosher salt and freshly ground black pepper
- 2 tablespoons vegetable oil
- 2 nice-sized catfish fillets, 6 to 8 ounces each

FOR THE SPICY TARTAR SAUCE

- 1 cup mayonnaise
- 1 tablespoon fresh lemon juice
- 1 tablespoon prepared horseradish
- 2 teaspoons hot sauce (I like Frank's Red Hot)
- 2 tablespoons dill relish
- Kosher salt and freshly ground black pepper

1 **Season the catfish.** In a small bowl, mix the paprika, garlic powder, onion powder, oregano, thyme, lemon zest, a pinch of salt, and a few grinds of pepper. Coat each piece of fish on both sides and allow to rest at room temperature at least 20 minutes.

2 **Cook the fish.** In a seasoned cast-iron pan, heat the oil over medium-high heat until it just begins to smoke. Gently add the fillets to the pan, laying them down away from you so there is less splatter. Cook until a peek beneath reveals a darkened crust, about 4 minutes. Flip and fry on the other side until cooked through, about 3 minutes more. Remove from the heat and rest at least 5 minutes.

3 **Make the spicy tartar sauce.** In a medium bowl, combine the mayonnaise, lemon juice, horseradish, hot sauce, dill relish, a tiny pinch of salt, and a few grinds of pepper. Taste and season with more salt, if needed.

4 **Assemble the sandwiches.** Cut each piece of fish in half crosswise. Split the bread in half lengthwise. Slather the bottom and top of each piece of bread with the tartar sauce. Layer each sandwich with lettuce and tomato, then top with fish. Spritz the fish with a squeeze of lemon. Serve warm or at room temperature.

FOR THE SANDWICHES

4 square loaves soft ciabatta bread (or 2 long ones, cut in half)

½ head iceberg lettuce, shredded into thin ribbons

1 Roma tomato, sliced

1 lemon, cut into wedges

tips! When adding small amounts of ingredients like seasonings to a filled bowl, as in this recipe, try to sprinkle them from a higher level than normal so the flavors distribute and blend easily once combined. ■ The tried and true way to store guacamole so it doesn't oxidize and turn brown is to cut a sheet of plastic wrap larger than the storage container, and gently press the plastic directly on top of the dip, making sure it touches and flattens the entire top surface. Cover that with a lid and the guacamole will maintain its green color. ■ This makes a great wrap with lots of shredded crisp romaine lettuce. The avocado won't brown if you close up the wrap nice and tight with plastic wrap. A perfect way to make lunch the night before.

this dip feeds a crowd; perfect for a big game day. I created it for a "Guac-Off" contest at Sirius/XM radio with hosts Covino and Rich, and it was the winner!. The addition of crab sealed the deal, with my secret ingredient, liquid smoke. It is water infused with actual smoke that adds hickory or mesquite flavor. I keep both flavors in my kitchen, and for this recipe, mesquite is what really makes this guac rock. **MAKES 13 CUPS**

smokey crab-a-mole

2 poblano peppers, tops removed and seeded

1 tablespoon olive oil

Kosher salt and freshly ground black pepper

10 ripe avocados, halved and flesh removed

¾ cup finely chopped red onion

1 bunch fresh cilantro (about 3 ounces), leaves only, chopped

¼ cup fresh lime juice

1½ cups Mexican crema

1½ teaspoons ground cumin

1½ teaspoons Hungarian or hot paprika

2 teaspoons liquid smoke (mesquite or hickory)

2 tablespoons hot sauce (I like Frank's Red Hot)

8 to 10 pickled jalapeño slices, or one whole pickled jalapeño, finely chopped

¼ cup pickled jalapeño juice

1 pound lump crabmeat, cleaned of all shells and debris

Tortilla chips, to serve

1 **Roast the peppers.** Preheat the oven to 400°F. Rub each poblano pepper with olive oil and place on a baking sheet. Roast until charred on one side, then flip. Do this until all sides are charred, 15 to 18 minutes total. Remove and immediately place on a plate in the refrigerator or freezer until cooled to loosen the thin skin. Once cooled, remove and discard the blistered skin and finely chop the flesh. Put in a large bowl and season with a pinch of salt and a grind of pepper.

2 **Mix the guacamole.** To the bowl with the peppers, add the avocados, red onion, cilantro, lime juice, crema, cumin, paprika, liquid smoke, hot sauce, pickled jalapeños, and jalapeño juice. Mash vigorously with a potato masher until smooth. Fold in the crab, then taste and season with a nice pinch of salt and a few grinds of pepper. Serve with tortilla chips.

will make quesadillas out of anything and use them to eat up leftovers, but when I have the chance, I pay close attention to the balance. The only requirement is melting cheese to hold the tortillas together like glue. Every holiday season in New York City, Union Square is packed with vendors selling ornaments, gifts, and food. A crepe stand there makes this simple but rewarding flavor combination of bacon and cheese, served with a drizzle of maple syrup. I love making crepes, but in a pinch a quesadilla does the trick. This recipe hits so many marks—it's sweet, savory, spicy, smoky, tangy, and gooey, and the toasted tortilla becomes the last needed texture note, crunchy. **MAKES 2**

maple bacon and chicken quesadillas

FOR THE CHICKEN

½ pound boneless, skinless chicken breast

1 teaspoon sweet paprika

1 teaspoon dried oregano

2 teaspoons liquid smoke

1 garlic clove, smashed

1 tablespoon fresh lemon juice

1 tablespoon olive oil

Kosher salt and freshly ground black pepper

FOR THE BACON

8 strips bacon, cut into 1-inch sections

¼ cup grade A maple syrup

½ cup finely chopped red onion

Kosher salt and freshly ground black pepper

1 **Marinate the chicken.** Place the chicken, paprika, oregano, liquid smoke, garlic, lemon juice, and olive oil in a resealable plastic bag with a pinch of salt and a few grinds of black pepper. Rest for 2 hours at room temperature, tossing the bag a bit halfway through.

2 **Grill the chicken.** Heat a seasoned grill or grill pan to medium-high. Remove the chicken from the plastic bag and shake off the excess marinating liquid. Place the chicken on the grill, smooth side down. Cook on one side until the chicken releases easily from the grill without sticking and has grill marks, 4 to 5 minutes. Flip, then cook 3 to 4 minutes more or until juices run clear. Transfer to a cutting board and let rest at least 15 minutes before roughly chopping.

3 **Cook the bacon.** Combine the bacon, syrup, onion, a pinch of salt, and a few grinds of pepper in a skillet over medium heat. Cook, stirring, until all the fat is rendered and the bacon is cooked and sticky, 6 to 8 minutes.

4 **Assemble the quesadillas.** Heat a grill pan to medium heat. In a medium bowl mix the Cheddar and Jack cheeses. Place 2 tortillas on the grill. Divide the cheese into 4 equal portions and sprinkle one quarter over each tortilla. Top each evenly with the bacon mixture. Next, evenly distribute all the chicken, then sprinkle with the remaining cheese. Finish by placing the 2 remaining tortillas on top.

5 **Cook the quesadillas.** Gently press the quesadillas as they grill. After 2 to 3 minutes, take a peek underneath and if there are visible grill marks, give the quesadillas a quarter turn to produce hash marks. Grill until the desired pattern appears. With one hand on top, carefully flip each with a spatula and continue to cook in the same manner until the cheese is melted and grill marks are set. Serve warm.

FOR THE QUESADILLAS

- **8 ounces shredded Cheddar cheese**
- **8 ounces shredded Monterey Jack cheese**
- **Four 10-inch flour tortillas**

Curry ketchup is a street food condiment I was introduced to on the streets of Bad Kreuznach, Germany. It's not as thick as what we're familiar with in the U.S., is a bit sweeter, and has a nice undertone of curry. I squirted it on bratwurst and French fries at the stands there called *schnell imbiss,* which translates as "fast food." Even at ten years old, I found the flavor combination of curry and ketchup pretty interesting. I now order bottles online and sometimes even make my own version. I love the marriage of the two flavors that complement each other like they are staring across the center of a color wheel. I've taken that contrasting flavor inspiration and put the curry in the burger, then topped it with an easy-to-make, spicy ketchup. Even the "only salt and pepper go in my burger" purists have tried this version and loved it. **MAKES 6**

curry pork burgers WITH SPICY KETCHUP

FOR THE PATTIES

2½ pounds ground pork, crumbled

2 teaspoons ground coriander

2 teaspoons yellow curry powder

2 teaspoons Worcestershire sauce

1 teaspoon cayenne pepper

3 scallions, finely chopped (white and green parts)

2 garlic cloves, finely chopped

2½ teaspoons kosher salt

Freshly ground black pepper

2 tablespoons olive oil, plus more as needed for cooking the burgers

1 **Season the pork.** In a large bowl gently combine the pork, coriander, curry powder, Worcestershire, cayenne pepper, scallions, garlic, salt, and a few grinds of black pepper. Make 6 even patties and refrigerate for 4 to 6 hours on a plate covered with plastic wrap or let rest at room temperature for up to 2 hours. If refrigerating, allow to come to room temperature before cooking.

2 **Make the spicy ketchup.** In a small saucepan over low heat, lightly cook the red pepper flakes and garlic in butter until tender and fragrant, 3 to 4 minutes. Stir in the ketchup and cayenne. Cook another 5 minutes. Remove from heat and stir in the scallion. Store in an airtight container in the refrigerator and serve at room temperature.

3 **Cook the burgers.** Heat a large frying pan over medium-high heat and coat with oil. Sear the patties until golden brown on both sides and cooked through, about 5 minutes per side. Cook in batches, if necessary.

4 **Assemble the burgers.** Place a burger on each bun and top with lettuce, tomato, and a generous squirt of the spicy ketchup.

tip! In a large straight-sided pan, cook the seasoned ground pork with a bit of oil, then add ½ pound of your favorite cooked pasta, a spoonful or two of the pasta water, and a sprinkle of your favorite cheese and stir to combine for a one-pot meal.

FOR THE SPICY KETCHUP

½ teaspoon crushed red pepper flakes

1 garlic clove, grated on a rasp or finely minced

1 tablespoon unsalted butter

1 cup ketchup

¼ teaspoon cayenne pepper

1 scallion, finely chopped (white and green parts)

FOR THE BURGERS

6 potato hamburger buns

1 head Boston, Bibb, or other butter lettuce, cleaned, leaves separated and patted dry

2 Roma tomatoes, sliced lengthwise

Me at home cooking on my one day of leave during basic military training. **(San Antonio, TX, 1993)**

this sandwich is great for special lunch guests or a nice lunch in the park. Whenever I have friends over for lunch I do either a scaled-down dinner or a salad or soup paired with a sandwich. This is tasty and just different enough to serve as a special sandwich for lunch. Even though I typically buy thicker chops for dinner, I also buy the thinner ones when I see them on sale. When marinated and chopped, thin chops are a great buy and go a long way. **MAKES 4**

chopped chops and goat cheese sandwiches

FOR THE CHOPS

- **4 thin-cut pork chops**
- **1 tablespoon olive oil**
- **2 teaspoons fresh lemon juice**
- **Kosher salt and freshly ground black pepper**

FOR THE GOAT CHEESE SPREAD

- **6 ounces goat cheese**
- **7 sprigs fresh thyme, leaves finely chopped**
- **3 sprigs fresh oregano, leaves finely chopped**
- **¼ cup dried cranberries, finely chopped**
- **¼ cup walnuts, toasted and finely chopped**
- **2 teaspoons fresh lemon juice**
- **Grated zest of 1 lemon**
- **Kosher salt and freshly ground black pepper**
- **8 slices of olive loaf or whole-grain bread, gently toasted**
- **2 cups chopped fresh spinach**

1 Marinate the chops. In a resealable plastic bag, combine the pork chops, oil, lemon juice, a pinch of salt, and a grind or two of pepper. Squeeze out as much air as possible, toss to fully coat the chops, and rest on the counter for at least 30 minutes, but no longer than 1 hour.

2 Grill the chops. Heat a seasoned grill or grill pan to medium-high heat. Remove the chops from the bag and shake off any excess marinade. Place on the grill and cook on one side until each chop easily releases from the grill without sticking, about 3 minutes. Flip and cook just 2 minutes more. Remove from the grill and allow to cool completely, then remove the meat from the bone and chop.

3 Make the spread. In a small bowl, mix together the goat cheese, thyme, oregano, dried cranberries, walnuts, lemon juice, and lemon zest. Season to taste with salt and pepper.

4 Assemble the sandwiches. Spread the cheese mixture on 4 pieces of the toasted bread and add the spinach and layer with 2 heaping spoonfuls of the chopped meat. Top each sandwich with another slice of toasted bread. Cut in half and serve.

tips! Something simple like cutting the bread creatively can take your sandwich experience to a new level. After assembling the sandwiches, try cutting off the crusts to make squares. Then cut each one into 4 smaller squares. ■ Don't count out lamb chops here; they are a great substitute for the pork.

I ate about a jillion of those dumplings, or *yaki mandu*, from various purveyors in a shopping and nightclub district of Seoul, South Korea, called Itaewon ("EAT-ay-won"). It was right outside the military base and the local haunt of many of my fellow military members on Yongsan army base. They took me to this Americanized district my first night in the country, and if it weren't for the fried dumplings on a skewer on the way home, I might not have made it through the next day. It was definitely one of those times when you promise never to have a drink again. These were the perfect street food to introduce me to Korean flavors in a tiny package. At home I leave the skewers alone and add a dipping sauce, followed by a chug of beer (Korean beer if I have my act together).

MAKES 35 TO 40

korean fried dumplings

FOR THE DIPPING SAUCE

- 1 tablespoon white sesame seeds
- 1 teaspoon crushed red pepper flakes
- ¼ cup soy sauce
- 2 teaspoons unseasoned rice vinegar
- 1 teaspoon toasted sesame oil

FOR THE DUMPLINGS

- 1 pound ground pork
- 2 garlic cloves, minced
- ¼ cup shredded carrot (about 1 small)
- 2 scallions, finely chopped (white and green parts)
- ½ teaspoon toasted sesame oil
- 1 teaspoon hot sauce (I like Frank's Red Hot)
- 1 egg, beaten

1 **Make the dipping sauce.** In a small pan over medium heat, combine the sesame seeds and red pepper flakes. Toss and stir until the sesame seeds are shiny, slightly golden, and fragrant, about 1 minute. Transfer to a plate and allow to cool. In a small bowl, stir together the soy sauce, rice vinegar, sesame oil, and cooled sesame seeds and red pepper flakes.

2 **Make the filling.** In a large bowl, combine the pork, garlic, carrot, scallions, sesame oil, hot sauce, egg, red pepper flakes, salt, and a few grinds of pepper. Mix well with your hands.

3 **Assemble the dumplings.** Fill a small bowl with water. Place a wonton wrapper floured side up on a flat surface. Place 1 to 2 teaspoons of the pork mixture in the center of the wrapper. Dip your finger in the water, then trace and wet the outer edge of the wrapper, folding it over to make a half circle. Press the dough together to seal, pushing air out as you work around the edge. Repeat with the remaining dumplings.

- 1 teaspoon crushed red pepper flakes
- 1 teaspoon kosher salt
- Freshly ground black pepper
- 40 round dumpling (potsticker/gyoza) wrappers
- Vegetable or peanut oil

4 **Fry the dumplings.** Heat ¼ inch of oil in a heavy-bottomed skillet with a lid over medium-high heat. Fry the dumplings in batches until golden on the bottom, about 3 minutes. Add 1 ice cube, then quickly put the lid on the pan to steam the dumplings until tender, about 4 minutes. Transfer to a plate. Serve with the soy dipping sauce. Store any extra dipping sauce in the refrigerator.

tips! These dumplings work well with beef or ground dark meat chicken. ■ These are great for a partial fry and steam. In a medium pan with a lid, heat 1 tablespoon oil over medium-high heat until hot, then add the dumplings. Cook until golden on the bottom, about 4 minutes. Add 2 ice cubes and quickly cover with the lid to steam for 4 to 6 more minutes.

Saving money in the kitchen is always a benefit, especially if guests are coming over. Less money on food means a better booze budget! Stretching a more expensive ingredient over lots of small bites is one of the first ways I think of to stretch a dollar. In this recipe, a pound of ground meat rolls into several crowd-pleasing juicy meatballs studded with scallions and Parmesan. As an appetizer they're tasty enough with just a toothpick and a napkin square, sauce need not apply. If you want to make them into a meal, add a simple pasta, rice, or orzo tossed with pesto. **MAKES 40**

mini scallion and parmesan meatballs

1 pound ground beef chuck (80% meat, 20% fat)

3 ounces grated Parmesan cheese

2 garlic cloves, grated on a rasp or finely minced

2 scallions, finely chopped (white and green parts)

1 teaspoon Hungarian or hot paprika

1 egg, beaten

2 tablespoons sour cream

1 teaspoon kosher salt

½ cup panko

Freshly ground black pepper

1 **Season the beef.** Break up the beef into small chunks and put them in a large bowl. Sprinkle the Parmesan cheese, garlic, scallions, and paprika over the entire bowl. In a small bowl, combine the egg, sour cream, and salt, and whisk until the salt is dissolved. Stir in the panko and pepper. Pour the mixture over the beef and gently mix into the beef with one hand, using your fingers like a pitchfork.

2 **Make the meatballs.** Divide the meat into quarters and make 10 mini meatballs per quarter, for a total of 40. Refrigerate the meatballs on a large plate for 20 minutes. Preheat the oven to 375°F.

3 **Bake the meatballs.** Line a baking sheet with parchment paper and set the meatballs at least ½ inch apart on the sheet. Bake for 20 minutes. Remove and rest at least 10 minutes before inserting toothpicks to serve. Serve warm or at room temperature.

brooklyn is a mix of ethnic neighborhoods and foods. A beef patty in Flatbush is a *bureka* in Midwood or a *pastelillo de carne* in Sunset Park. I've lived in all three neighborhoods and love all versions of what is basically ground beef spiced, then folded into a pastry and fried or baked. In Sunset Park, I often get these at a late-night street vendor just a few blocks from my place. My recipe combines traditional Jamaican beef patty flavors with additions of my own. **MAKES 12 TO 14**

brooklyn beef patties

1 tablespoon olive oil

1 medium russet potato, diced

½ small onion, finely chopped

2 garlic cloves, grated on a rasp or finely minced

½ pound ground beef chuck (80% meat, 20% fat)

½ teaspoon ground cumin

½ teaspoon curry powder

½ teaspoon chili powder

¼ teaspoon allspice

¼ teaspoon dried thyme

Pinch of cinnamon

1 teaspoon kosher salt

Freshly ground black pepper

½ cup corn kernels

14 6-inch empanada wrappers

Vegetable or peanut oil, for deep frying

tip! Dip the fork in flour or oil if it sticks to the pastry. Use a sliding-out motion to release it.

1 **Cook the potatoes.** Heat the olive oil in a large pan over medium-high heat. When warm, add the potatoes. When golden on one side, toss in the onion. Sauté until softened, about 3 minutes. Add the garlic and cook until fragrant, just 1 minute more. Transfer with a slotted spoon to a plate or bowl.

2 **Cook the beef.** In that pan, combine the beef, cumin, curry, chili powder, allspice, thyme, cinnamon, salt, and a few grinds of pepper. Cook, stirring often to break up the beef, until it browns, about 10 minutes. Remove from the heat and stir in the corn and reserved potato-onion mixture. Let cool.

3 **Assemble the patties.** When the beef filling is cool to the touch, work with 1 wrapper at a time and scoop 2 heaping tablespoons of filling into the center, then fold the dough over to form a half circle. Press out the air with your fingertips, from the filled sides to the edges. Press the tines of a fork along the edges to seal, creating a border about ½ inch wide. Repeat with more filling and wrappers.

4 **Fry the patties.** In a large pot or deep fryer, heat 4 inches of oil to 360°F. so the oil rests at 350°F. when the patties are added. In batches of 2 or 3, fry until golden brown, 4 to 6 minutes for each batch. Allow the oil to rise to 360°F. before beginning a new batch. Transfer the patties to a paper towel–lined plate. Serve warm or at room temperature.

I have a small but coveted backyard in Brooklyn and during my first year there, I spent sweaty days out back turning soil and picking weeds. I'd take a beer break when the going got tough and make lunch. I made these wraps one day and repeated them a few days in a row, which for me is the sign of a great new recipe! The overnight marinade really intensifies the flavors, but in a pinch, this can marinate on the counter for just two hours before you grill it. This sandwich, alongside some pork rinds and a beer (or two), fueled the cleanup and planting efforts. Now every summer I break out this wrap for a little backyard snack, whether I'm planting or lounging. **MAKES 4**

southwestern carne asada wraps

FOR THE BEEF

- 1 **pound thinly sliced top round beef**
- 1 **packet (about 1¼ teaspoons) Sazon seasoning**
- 1 **tablespoon ground cumin**
- 1 **tablespoon hot sauce (I like Frank's Red Hot)**
- 1 **tablespoon olive oil**
- 2 **scallions, finely chopped (white and green parts)**
- 2 **garlic cloves, smashed**
  Kosher salt and freshly ground black pepper
- 1 **tablespoon fresh lime juice**

1 **Marinate the beef.** In a resealable plastic bag combine the beef, Sazon, cumin, hot sauce, olive oil, scallions, garlic, a pinch of salt, and a few grinds of pepper. Tightly seal the bag, pressing out as much air as possible. Squish it around a bit to mix the seasonings and coat the beef, then refrigerate overnight, or at least 6 hours. Two hours before you are ready to grill the beef, remove the bag from the refrigerator, give it a toss and rest the bag on the counter at room temperature.

2 **Grill the beef.** Heat a seasoned grill or grill pan to medium-high. Remove the beef from the bag and shake off any excess marinade. Place the beef on the grill and cook on one side until the beef releases, about 6 minutes. Flip, then cook just 3 to 4 minutes more. Transfer from the grill to a cutting board and let rest at least 15 minutes. Roughly chop, then sprinkle the lime juice over the pile of chopped beef. Set aside.

3 **Make the avocado spread.** In a large bowl, combine the avocado flesh, crema, cilantro, tomatoes, jalapeños, and jalapeño juice. Mash with a fork or potato masher until relatively smooth. Taste and season with a pinch of salt if needed.

4 **Assemble the wraps.** Make sure the tortilla wraps are pliable. If not, warm them in the oven at 100°F. to 200°F. or zap them for a few seconds in the microwave. Place a tortilla wrap on a flat surface, layer several lettuce leaves along the center of each without going over the edges, and sprinkle with cilantro. Dollop a quarter of the avocado spread in a row along the center of the wrap, then top with a quarter of the beef and another layer of lettuce. Tuck in both sides with your hands, then fold the side closest to you over the filling and away from you, while tucking the filling under the tortilla flap. Be sure to keep the lettuce as a barrier between the wrap and the beef or spread as you roll it up. Secure with a toothpick or wrap tightly in parchment paper, then slice. Serve at room temperature or chilled.

FOR THE AVOCADO SPREAD

2 ripe avocados

¼ cup Mexican crema

½ cup chopped fresh cilantro

2 Roma tomatoes, seeded and finely chopped

6 to 8 pickled jalapeño slices, chopped

2 tablespoons pickled jalapeño juice

Kosher salt

FOR THE WRAPS

4 10-inch tortilla wraps (spinach wraps are fun if you can find them)

1 head Boston or Bibb lettuce, cleaned, leaves separated and patted dry

½ cup chopped fresh cilantro

I like to start the grilling season by trying something new. I grill outside year round, even in the snow, with my trusted tiny grill. Ground lamb is perfect for kabobs and I often make these instead of burgers because it's easier to mingle and chat with food on a stick. Plus they taste great in a grilled flatbread with plenty of char and a drizzle of cucumber mint sauce.

SERVES 4 TO 6; MAKES 2½ CUPS SAUCE

ground lamb kabobs
WITH CUCUMBER MINT SAUCE

FOR THE KABOBS

12 6-inch wooden skewers, soaked in water for 30 minutes

1½ pounds ground lamb

2 scallions, finely chopped (white and green parts)

2 teaspoons onion powder

2 teaspoons chopped fresh oregano leaves

1 teaspoon chopped fresh rosemary leaves

1 teaspoon garlic powder

1 teaspoon ground cumin

½ teaspoon dried thyme

1½ teaspoons kosher salt

Freshly ground black pepper

Vegetable oil, for brushing

At least 6 loaves flatbread

1 **Mix the lamb.** In a large bowl combine the lamb, scallions, onion powder, oregano, rosemary, garlic powder, cumin, thyme, salt, and a few grinds of black pepper. Form meat around the skewers, making an oblong shape, 4 to 6 inches long, pressing and securing firmly. Place on a parchment-lined tray and rest at room temperature for 30 minutes.

2 **Make the sauce.** In a food processor, combine the yogurt, mint, cucumber, garlic, hot sauce, paprika, honey, lemon zest, and lemon juice. Blend until smooth, then taste and season with salt and pepper. Refrigerate for at least 30 minutes before serving.

3 **Grill the kabobs and flatbread.** Heat the grill to high and brush or drizzle the kabobs with oil and grill until charred on the outside and cooked, medium rare, turning only once, about 3 minutes on each side. Transfer from the grill to a plate, cover loosely with aluminum foil, and rest for 10 minutes. Brush the flatbread lightly with oil and grill on both sides until warm and charred. Remove the lamb kabobs from the skewers and place 1 or 2 on each piece of bread breaking into chunks. Drizzle with sauce and serve folded like a soft taco.

tips! Instead of forming the meat on a skewer, shape it into burgers and use the sauce to top them like ketchup.
■ Chop leftover kabobs and toss them and the sauce with couscous or rice.

FOR THE SAUCE

2 cups whole-milk Greek yogurt

½ cup loosely packed mint

1 6- to 8-inch cucumber, seeded and diced into small cubes

1 garlic clove, grated on a rasp or finely minced

2½ teaspoons hot sauce (I like Frank's Red Hot)

½ teaspoon sweet paprika

2 teaspoons honey

Grated zest of 1 lemon

1 teaspoon fresh lemon juice

Kosher salt and freshly ground black pepper

burger with a surprise of gooey cheese inside sets this recipe off on a good start, then I top it with my equivalent of candy. Roasted garlic and onions are truly sweet and I twirl them with pasta and spread them on crostini and steaks, so why not pile them high on a juicy burger with a secret. Make these for the perfect summer cookout with friends or even cook them indoors. The liquid smoke guarantees that no matter what, they'll taste and smell like summertime.

MAKES 4

gouda-stuffed burgers

WITH ROASTED GARLIC AND ONIONS

FOR THE GARLIC AND ONIONS

- 20 garlic cloves, ends trimmed
- 20 pearl onions, halved
- ½ teaspoon kosher salt
- Olive oil, to cover

FOR THE BURGERS

- 1½ pounds ground beef chuck (80% meat, 20% fat)
- 1 tablespoon Worcestershire sauce
- 1½ teaspoons liquid smoke, hickory scent
- 1½ teaspoons kosher salt
- Freshly ground black pepper
- 4 sesame seed hamburger buns
- 8 ounces smoked gouda cheese, shredded

1 **Roast the garlic and onions.** Preheat oven to 375°F. In a small ramekin or oven dish add the garlic, onions, salt, and enough olive oil to just cover them. Roast uncovered until golden brown and tender, about 20 to 24 minutes. Remove from the oven and using a slotted spoon, transfer the garlic and onions to a paper towel-lined plate. Reserve the oil for many uses, including toasting the buns below.

2 **Season the beef.** In a large bowl break up the beef and sprinkle the Worcestershire sauce, liquid smoke, salt, and pepper over the top. With your less dominant hand, gently mix the entire bowl using pitchfork fingers.

3 **Form the patties.** Either use a gadget made for stuffed burgers, placing 2 ounces of gouda in the center, or make 8 thin patties and place 2 ounces of cheese between the center of 2 patties. Press and crimp the ends to seal. Let rest at room temperature for 20 minutes.

continues

4 **Grill the patties and toast the buns.** Preheat a grill to medium-high heat. Pour some of the reserved roasting oil in a small bowl and brush the insides of each hamburger bun with oil, then the top of each patty as well. Place the burgers on the grill, oiled side down and cook until the burgers release, about 5 minutes. Flip only once and cook on the other side until it reaches the desired doneness. Remove the burgers from the grill to a plate and cover with aluminum foil for 5 minutes. Meanwhile, place the buns on the grill, oiled side down and toast until golden, about 2 minutes each.

5 **Assemble the burgers.** Place a patty on each bottom half of the buns, then top with a heaping portion of the roasted garlic and onions. Top with the other bun half and eat.

In the mid-1980s, we took a family road trip to Denmark to see tulips and Legoland. For lunch, I ordered a grilled cheese and it wasn't Mom's, with white bread and American cheese. It was crusty, toasted brioche slices, and gooey mozzarella cheese, served with a squirt of ketchup on the side. It blew my mind! This is also great with my Fastest Chunky Tomato Cream Soup (page 99). **MAKES 4**

pepper jack grilled cheese

FOR THE TOMATOES

2 Roma tomatoes, sliced ¼ inch thick

1 tablespoon olive oil

Kosher salt and freshly ground black pepper

FOR THE CILANTRO MIX

¼ cup chopped fresh cilantro

¼ cup chopped red onion

Grated zest of 1 lime

Kosher salt

FOR THE SANDWICHES

8 slices stale white bread

6 tablespoons salted butter, room temperature

8 1-ounce slices pepper Jack cheese

1 **Season and roast the tomatoes.** Preheat the oven to 400°F. Place the tomatoes on a baking sheet lined with nonstick aluminum foil or parchment paper and drizzle with olive oil. Sprinkle with salt and pepper, then roast until they begin to darken and caramelize on the edges, about 20 minutes. Remove and let cool, then gently chop.

2 **Make the cilantro mix.** On a cutting board, pile the cilantro, onion, lime zest, and a pinch of salt, then chop vigorously until fine and well combined.

3 **Assemble the sandwiches.** Preheat a griddle over medium-high heat. Butter one side of each piece of bread. Place 4 slices on the griddle, buttered side down. Add a slice of cheese to each. Evenly sprinkle the cilantro-onion mixture and the tomatoes over the slices. Finish with another layer of cheese, then add the second piece of bread, buttered side up.

4 **Grill the sandwiches.** Check the bottom of the sandwich. If golden brown and the cheese is melting, gently flip. Reduce the heat if the bread is toasting too fast and the cheese has yet to melt. Remove after the second flip when the bottom shows golden brown and fully melted cheese, 4 to 6 minutes total. Transfer to a cutting board and let rest for 1 minute. Cut in half and serve.

⊥his is a fast and pretty tart. I love pesto and think a quick basil pesto should be in every cook's repertoire. It's perfect with pasta or on garlic bread, and here it's a great match with roasted tomatoes. Buying the piecrust makes this perfect for a potluck or invited guests. Shortcuts like that leave you more time to tidy up your place—or enjoy cook's treats and a coffee for the long night before guests arrive.

MAKES TWO 9-INCH ROUND TARTS OR THREE 14 × 4½-INCH RECTANGULAR TARTS

tomato and pesto tarts

FOR THE TARTS

- 2 premade piecrusts
- Nonstick cooking spray
- 10 to 12 ripe Roma tomatoes, sliced ¼-inch thick
- 2 tablespoons olive oil
- Kosher salt and black pepper
- ¼ cup grated Parmesan cheese, for garnish

FOR THE PESTO

- 1 bunch flat-leaf or curly parsley, roughly chopped (1 lightly packed cup), including stems
- 1 bunch basil, roughly chopped (1 lightly packed cup), including stems
- 10 sprigs fresh thyme, leaves stripped
- 4 garlic cloves
- ½ cup grated Parmesan cheese
- ½ cup almond slivers
- Grated zest of 2 lemons
- 2 tablespoons fresh lemon juice

1 Set the crusts. Unroll and press the piecrusts into two 9-inch tart pans. If using rectangular pans, just trim one-third of each crust and press the pieces together to fit. Then, use your pointer finger to press the dough into the sides of the tart pan. Use a knife to remove the excess crust along the top edges and discard the scraps. Using a fork, prick the bottom of the crust a few times to allow for venting (maybe 3 pricks per quadrant). Chill for 30 minutes. Preheat the oven to 425°F.

2 Prebake the crusts. Spray the shiny side of 2 pieces of aluminum foil with a bit of nonstick spray and press into the tart shells, sprayed side down. Fill with dried beans or pie weights and bake until the edges are golden and the sides are set, about 15 minutes. Remove the foil and beans and bake another 10 to 12 minutes, until cooked through. Remove from the oven and allow to cool to room temperature. Reduce the oven temperature to 375°F.

3 Make the pesto. Blend the parsley, basil, thyme, garlic, Parmesan, almonds, lemon zest, and lemon juice in a food processor until the ingredients resemble a rough paste. Taste the pesto and season with salt and pepper, if needed. To finish, slowly drizzle the olive oil into the feed tube while blending.

4 **Assemble and bake the tarts.** Divide the pesto equally and, using a rubber spatula, evenly spread it over the bottom of each prepared crust. Starting around the outer edges, place the tomatoes over the pesto, overlapping each slice slightly as you move around the tart pan. Then make a smaller circle of overlapping slices within the starter ring. Continue until the entire pan is covered in circles of tomato slices. Repeat for the second tart. Drizzle 1 table-spoon olive oil over the top of each tart and sprinkle with a pinch of salt and a few grinds of black pepper. Bake for 40 to 45 minutes, or until the tomatoes appear roasted in texture and the edges of the crust are golden brown. If the dough browns too quickly, tent the edges with foil.

5 **Garnish the tarts and serve.** Remove the tarts from their rings and sprinkle Parmesan on top. Serve warm, at room temperature, or cold.

Kosher salt and freshly ground black pepper

¼ cup olive oil

tips! Have a nut allergy? A great substitute for the texture and nutty flavor they provide in pesto is corn tortillas. Shallow-fry a few of them in an equal amount of unsalted butter and oil until they are a deep golden color, darker than tortilla chips. Let them cool on a paper towel–lined plate, then chop them down and measure them as you would the nuts in the recipe. ■ Leftover pesto is great on toasted baguettes, mixed into ground meat for burgers, scrambled into eggs, and of course tossed with pasta.

I love spinach and artichoke dip served with toasty bread for dipping. I started stuffing baguettes a couple of years ago when I found a good local bakery with crusty and uniformly rounded baguettes. This is perfect for a party, road trip, or day in the park because it's easy to prep the day before and is tasty at any temperature. I either bake, then chill it overnight to serve at room temperature the next day, or save baking for the day I need it and serve the slices warm.

MAKES 16 TO 20 1-INCH SLICES

spinach and artichoke–stuffed baguette slices

FOR THE FILLING

¼ cup chopped walnuts

2 demi baguettes (see Note)

½ cup crumbled tomato and basil–flavored feta cheese

1 cup grated Parmesan cheese

FOR THE VEGETABLES

¼ cup olive oil

1 cup chopped artichoke hearts (canned in water)

3 cups tightly packed baby spinach

¼ teaspoon chili powder

⅛ teaspoon grated nutmeg (5 or 6 scrapes of fresh nutmeg on a rasp)

1 **Toast the walnuts.** Heat a dry sauté pan over medium heat. Toss the walnuts in the hot pan until fragrant and a test bite is soft, warm, and a bit chewy. Transfer the walnuts to a large bowl (large enough to hold the filling) to cool. Preheat the oven to 350°F.

2 **Sauté the vegetables.** In the same pan, heat 2 tablespoons of the oil over medium heat. When the oil begins to swirl a bit, add the artichokes, spinach, chili powder, and nutmeg. Using tongs, toss until the spinach is wilted, about 5 minutes. Add to the bowl with the walnuts and allow to cool.

3 **Prepare the baguettes.** With a serrated knife, cut about 2 inches off one end of each baguette and reserve. Use the knife to hollow out the inside of each baguette, leaving just ⅛ inch of bread as a shell. Be careful to not puncture the outside of the bread from the inside while hollowing each baguette. Save the bread for bread crumbs.

continues

Note: If using a regulation-sized baguette instead of demi baguettes, cut it in half or in thirds to make it easy to hollow out. Leave the ends intact and, in the absence of trimmed ends to plug the fillings, just tightly wrap each baguette section. Also, whether using demi or standard baguettes, pick out ones that are more rounded than flat, so they're easier to stuff.

4 **Combine the filling.** Add the feta and Parmesan cheese to the large bowl. Stir to combine. Give a taste (cook's treat); everything should be salty enough courtesy of the cheese.

5 **Stuff and bake the baguettes.** Use a spoon to stuff each baguette with the filling, then use the handle of a wooden spoon or something similar to pack the stuffing in tight. When done with each, invert the untrimmed, tapered end of each baguette into the open end to seal in the filling. Tightly wrap each baguette in aluminum foil and bake for 25 minutes. Remove from the oven and raise the temperature to 400°F. Open the aluminum foil and brush both baguettes with the remaining oil. Return to the oven uncovered and cook until golden, 5 to 8 more minutes.

6 **Rest, slice, and serve.** Allow the baguettes to cool until just warm. Using a serrated knife, cut 1-inch slices along the length of each baguette. If transporting the baguettes to a party, keep the slices in the form of a baguette and wrap them back up in the same aluminum foil. These are also great cold or at room temperature. Feel free to slice, cool completely, then rewrap and refrigerate.

this is simplicity and flavor combined. Plus it's real easy on the eyes. I make this mostly for dinner guests, because it's so easy it almost shouldn't be a recipe. It comes together very quickly as well, so I love having as an option for last-minute planning. Here I serve it with bread slices; you could also scoop a few tomatoes and a bit of cheese to mash into rice or potatoes, or just pile everything on top of a juicy steak. **SERVES 4 TO 6**

vine-on roasted tomatoes and goat cheese

½ cup goat cheese

20 to 24 vine-on cherry tomatoes

¼ cup olive oil, for drizzling

½ teaspoon garlic powder

1 teaspoon dried basil

Kosher salt and freshly ground black pepper

1 loaf of crusty, chewy bread, cut into ¼-inch slices

1 **Assemble the dish.** Preheat the oven to 400°F. In an ovenproof dish, distribute dollops of goat cheese. Keeping the vines and tomatoes intact, place them over the goat cheese, pushing them down into the cheese to make them level. Drizzle with olive oil and sprinkle with the garlic powder, basil, a nice pinch of salt, and a few grinds of black pepper.

2 **Roast and serve.** Place the dish in the oven and roast until the tomato skins begin to blister, 30 to 35 minutes. Scoop out a bit of oil, cheese, and tomato and spread on bread slices. Enjoy!

SOUPS & SALADS

Things in a bowl. Really, that's what this is all about. I have to fess up, if I'm at home by myself, I don't set the table, I just hang out on the couch and enjoy dinner while watching television. I don't even pull out the TV tables. I think that's why I make so many sauces—if it's drippy, it belongs in a bowl, and cradling a big bowl of something is so comforting. I can bring it up to my chest and just scoop away. Every culture has its own version of a restorative soup, and I've included some hearty, cold-curing flavors I've picked up with each move. Chili from Detroit, ramen from Korea and Brooklyn combined, and of course, chicken soup.

On the lighter side are the salads, also perfect for piling into a bowl and enjoying their texture and personality. These too bring me comfort. Feel free to take these recipes from the couch to the dinner buffet for guests and to work for lunch. I hope you're also inspired to visit a farmers' market. I sometimes visit mine in the summer; it was a benefit to moving into my neighborhood, fresh produce just blocks away. Get inspired by what is in season and if that doesn't work, take a look in your grocer's freezer section. Grandma Williams taught me, it sometimes holds better produce than you can find in season. Picked fresh or frozen, ready for your bowl.

Spicy Spinach Panzanella (PAGE 115)

I was introduced to big, hot bowls of spicy noodle soup during my year in Korea. Each restaurant had its own blend of ingredients, and many would have a huge pot of soup cooking out front on the sidewalk. So you could stroll along all of the storefronts to see what was cooking, then go inside to eat whatever looked good to you—way more inviting than a printed menu in the window. Now, in my Brooklyn 'hood, just six blocks away is a Vietnamese place that makes the best pho, their version of spicy noodle soup. Being a short walk from my soup pharmacist is quite a dream. I've adapted this soup to make at home. After all, cold weather sometimes means staying in and playing video games all day, right? And don't underestimate the lime wedge on the side; it cuts the oil and the heat. This is a dish that's spicy with no apologies. **SERVES 4 TO 6**

spicy noodle bowl

FOR THE SEASONING BASE

2 tablespoons olive oil

2 Vidalia onions, chopped

1 teaspoon ground fennel

1 teaspoon ground cardamom

2 teaspoons crushed red pepper flakes

1-inch piece of fresh ginger, skin removed, grated on a rasp

Kosher salt and freshly ground black pepper

2 garlic cloves, grated on a rasp or finely minced

½ cup sriracha hot chili sauce

1 **Cook the seasoning base.** In a large pot over medium heat, combine the oil, onions, fennel, cardamom, red pepper flakes, ginger, a nice pinch of salt, and few grinds of black pepper. Cook until the onions are tender and fragrant, 8 to 10 minutes. Add the garlic and cook another 5 minutes, being careful to not brown the garlic. Add the sriracha and cook, stirring, until it turns a deep reddish brown, about 5 minutes more.

2 **Add the broth and noodles.** Add the broth to the seasoning base and bring to a boil, then reduce to a simmer and cook for 15 minutes. In a separate large pot, prepare the noodles as directed on the package. Strain in a colander and rinse under cold water until the water runs clear. Shake off the excess water and add them to the simmering soup pot; simmer to reheat the noodles, about 2 minutes.

continues

6 cups beef broth

2 pounds rice noodles

1 pound flank steak or tri tip, frozen for 20 minutes, then sliced as thin as possible

3 scallions, finely chopped (white and green parts)

FOR THE EGGS (OPTIONAL)

4 to 6 tablespoons unsalted butter

4 to 6 large eggs

FOR THE GARNISH

1 bunch Thai basil, leaves only

1 bunch cilantro, leaves only

1 bunch bean sprouts

4 limes, cut into wedges

3 **Make the eggs (optional).** In a small pan over medium heat, melt 1 tablespoon of butter without browning it. Crack 1 egg in the center and raise the heat slightly. Cook until the white is set and the yolk is still runny, about 5 minutes. Transfer to a plate and repeat the process for the rest of the eggs.

4 **Finish the soup.** Add the beef and scallions to the pot and stir until the beef is almost cooked through. Depending on how thin your beef slices are, this should take 4 to 6 minutes. Serve hot in a soup bowl topped with an egg, if using, and some Thai basil, cilantro, bean sprouts, and a lime wedge on the side. Add these garnishes to the bowl as you eat the soup or all at once, squeezing the lime juice over the top and stirring it in.

tips! Broth is important to use here instead of stock. Stock is made with veggies, bones, and trim. Broth is made with the same including actual pieces of meat. Broth has slightly a richer flavor, which is perfect for this minimal ingredient soup. ■ Swap shredded rotisserie chicken and chicken stock for the beef and beef broth to change this to a chicken soup. ■ If you're planning to enjoy this on a second or third day, store the noodles in a separate airtight container or plastic bag in the refrigerator. Then, when making future servings, add them back to the soup halfway through the reheating process.

I think I had potatoes every way you can have them when we lived in Germany—even something called *kartoffel küchen,* or potato cake. It was like a coffee cake topped with tons of streusel, but the cake part was potato based. German food really is all about meat and potatoes. Because of that and likely the DNA from my dad, I'm a real meat and potatoes girl and truly love a good potato soup. I've had some gloppy ones and still devoured them because I just truly love potatoes. This is how to make a sack of potatoes look good and taste delicious. **SERVES 4 TO 6**

Digging in to knackwurst and pommes frites, one of several German meat and potato combos. **(Bad Kreuznach, Germany, 1986)**

potato and leek soup

- 4 strips bacon, cut into 1-inch pieces
- 1 tablespoon unsalted butter
- 2 cups chopped onions
- 3 leeks, trimmed, rinsed, and chopped
  Kosher salt and freshly ground black pepper
- 4 garlic cloves, smashed
- 1 tablespoon dry mustard
- 8 sprigs fresh thyme
- 1 pound russet potatoes, peeled and cut into 1-inch cubes
- 2 cups chicken stock
- 1 cup heavy cream
- 2 scallions, finely chopped (white and green parts), for garnish

1 Crisp the bacon. In a large pot over medium heat, cook the bacon until the fat is rendered. Transfer with a slotted spoon to a paper towel–lined plate, leaving the rendered fat in the pot.

2 Sweat the veggies. In the same pot, add the butter, onions, leeks, a nice pinch of salt, and a few grinds of pepper. Cook until the onions and leeks are tender, 8 to 10 minutes. Add the garlic, mustard, and thyme and cook until the garlic is tender and the pot smells good, 6 to 8 minutes.

3 Finish the soup. Add the potatoes and stock. Raise the heat and bring the soup to a boil, then reduce to a simmer and cook until the potatoes are fork tender, 14 to 16 minutes total. Remove the thyme sprigs. Turn off the heat and blitz with an immersion blender, leaving a few chunks. Stir in the heavy cream and return the heat to low, cooking for just a few minutes more to reheat the soup. Serve warm, garnished with scallions and the reserved bacon.

Instead of chicken soup for my soul, I do chowder. Chowder is fun because it can have plenty of personality and chunky goodness. That means less detail on the chopping and more detail on the chomping. Chunks of juicy dark meat, plump hominy kernels, and knobs of potato all fighting for room on my spoon with each scoop is why I love this recipe. And the secret is out: dark meat is really flavorful. Not only is this soup comforting, but it also comes together faster than old-school chicken soup, and if you're under the weather, that means less time outside of your blanket cocoon. **SERVES 4 TO 6**

chunky chicken chowder

4 chicken thighs, bone in, skin removed

Kosher salt and freshly ground black pepper

¼ cup (½ stick) unsalted butter

1 tablespoon vegetable or olive oil

1 cup roughly chopped Vidalia or sweet onions

10 to 12 sprigs fresh thyme, tied in a bundle

2 bay leaves

4 garlic cloves, grated on a rasp or finely minced

1 quart chicken stock

2 russet potatoes, peeled and cut into bite-sized cubes

8 ounces white hominy, drained if from the can and thawed if frozen

2 tablespoons all-purpose flour

2 cups whole milk

1 cup heavy cream

1 lemon, cut into wedges

1 **Prepare the chicken.** Cut the flaps from the thighs and cube the meat, leaving some meat on the bone. Season the chicken with salt and pepper. Heat 2 tablespoons of the butter and all the oil in a stockpot over medium-high heat. When the butter is melted and the oil hot, add the thigh bones and cubed meat. Brown on all sides, 8 to 10 minutes. Use tongs or a slotted spoon to transfer all the meat, bones included, to a plate.

2 **Sweat the veggies.** Reduce the heat slightly and add the onion, thyme, bay leaves, a pinch of salt, and a few grinds of pepper. Cook until the onion is tender, about 5 minutes. Add the garlic and cook, stirring, until the garlic smells great but isn't browned, 2 to 4 minutes.

3 **Build the soup.** Stir the chicken and bones back into the pot and add the stock. Bring the soup to a boil, then reduce and simmer for 20 minutes. Add the potatoes, hominy, and another pinch of salt. Bring to a boil, then reduce the heat to a simmer and cook until the potatoes are tender, 20 to 25 minutes more, depending on how small you chopped them.

4 **Finish the soup.** Use tongs to fish out the thyme sprigs and bay leaves. In a small bowl or plastic bag, make a paste with the remaining 2 tablespoons butter and the flour. Reduce the heat and add the milk, cream, and flour paste in bits. Bring the soup to a simmer and stir to make sure the flour paste breaks up as the soup cooks. When the soup thickens, 6 to 8 minutes, taste and season with salt if needed. Serve with bones included in the bowls for nibbling and a wedge of lemon to spritz over the soup.

Although canned tomato soup has been the de facto spouse of grilled cheese for years, have you looked at the sodium content on those cans lately? I sure never thought about it as a kid, devouring this combo on many occasions while watching an after-school special on TV. So I say give this a go; a homemade soup is easy and tastes way better, plus you might have leftovers—more than I can say for the can. Pair this with my Pepper Jack Grilled Cheese, page 81, or my Maple Bacon and Chicken Quesadilla, page 62. **SERVES 4 TO 6**

fastest chunky tomato cream soup

1 tablespoon olive oil

½ cup chopped Vidalia onion

8 to 10 sprigs fresh thyme

1 teaspoon sweet paprika

1 serrano pepper, seeded and chopped

Kosher salt and freshly ground black pepper

2 garlic cloves, smashed

1 tablespoon plus 1 teaspoon tomato paste

8 Roma tomatoes, cut into big chunks

1 quart chicken stock

½ cup heavy cream, at room temperature

tip! If using a blender, remove a few chunks of tomato from the pot with a slotted spoon and set aside. Blitz the remaining soup in batches, filling the blender only a third of the way with soup. Any more than that and the blender could burst with pressure upon blending. Be safe! It's hot! Return the blended soup and reserved tomato chunks back to the pot and serve warm.

1 Sweat the veggies. In a stockpot over medium heat, combine the olive oil, onion, thyme, paprika, serrano pepper, a pinch of salt, and a few grinds of black pepper. Stir with a wooden spoon and cook until the onion is tender but not browned, 5 to 8 minutes. Add the garlic and tomato paste, stirring to coat everything in the pot. Cook, stirring, over medium heat until the paste turns a deep red color, 8 to 10 more minutes.

2 Cook the tomatoes. Add the tomato chunks and bring to a simmer. Cook, stirring the tomatoes to ensure a bit of that moisture evaporates, but they don't burn. Cook this way until the tomatoes are tender and the skins are peeling off, about 5 minutes.

3 Finish the soup. Add the chicken stock and bring to a boil, then reduce to a simmer and cook for just 10 more minutes. Remove the pot from the heat and, using tongs, remove the thyme. Using an immersion blender, blitz the soup in the pot, leaving a few chunks of tomato for texture. Return to low heat and slowly stir in the cream. Serve warm.

I do believe chili can cure a cold just like chicken soup. In Detroit, snow always seemed so sudden and brutal, laying a blanket of white over the city. At the first snow, I'd hop in my truck and circle the parking lot of the National Coney Island diner, waiting for a plowed parking space. I ordered the same thing every time: "Large fries and bowl of chili with onions, cheese, and mustard, please." I make a number of chilis and this one's a favorite. It's already chunky from the beef, and then in a moment of fall inspiration I glanced at a butternut squash and decided to give it a try. The squash soaks up the flavor and adds texture in this chili. It's hearty and it's perfect to make a day before the big game or at the first sign of a cold spell. **SERVES 6 TO 8**

beefy butternut squash chili

FOR THE SEASONING BLEND

- 1 tablespoon ground cumin
- 1 tablespoon chili powder
- 1 teaspoon pumpkin pie spice
- 2 teaspoons dried oregano
- 2 teaspoons kosher salt
  Freshly ground black pepper

FOR THE CHILI

- 3 tablespoons olive oil
- 1 pound beef chuck or stewing beef, cut into 1-inch cubes
- 1 cup finely chopped Vidalia or sweet onions
- 1 red bell pepper, seeded and chopped
- 3 garlic cloves, grated on a rasp or finely minced
- 3 tablespoons tomato paste
- 2 tablespoons hot sauce

1 **Make the seasoning blend.** In a small bowl, combine the cumin, chili powder, pumpkin pie spice, oregano, salt, and a few grinds of black pepper. Set aside.

2 **Sear the beef.** Heat the olive oil in a large pot over high heat until it begins to swirl. Add the beef cubes and sprinkle with half of the seasoning blend. Cook, stirring intermittently, until the beef is browned on all sides but not cooked through, about 5 minutes. Remove the beef chunks with a slotted spoon and set on a plate.

3 **Build the flavor.** Reduce the heat to medium and add the onions, bell pepper, garlic, tomato paste, and hot sauce. Cook, stirring, until everything turns a dark reddish brown, about 10 minutes.

4 **Complete the chili.** Add the ground beef and sprinkle with the remaining half of the seasoning blend. Cook, stirring, until the beef is browned, then add the reserved beef chunks back to the pot along with the cornmeal, stock, wine, and squash. Bring to a boil, then reduce to a simmer and cook until the chili is thick and the liquid reduced, 40 to 50 minutes. Taste and season with another pinch of salt if needed, but the seasoning blend you've made should have this tasting perfect for you. If using cinnamon, add the stick 20 minutes before the chili is done, then remove before serving. Serve warm.

(I like Frank's Red Hot here)

1 pound ground beef chuck (80% meat, 20% fat)

2 tablespoons fine cornmeal

1½ cups beef stock

1½ cups red wine (any inexpensive chianti will do)

1 butternut squash, peeled, seeded, and cut into ½-inch cubes

Kosher salt

1 cinnamon stick (optional)

tip! If you don't have butternut squash, substitute 2 or 3 sweet potatoes for equally tasty results.

tips! Make meatball soup using 1 pound of ground beef (80% meat, 20% fat) and the same amount of seasoning as you would for the steak. Roll meatballs the size of golf balls and use the olive oil to pan-fry them over medium-high heat until golden on all sides. Then drop them in the soup to finish cooking. Jiggle, and don't stir the pot while cooking to avoid breaking up the meatballs.

This is a soup you can eat with a fork, then just tilt the bowl toward you to sip the rest. For such complex flavors, it's very simple to put together. I even made it once with leftover steak from a restaurant. Perfect for a winter day, it can actually stand alone as meal. **SERVES 4 TO 6**

steak and tortilla soup

FOR THE TORTILLA STRIPS

Peanut or vegetable oil

8 corn tortillas, sliced into ¼-inch strips

Kosher salt

FOR THE STEAK

2 teaspoons ground cumin

2 teaspoons garlic powder

1 teaspoon dried thyme

1 teaspoon kosher salt

1 teaspoon freshly ground black pepper

1 pound flank steak

1 tablespoon olive oil

FOR THE SOUP

2 to 3 tablespoons olive oil

½ cup chopped Vidalia or sweet onion

½ pound button mushrooms, sliced

1 garlic clove, minced

1 quart beef broth

¼ cup sliced pickled jalapeños

1 cup canned crushed tomatoes, juices included

11 ounces baby spinach

1 **Fry the tortilla strips.** Heat at least 2 inches of oil in a pot or deep fryer until it reaches 360°F. Fry the tortilla strips in batches until golden brown and crisp, 3 to 4 minutes per batch. Maintain the frying temperature at 350°F., allowing it to come back to 360°F. between batches. Transfer to a paper towel–lined plate and sprinkle with salt.

2 **Season and rest the beef.** In a small bowl, combine the cumin, garlic powder, thyme, salt, and pepper. Rub the spice blend over all of the steak and drizzle with the olive oil. Let rest at room temperature for about 15 minutes.

3 **Start the soup.** In a large pot, heat 2 tablespoons olive oil over medium heat. Add the onion and sauté until tender, about 4 minutes. Stir in the mushrooms and garlic and sauté until the mushrooms are tender, adding extra oil if needed. Pour in the broth, jalapeños, and tomatoes. Bring to a boil, then reduce the heat and simmer for 15 minutes.

4 **Grill the steak.** Preheat a grill to medium-high. Sear the steak until golden brown on both sides, about 5 minutes per side. Place on a cutting board and let rest 10 minutes. Cut the beef against the grain into strips and add to the soup along with the spinach, stirring until the spinach wilts. Season to taste. Serve topped with the fried tortilla strips.

This soup is light and filling with minimal ingredients. Sometimes you just have to let the ingredients do the talking. Here, the hint of licorice flavor from the tarragon gets smoothed out by the heavy cream; then the lemon comes along and makes everything bright. It's a simple combination that tastes totally classy—five-star taste attainable in your kitchen. **SERVES 4 TO 6**

lemon and tarragon cream soup WITH GARLIC-PEPPER CROSTINI

2 tablespoons unsalted butter

1 cup finely chopped Vidalia onions

2 celery stalks, finely chopped

Kosher salt

2 garlic cloves, smashed

Grated zest of 2 lemons

6 to 8 fresh tarragon leaves

1 quart chicken stock

2 tablespoons fresh lemon juice

2 cups heavy cream

FOR THE CROSTINI

1 cup olive oil

4 garlic cloves, smashed

1 teaspoon kosher salt

1 tablespoon freshly ground black pepper

1 baguette, cut on the bias into ¼-inch slices

1 **Sweat the veggies.** Melt the butter in a large pot over medium heat. Add the onions, celery, and a pinch of salt. Stir and cook until the onions are tender, 6 to 8 minutes. Add the garlic, lemon zest, and tarragon and cook, stirring, until the garlic is tender and fragrant but not browned, about 5 minutes.

2 **Add the stock.** Add the chicken stock and lemon juice. Bring to a simmer and cook for just 5 minutes. Turn off the heat and remove the tarragon leaves. Using an immersion blender, blend the soup until smooth.

3 **Prep and bake the crostini.** Preheat the oven to 400°F. In a small pan over very low heat, combine the oil, garlic, salt, and pepper. Cook for 20 minutes or until a taste reveals the flavor of garlic and pepper. Season with more salt if desired. Brush both sides of each bread slice with the flavored oil and place on a baking sheet. Set the sheet in the center of the oven and bake the crostini until the edges are golden brown, 10 to 12 minutes.

4 **Finish the soup.** Add the heavy cream and bring to a simmer again for a few minutes. Taste the soup and season with salt, if needed. Serve warm with the crostini.

o me, squash is neutral. Sure it has flavor, but not so much that it can't be pushed around in the kitchen; I find it accepts flavor very easily. I'm in an area of Brooklyn that always has tomatillos on sale, so it was only a matter of time before I worked them into a soup instead of a salsa. Quite honestly, all I was thinking about was color. Green squash, green tangy tomatillos, green soup. It turned out pretty and tasty at the same time; score one for nature's color coordination. **SERVES 4**

zucchini and tomatillo soup

FOR THE ZUCCHINI

2 cups chopped zucchini flesh (about 4)

1 cup vegetable stock

2 garlic cloves, smashed

4 sprigs fresh thyme

Kosher salt

FOR THE TOMATILLOS

½ pound tomatillos (about 4), husked and cleaned

½ small red onion, cut in half again

2 tablespoons olive oil

Kosher salt and freshly ground black pepper

¼ cup fresh cilantro leaves, for garnish

1 **Cook the zucchini.** Preheat the oven to 400°F. In a medium pot, combine the zucchini, stock, garlic, thyme, and a pinch of salt. Bring to a simmer and cook 20 minutes. Remove the thyme and discard.

2 **Roast the tomatillos and onion.** Place the tomatillos and onion on a rimmed baking sheet and drizzle with olive oil. Toss with your hands to coat all sides, then season with a sprinkle of salt and freshly ground black pepper. Roast until golden but not charred, 20 to 24 minutes.

3 **Blend the soup.** Put the tomatillos and onion along with any remaining oil on the roasting sheet in a blender. Add a spoonful from the cooked zucchini mixture and blend until smooth. Add a few more scoops and blend, continuing until all of the pot contents are blended. Pour everything back into the pot and bring to a simmer for 5 minutes to serve warm or refrigerate to serve chilled. Garnish with cilantro.

When people say that kids hate Brussels sprouts, I feel like an outsider. I actually loved them growing up, and that was back when people just boiled them, maybe with some onions. For this recipe I love the sprouts in all their green crunchy glory. This came from making cabbage in a similar way and then one day thinking, wait a minute, Brussels sprouts are just tiny cabbages, so why not? I implore you to try this salad! I can eat the entire recipe in one sitting. This takes all of ten minutes to pull together. **SERVES 4**

crunchy-sweet brussels sprout salad

½ cup chopped walnuts

1 pound Brussels sprouts

2 tablespoons olive oil

½ cup chopped red onion

½ teaspoon grated nutmeg

Kosher salt and freshly ground black pepper

½ cup dried cranberries

1 Toast the walnuts. In a large dry skillet over medium heat, toast the walnuts, tossing them until fragrant and a test bite (cook's treat!) reveals a creamy texture, about 5 minutes. Transfer to a plate and reserve the pan.

2 Prepare the Brussels sprouts. Shred the Brussels sprouts by removing the core and thinly slicing or passing them through a food processor fitted with the slicing disc.

3 Cook the Brussels sprouts. Warm the olive oil in the same pan over medium-high heat until it begins to swirl. Add the Brussels sprouts, red onion, nutmeg, a pinch of salt, and a nice grind of pepper, to taste. Cook, stirring or tossing, until the Brussels sprouts are bright green and only slightly wilted, 2 to 3 minutes.

4 Finish the salad. Remove from the heat. Add the toasted walnuts and dried cranberries and toss to combine. Taste the salad and season with more salt if needed. Serve warm or chilled.

In my neighborhood, Sunset Park, Brooklyn, I look forward to the street food that appears each summer. More specifically, *elotes*, which is simply a word for corn. But in Sunset Park it comes grilled on a stick and loaded with toppings. Seeing elotes is more a sign of summer to me than any weather forecast. I order my grilled corn on the cob "con todo" (with everything). It gets slathered with mayo, coated with cotija cheese (a salty, crumbly cow's milk cheese), then hit with a sprinkle of cayenne pepper and, finally, a squirt of fresh lime juice. Some vendors will pile all the kernels and toppings for the corn into a cup with a spoon sticking out—then you don't need a toothpick! This salad is my nod to summertime, featuring my own version of "con todo." No toothpicks needed. **SERVES 4**

sunset park salad

2 carrots

4 ears fresh corn, shucked

2 heads Belgian endive, cut in half lengthwise

3 to 4 tablespoons olive oil

Kosher salt and freshly ground black pepper

1 bunch cilantro (about 3 ounces), leaves only

½ small red onion, thinly sliced

½ cup crumbled feta cheese

2 teaspoons fresh lime juice

½ teaspoon ground cumin

¼ teaspoon cayenne pepper, or to taste

tip! A great substitution for the endive is a heart of romaine lettuce cut into quarters lengthwise. Grill the romaine spears for the same time as you would the endive, until both cut sides are charred, then chop the same way as the endive.

1 **Grill the veggies.** Preheat a grill or grill pan to medium-high. Cut the carrots in half. Then cut the smaller end of the carrots into fourths lengthwise and the larger half into sixths or eighths. The key is to make all the spears about the same size. Place the carrot spears, corn, and endive on a baking sheet or cutting board and drizzle all sides with olive oil, then season with a pinch of salt and black pepper. Place the vegetables on the grill, the endive's flat side down first, and cook until charred on all sides, 3 to 4 minutes total for the endive, 5 to 6 minutes for the corn, and 10 to 12 minutes for the carrots. Remove from the grill and allow to cool.

2 **Make the rest of the salad.** In a medium bowl, combine the cilantro, red onion, feta, lime juice, cumin, and cayenne pepper and toss gently.

3 **Add the veggies.** Slice the endive crosswise into ¼-inch pieces, chop the carrot spears, trim the kernels off the cobs, and add all to the bowl. Toss and taste, then add a pinch of salt, if needed. Serve at room temperature or chilled.

ometimes I just buy a basketful of fruits and vegetables and try to figure out something new. The crisp vibe of cucumbers with the tart but sweet orange sections is great with just a tiny sprinkle of salt, and a sprinkle of apple cider vinegar. I learned that simple way to enjoy cucumbers from my dad, and I've made it many times as a snack. But to make it a real salad instead of a break in my kitchen, I toss it with my sweet and creamy pineapple dressing. Adding the scent and flavor of toasted coconut flakes makes this salad seriously taste like time off. **SERVES 4 TO 6**

cucumber and orange salad
WITH CREAMY PINEAPPLE DRESSING

FOR THE DRESSING

- ½ cup canned crushed pineapple, undrained
- ¼ cup sour cream
- 2 tablespoons apple cider vinegar
- 2 teaspoons sugar
- Kosher salt

FOR THE SALAD

- 2 tablespoons sweetened coconut flakes, for garnish
- 2 oranges
- 2 English cucumbers, peeled, halved lengthwise twice to quarter them, then sliced ½-inch thick
- ½ cup finely chopped red onion

1 **Make the dressing.** In a large bowl, combine the pineapple, sour cream, apple cider vinegar, and sugar. Stir until the sugar dissolves and is not gritty. Taste and season with a tiny pinch of salt. Refrigerate for at least 30 minutes.

2 **Toast the coconut flakes.** In a small, dry pan over medium heat, toast the coconut flakes, tossing them until fragrant and slightly golden, 3 to 4 minutes. Set aside.

3 **Prepare the oranges.** Slice off the top and bottom of each orange to create a flat surface on each end. With the orange resting on one cut side, use a knife to cut between the flesh and white pith of the peel, angling the knife to expose the flesh from top to bottom. Hold an orange in one hand over a large bowl and carefully remove the segments with the other by sliding the knife between the flesh and the membrane that separates each wedge. Repeat with the second orange.

4 **Toss the salad with dressing.** Add the cucumber, red onion, and dressing to the oranges. Gently toss, then serve chilled or at room temperature with a sprinkle of toasted coconut.

I cook because I like to eat, I'm impatient, and I like to make my own portions, which are sometimes bigger or smaller than a restaurant's depending on the dish. I'm also a food detective, and this salad is one of my great detective cases, made for a friend who lived far from the restaurant where he fell in love with the dish. After just a few visual notes, ingredient clues, and a walk through his local grocery store, the rest was up to me. It turned out just as he remembered and now, happily, this salad is one of my favorite solved mysteries in the kitchen. It's served perfectly in lettuce cups, with crackers, or on crostini. **SERVES 4 TO 6**

creamy shrimp and dill salad

FOR THE SHRIMP

¼ cup finely chopped dill

2 garlic cloves, smashed

Kosher salt and freshly ground black pepper

1 pound (26 to 30 count) shrimp, peeled and deveined

FOR THE DRESSING

1 cup chopped fresh dill

1 garlic clove, grated on a rasp or finely minced

1 cup mayonnaise

½ cup sour cream

½ cup whole-milk Greek yogurt

1 cup diced seedless cucumber (about 1 large cucumber)

¾ cup finely chopped red onion

Grated zest of 1 lemon

2 teaspoons sugar

Kosher salt and freshly ground black pepper

1 **Prepare an ice bath and blanch the shrimp.** Fill a large bowl with water and add plenty of ice. Set aside. Fill a large pot halfway with water. Add the ¼ cup dill, the garlic, a nice pinch of salt, and a few grinds of black pepper. Bring to a boil and simmer until the pot is fragrant, about 5 minutes. Add the shrimp and remove the pot from the heat. Stir, allowing the shrimp to cook until pink and opaque, 2 to 3 minutes. Drain the pot and pour the shrimp into the ice bath to cool.

2 **Make the dressing.** In a large bowl, combine the dill, grated garlic, mayonnaise, sour cream, yogurt, cucumber, onion, lemon zest, and sugar. Taste, then season with a pinch of salt and a few grinds of black pepper.

3 **Finish the salad.** Remove the shrimp from the ice bath and dry gently with a paper towel. Lightly chop and stir into the dressing. Cover and refrigerate for at least 2 hours. Serve cold or at room temperature.

When I moved from Indianapolis to Seoul, South Korea, to serve in the air force, my mom gave me a pickled onion recipe. I jotted it down in my first recipe journal and used it in many forms over the years, even as a caterer. The recipe now costars radishes, which I never really liked; then all of a sudden I loved them. That's why I ask people to continue to try foods they haven't liked in the past, because you never know how your palate can change and grow with time. I find myself adding this salad to a plate that needs something with acid to cut the fat, or piling it on top of tacos, steaks, hot dogs, or burgers. Plus it keeps well in the fridge if you can get over the red in the radishes bleeding.

SERVES 4 TO 6

onion and radish salad

1 small Vidalia onion, halved and thinly sliced on a mandoline

¼ cup apple cider

¼ cup orange juice

¼ cup fresh lime juice

1 teaspoon apple cider vinegar

2 teaspoons sugar

Kosher salt and freshly ground black pepper

12 ounces radishes, thinly sliced on a mandoline or in a food processor with the slicing disc

¼ cup fresh cilantro leaves

1 Cook the onion. In a medium pot, combine the onion, cider, orange juice, lime juice, vinegar, sugar, a pinch of salt, and a grind of pepper. Heat to a simmer, stirring, to dissolve the sugar and slightly wilt the onion, 4 to 6 minutes. Remove from the heat, transfer to a bowl, and refrigerate until cool, about 30 minutes.

2 Finish the salad. Once the onion mixture is cool, drain and discard the liquid. Add the radishes and cilantro, and refrigerate for 30 minutes, tossing halfway through. Serve chilled or at room temperature.

My parents visiting my barracks on basic training graduation day, Lackland Air Force Base. (San Antonio, TX, 1993)

made this for an old-school Italian grandma who invited me and a camera crew over for dinner while we were taping *Home Made in America*. She was cooking from a handwritten book her mother had penned in the 1940s in Sicily, so there's no way I could show up with just a bottle of wine in return for her family's Sunday gravy. I'd made this panzanella a few times at home for myself and knew it would travel well, but the true test of a native dish is feeding it to the natives. Luckily, it was devoured along with the rest of the abundant spread, and everyone wanted the recipe. I love it when that happens. It's moved to the top of my list for potlucks and for guests stopping by for a bite. **SERVES 4 TO 6**

spicy spinach panzanella

1 baguette, split and cut into bite-sized cubes

3 tablespoons olive oil

Kosher salt and freshly ground black pepper

FOR THE VINAIGRETTE

2 teaspoons whole-grain mustard

Grated zest of 1 lemon

3 tablespoons fresh lemon juice

⅓ cup olive oil

Salt and freshly ground black pepper

10 to 12 pickled jalapeño slices, chopped

10 to 12 super-thin slices of red onion, cut in half

FOR THE SALAD

10 ounces baby spinach

4 heirloom tomatoes, chopped into chunks

¼ cup sliced black olives, lightly chopped

1 **Toast the baguette cubes.** Preheat the oven to 400°F. Put the baguette cubes in a large bowl and drizzle with olive oil. Toss until the bread is coated. Sprinkle with a pinch of salt and a few grinds of pepper, then toss again. Spread on a nonstick baking sheet and toast until golden on all sides, removing from the oven to toss every 3 to 4 minutes. This should take 12 to 14 minutes. Remove and allow the cubes to cool slightly before tossing back into the large bowl.

2 **Make the vinaigrette.** In a medium bowl, combine the mustard, lemon zest, and lemon juice. Slowly whisk in the olive oil. Season to taste with salt and pepper. Add the jalapeños and onion, and allow them to soak in the vinaigrette for 10 minutes.

3 **Build the salad.** Add the baby spinach, tomatoes, and black olives to the bowl of baguette cubes. Pour the vinaigrette over the salad and toss with your hands to massage and wilt the spinach until everything is combined. Serve at room temperature.

**Flank Steak Fajitas with
Chimichurri and Drunken Peppers**
(PAGE 120)

BEEF

Flank Steak Fajitas
  with Chimichurri and Drunken Peppers

Una de Cada Enchilada Casserole

Honey BBQ Short Ribs

Brewed Awakening Coffee Rib Roast

Chimichanga Alamo

BK Jaegerschnitzel

Spicy Garlic-Studded Meatloaf

Caprese Steak

Easy Beef and Ginger Lettuce Wraps

Easy Cheesy Beefy Ravioli
  with Chunky Vodka Sauce

Oxtail Stew and Rice

I'm easily a meat and potatoes woman.

I once went on a silly crash diet that involved only lemon juice, maple syrup, water, and cayenne pepper as the foundation. I only did it for a week and sure, I dropped a few pounds, but it came at a cost: I lost my craving for beef. Weeks after the diet, I wanted to know when my brain was going to tell me to have steak again. I was really mad at myself. Finally my carnivore ways returned, and I immediately celebrated by going out and buying the most beautiful roast at the butcher and roasting, then carving it into steaks to serve. Beef is great that way, it's perfect for a celebration. It's great with friends and families at cookouts, on game day, roasts for the holidays, and steak on special occasions at home. Great raw, roasted, braised, grilled, fried, or baked, beef is a versatile meat. This is a shout-out to the meat nation. And yes, some of my best friends are vegan.

Flank Steak Fajitas with
Chimichurri and Drunken Peppers (PAGE 120)

Sometimes I cook because I'm lazy and impatient. Going out to eat means getting myself put together and then waiting on everything—the traffic, a table, ordering—then more waiting. So I prefer to stay home most nights for dinner. Given my lack of time and patience, one of the easiest cuts of beef I use is the flank steak. It's thin, so it gets to room temperature fast, and it's juicy and tender when medium rare. That means a fast cooking time. Paired with a quick and easy no-cook sauce and peppers drunk from a beer bath, this meal is done faster than a waiter can ask you, "Still or sparkling?" **SERVES 4 TO 6**

flank steak fajitas
WITH CHIMICHURRI AND DRUNKEN PEPPERS

FOR THE CHIMICHURRI

- 1 bunch fresh flat-leaf or curly parsley, leaves only
- 1 bunch fresh cilantro, leaves only
- 5 garlic cloves
- ½ cup roughly chopped red onion
- 2 teaspoons Hungarian or hot paprika
- 2 tablespoons sherry or red wine vinegar
- ½ cup olive oil
- 1 tablespoon kosher salt
- 1 teaspoon freshly ground black pepper

FOR THE FAJITAS

- 2 pounds flank steak
- Kosher salt and freshly ground black pepper
- 12 8-inch flour tortillas

FOR THE PEPPERS

- 2 tablespoons olive oil
- 2 poblano peppers, seeded and cut into strips

1 **Make the chimichurri.** In a food processor, combine the parsley, cilantro, garlic, red onion, paprika, vinegar, olive oil, salt, and pepper. Blend until smooth. Reserve half for drizzling on the fajitas. Place the remaining half in a large resealable plastic bag.

2 **Marinate the steak.** Place the steak in the bag with the marinade, squeeze out excess air, and seal. Rest at room temperature for up to 2 hours.

3 **Make the peppers.** In a large straight-sided pan with a lid, heat the oil over medium-high heat. When the oil begins to swirl, add the poblano, bell, and jalapeño peppers, and the onion. Season with a pinch of salt and a few grinds of pepper. Cook, stirring, until softened and slightly caramelized around the edges, 6 to 8 minutes. Add the beer, cover, and reduce the heat to medium. Cook until all the vegetables are plump and tender, about 10 minutes. Remove from the heat.

4 **Grill the steak.** Preheat a grill or grill pan to medium-high. Remove the steak from the marinade and discard the marinade. Season the steak with a pinch of salt and a few grinds of pepper on both sides. Grill the steak, flipping just once, until cooked to medium rare, 5 to 6 minutes per side. Transfer the steak to a plate, cover loosely with aluminum foil, and let rest for 10 minutes before slicing.

5 **Warm the tortillas.** Preheat the oven to 200°F. Wet your hands and rub each side of the tortillas with your hands, then stack the tortillas, wrap them tightly in aluminum foil, and place on the center rack of the oven until steamy, about 10 minutes (or place them in a warmer).

6 **Assemble the fajitas.** Slice the steak into thin slices on the bias, against the direction of the muscle. Place a few strips of meat on each warmed tortilla and top with the peppers. Drizzle the reserved chimichurri over the top and fold loosely like a soft taco.

2 green bell peppers, seeded and cut into strips

2 red bell peppers, seeded and cut into strips

2 jalapeño peppers, seeded and cut into strips

1 large Vidalia or sweet onion, thinly sliced

Kosher salt and freshly ground black pepper

16 ounces pale ale or pilsner beer

tips! These peppers keep well in an airtight container in the refrigerator and are great with scrambled eggs in the morning, over grilled chicken or pork, or on a hot dog. ■ Add a few capfuls of apple cider vinegar while you cook the peppers and serve them with fried fish.

I f con todo (with everything) is my favorite two-word phrase in Spanish, then it's only right that *una de cada* is my favorite three-word phrase. It means "one of each," and I use it every time I order enchiladas at restaurants in my Sunset Park neighborhood in Brooklyn. Typically they come in chicken, beef, or cheese, and it's hard to choose. So, with a big smile, I conjure up a sentence including the phrase that pays and ask for one of each instead of getting a plate of three identical enchiladas. Ordering off the menu usually works if you ask kindly, but again, another reason to cook at home! It's your kitchen, your rules. In my kitchen I often skip the step of rolling three different types and stack everything in one deep casserole dish, kind of like lasagna. **SERVES 10 TO 12**

una de cada enchilada casserole

2 tablespoons unsalted butter

FOR THE ENCHILADA SAUCE

1 tablespoon olive oil

½ cup finely chopped Vidalia or sweet onion

Kosher salt and freshly ground black pepper

2 tablespoons tomato paste

1 garlic clove, grated on a rasp or finely minced

1 teaspoon ground cumin

½ teaspoon dried thyme

1 28-ounce can crushed tomatoes

¾ cup beef broth

FOR THE BEEF LAYER

2 tablespoons olive oil

½ cup finely chopped Vidalia or sweet onion

½ cup finely chopped green bell pepper

1 **Prepare the baking dish.** Use the butter to coat the bottom and sides of a lasagna-deep 13 × 9-inch baking dish. Set aside.

2 **Make the sauce.** In a medium pot over medium heat, combine the oil, onion, a pinch of salt, and a few grinds of pepper. Cook until the onion is tender and fragrant, about 8 minutes. Raise the heat to medium-high and add the tomato paste, stir with a wooden spoon, and cook until it deepens in color, 4 to 6 minutes. Add the garlic, cumin, and thyme. Cook, stirring, until combined and fragrant, about 5 minutes, then add the crushed tomatoes and beef broth. Bring the pot to a boil, reduce to a simmer, simmer, covered, for 20 minutes. Keep warm over low heat.

3 **Cook the beef.** Preheat the oven to 350°F. In a large straight-sided pan, heat the olive oil over medium-high heat. When the oil begins to swirl, add the onion and the green and red bell peppers.

continues

½ cup finely chopped red bell pepper

Kosher salt and freshly ground black pepper

3 garlic cloves, grated on a rasp or finely minced

1½ pounds ground beef chuck (80% meat, 20% fat)

1 teaspoon onion powder

1 teaspoon ground cumin

1 teaspoon dried thyme

1 packet (about 1¼ teaspoons) Sazon seasoning

2 Roma tomatoes, seeded and chopped

¼ cup beef broth

FOR THE CHICKEN LAYER

1 rotisserie chicken, skin and bones discarded, meat shredded

½ cup shredded Cheddar cheese

½ cup shredded pepper Jack cheese

FOR THE CASSEROLE

1½ cups shredded Cheddar cheese

1½ cups shredded pepper Jack cheese

20 to 24 6-inch yellow corn tortillas, cut in half

Sprinkle with a nice pinch of salt and cook until the onion and peppers are tender but not browned, about 8 minutes. Add the garlic and cook until fragrant, about 4 minutes more. In this order add the beef, onion powder, cumin, thyme, Sazon, tomatoes, and broth, allowing time between each addition to blend. Cook for another 8 to 10 minutes, stirring to break down the beef into bits. When the beef is cooked through, taste and season with a pinch of salt and a grind or two of pepper. Sazon adds salt, so be careful not to overseason. Set aside.

4 **Prepare the chicken layer.** In a large bowl, toss together the shredded chicken, ½ cup of the enchilada sauce, and the Cheddar and pepper Jack cheeses. Set aside.

5 **Assemble and bake the casserole.** In a small bowl toss the shredded cheeses together. Pour 1 cup of enchilada sauce into the prepared dish. One piece at a time, dunk the tortilla slices in the still-warm enchilada sauce in the pot and layer them on the bottom using the straight edges to line the sides, overlapping where needed and covering the entire bottom of the dish. Next, add ½ cup of the shredded cheese blend, all of the beef, another ½ cup of the shredded cheese blend, a new layer of tortillas dunked in the enchilada sauce, all of the chicken and a final layer of tortillas dunked in the enchilada sauce. Pour the rest of the sauce over all and top with the remaining shredded cheese blend. Bake until the cheese is melted and the sauce bubbles, 35 to 40 minutes. Let it rest a bit before you slice it, just like lasagna. It's nice to look at the layers.

I say pretty much everything I do is easy because it is, but easy just isn't the right word for this recipe. This is truly the simplest way to get short ribs on the table. This BBQ classic doesn't disappoint, and for easy cleanup, you can make the rub for the beef ribs in the same dish used to slow-roast them. All you need is a fresh loaf of white bread for a quick sandwich or a pile of white rice to top with chunks of beef and a ladle of beef jus. **SERVES 4 TO 6**

honey bbq short ribs

¼ cup sweet paprika

1 tablespoon onion powder

1 tablespoon plus 1 teaspoon kosher salt

2 teaspoons dried oregano

2 teaspoons garlic powder

½ teaspoon cumin

¼ teaspoon cayenne pepper
Freshly ground black pepper

4 pounds bone-in short ribs (flanken), cut into 5- to 6-inch strips

½ cup honey

8 to 12 slices fresh white bread

1 Rub the ribs. In a small bowl, combine the paprika, onion powder, salt, oregano, garlic powder, cumin, cayenne pepper, and a few grinds of black pepper. Rub the mixture all over the beef and let rest at room temperature for an hour or so—2 hours at the most. As the meat finishes resting, preheat the oven to 275°F.

2 Cook the ribs. Place the ribs snugly in an 8 × 8-inch baking dish with the fat side of each rib facing up. Cover with aluminum foil very tightly; don't be afraid to top the dish with a baking sheet to ensure the seal! Slow-roast until the meat is falling off the bones, 2½ to 3 hours.

3 Glaze the ribs. Remove the ribs from the oven and, using tongs, flip to coat in the juices and move them around a bit. Drizzle honey evenly over each rib. Place back in the oven, this time venting one corner by peeling back a bit of the foil. Cook for 30 minutes more and serve with bread.

Rib roast is the king of roasts. It's marbled with rivers of white fat, meaning it swims in flavor when it cooks and the fat melts, making it tasty and juicy "as all get out," as my family would say. I've made this recipe with a T-bone or single rib-eye steak just for myself, but love the wow factor of a rib roast for guests. The sugar and coffee together in the rub build a balance of sweet and bitter in a caramelized crust that's perfect for beef. I gave this recipe to a friend and for the next few months she sent pictures or a text every time she made it. I finally had to break her pattern and send her another beef recipe to try. This is addictive.

SERVES 8

brewed awakening coffee rib roast

FOR THE BRINED ROAST

½ cup kosher salt

4 cups brewed French roast coffee

1 standing rib roast, 3 bones, about 6 pounds

FOR THE RUB

¼ cup packed dark brown sugar

1½ teaspoons ground sage

1½ teaspoons Hungarian or hot paprika

2 tablespoons chopped fresh flat-leaf or curly parsley

1½ teaspoons garlic powder

½ teaspoon freshly ground white pepper

¼ cup plain dried bread crumbs

1 **Brine the roast.** In a large bowl, combine 4 cups warm water, the salt, and coffee. Stir to dissolve the salt, then add the rib roast. If the liquid does not cover all of the meat, consider transferring everything to a large turkey brining bag, then sealing tightly so the roast is completely surrounded by the brine. If using a large bowl, flip the roast halfway through the brining time. Refrigerate for 8 hours.

2 **Make the rub.** In a small bowl, mix together the brown sugar, sage, paprika, parsley, garlic powder, white pepper, bread crumbs, coffee, salt, and a few grinds of black pepper.

3 **Rub and rest the roast.** Remove the roast from the refrigerator and discard the brining liquid. Pat the roast dry with paper towels. Using your hands, coat the roast on all sides with the rub, gently massaging it into the flesh. Let rest at room temperature, rib side down, for 2 hours. As the meat finishes resting, preheat the oven to 325°F.

4 Cook the roast. Place the beef in a roasting pan outfitted with a rack, rib side down. Cook until medium rare, about 1 hour and 40 minutes, or until the internal temperature is about 120°F. Remove from the oven and cover loosely with aluminum foil while the meat rests, 15 minutes. Slice between the ribs and serve warm.

¼ cup ground French roast coffee beans

1½ teaspoons kosher salt

Freshly ground black pepper

tex-Mex cooking is one of my favorite types of comfort food, with the chimichanga being one of the great creations of the blended cultures. Basically, it's a burrito on steroids, can I say that? The chimichanga is a beefed-up, pumped-up version of a burrito. It was 1989 in San Antonio, Texas, when I had my first burrito deep-fried and topped with a salad of sorts. The burrito gets more texture from the golden-fried flour tortilla wrap and even more from the crisp iceberg lettuce mounded on top. I covet the crunch in the layers of tucks and folds at each end, sometimes cutting them off and saving them both for last as I plow through the meaty center. **SERVES 4**

chimichanga alamo

FOR THE CILANTRO-AVOCADO CREAM SAUCE

- 1 cup chopped fresh cilantro
- 2 avocados, pitted and mashed
- 1 cup sour cream
- 2 tablespoons fresh lime juice

  Kosher salt

FOR THE BEEF FILLING

- 1 tablespoon vegetable or olive oil
- 1 cup finely chopped Vidalia or sweet onions
- 1 teaspoon kosher salt

  Freshly ground black pepper
- 1 teaspoon ground cumin
- 3 or 4 sprigs fresh thyme, leaves stripped and chopped
- 2 garlic cloves, grated on a rasp or finely minced
- 1 pound ground beef chuck (80% meat, 20% fat)

1 **Make the cilantro-avocado cream sauce.** In a blender, combine the cilantro, avocado, sour cream, lime juice, and a pinch of salt. Blend until smooth. Set aside.

2 **Make the beef filling.** Heat the oil in a large skillet over medium heat. When it begins to swirl, add the onions, salt, a few grinds of pepper, the cumin, and thyme. Cook, stirring, until the onions are tender, about 5 minutes. Add the garlic and cook until fragrant, about 5 minutes. Add the beef and break up with a spoon or spatula as it browns. When the meat is cooked through, taste and, if needed, season with a pinch of salt.

3 **Fill the chimichangas.** Warm the tortillas in a microwave for just a few seconds or in a 100°F. oven for a few minutes. Divide the refried beans into 4 equal portions. Using a rubber spatula or the back of a spoon, spread the beans in the center of each tortilla, making a rectangle with the rough dimensions of 6 × 3 inches. Using this as a guide add the beef directly over the beans. On a 10-inch tortilla, this leaves 2 inches of tortilla on the rectangle's short side of the filling, and 3½ inches of tortilla on the long sides.

continues

FOR THE CHIMICHANGAS

FOR THE CHIMICHANGAS

4 10-inch flour tortillas

1 15.5-ounce can refried black beans

Vegetable oil

FOR THE TOPPING

1 cup shredded Cheddar cheese

1 cup shredded pepper Jack cheese

1 head iceberg lettuce, shredded

4 Roma tomatoes, seeded and chopped

8 to 12 pickled jalapeño slices

4 radishes, thinly sliced

tips! Use this technique to make a breakfast or brunch chimichanga filled with black beans, scrambled eggs, cheese, and cooked sausage. ▪ Make smaller versions of this for kids using 6-inch soft taco shells.

4 **Roll the chimichangas.** With the length of the rectangle of fillings horizontal to you, use both hands to fold each end with the 2-inch border in and over the mound of beef. Then fold the 3½-inch flap closest to you over the beef, tuck it in gently, but tightly, and roll the burrito away from you. Set aside. Rest with the seam side down and continue with the remaining chimichangas.

5 **Fry the chimichangas.** Fill a large straight-sided pan with an inch of oil and bring it to 360°F. (The temperature will fall when the burritos are added.) When the oil is hot, add 2 burritos at a time, seam side down, keeping the temperature at 350°F. Cook until golden on the bottom, then roll and cook all sides, about 8 to 10 minutes total. Transfer each to a paper towel–lined plate. Repeat with the second batch.

6 **Top the chimichangas.** Turn on the broiler or preheat your oven to 500°F. Place each chimichanga on a baking sheet, seam side down. Mix the Cheddar and Jack cheeses in a bowl. Top each chimichanga evenly with an equal amount of cheese. Cook until the cheese melts, 2 to 3 minutes. Transfer each to a serving plate and top evenly with lettuce, avocado cream sauce, tomatoes, jalapeño slices, and radish slices.

Me cooking beef and learning how to hold cast iron safely.
(Norfolk, VA, 1985)

my final meal is such a list it should be a buffet. Jaegerschnitzel (meaning hunter's cutlet) always hovers at the top of the list behind family recipes from my elders. I was introduced to this breaded and fried veal chop with a deep brown mushroom sauce in Bad Kreuznach, Germany. At the end of our block was a restaurant called Rosie's, and our family went so much with our dog, Ginger, that we were quickly the recipient of a *stammtisch*, a table usually reserved for family members of the restaurant owners. Even on a busy night, the table stays empty awaiting your unannounced visit! I usually pair this dish with a traditional German egg noodle called spaetzle (Lemon-Thyme Spaetzle, on page 240) or mashed potatoes to cradle the gravy. Think of this as the German answer to Southern chicken-fried steak. **SERVES 4**

bk jaegerschnitzel

FOR THE CHOPS

4 shoulder veal chops, ¾ inch thick (about 3 pounds)

Kosher salt and freshly ground black pepper

Vegetable oil

FOR THE DREDGE

1 cup all-purpose flour

3 eggs, beaten

2 cups plain dried bread crumbs

2 teaspoons dried sage

2 teaspoons dried oregano

2 teaspoons garlic powder

2 teaspoons onion powder

1 teaspoon Hungarian or hot paprika

1 teaspoon ground cardamom

1 teaspoon kosher salt

1 teaspoon freshly ground black pepper

1 **Prepare the chops.** Use a rolling pin to flatten the chops to a little less than ½ inch. Season the veal chops on both sides with a pinch of salt and a grind of pepper.

2 **Set up a dredging station.** Place 3 large bowls in a row, with the last one closest to your stove. Next to the last bowl, place a larger plate to rest the chops after dredging. Put the flour in the first bowl. In the middle bowl, whisk the eggs with a splash of water. In the last bowl, combine the bread crumbs, sage, oregano, garlic powder, onion powder, paprika, cardamom, salt, black pepper, chili powder, and lemon zest. Stir with a fork.

3 **Dredge the chops.** Take each seasoned chop and dredge in the flour, shaking off the excess. Next, dip in the egg wash, then press into the breading mixture, making sure to completely cover both sides. Transfer each chop to the resting plate.

continues

½ teaspoon chili powder

Grated zest of 1 lemon

FOR THE GRAVY

3 tablespoons olive oil, if needed

2 cups chopped Vidalia or sweet onions

2 carrots, peeled and shredded

3 celery stalks, finely chopped

6 to 8 sprigs fresh thyme, leaves stripped and gently chopped

1 small bay leaf

Kosher salt and freshly ground black pepper

1½ cups red wine (I like merlot or cabernet)

2½ cups beef broth

3 tablespoons unsalted butter

8 ounces baby bella or button mushrooms, sliced

8 ounces mixed wild mushrooms, chopped

3 tablespoons all-purpose flour

1 tablespoon chopped fresh flat-leaf or curly parsley, for garnish

4 **Fry the chops.** Pour ½ inch of oil in a large pan over medium-high heat. Cook the chops until golden brown, 5 to 6 minutes per side. Remove from the pan and keep warm by covering loosely with aluminum foil (do not seal) or placing uncovered in a 100°F. to 150°F. oven.

5 **Start the gravy.** Reduce the heat to medium and in the same pan used to fry the chops, add 3 table-spoons oil if the pan is dry and half the onions, plus the carrots, celery, thyme, bay leaf, a pinch of salt, and a few grinds of black pepper. Cook, stirring, until everything is tender and fragrant, about 15 minutes. Raise the heat and add the wine, using a wooden spoon to scrape up the brown bits that cling to the bottom of the pan. When the wine has reduced by about half, add the broth, bring to a simmer, and reduce by half, about 10 minutes. Pour the sauce through a sieve into a bowl, pressing down with a spoon or rubber spatula to get as much liquid out of the solids as possible. Discard the solids and set the liquid aside.

6 **Finish the gravy.** Wipe the pan clean with a paper towel. Over medium heat, melt the butter, but don't brown it. Then add the remaining onion, all the mushrooms, a pinch of salt, and a few grinds of pepper. Cook, stirring, until tender, about 5 minutes. Sprinkle with the flour and stir while cooking a few more minutes until the veggies soak up the flour. Add the reserved sauce back to the pan and bring to a simmer. Cook, stirring, until thickened, about 10 minutes. To serve, pour the gravy over the chops and sprinkle with parsley.

I love garlic, and if it's one of your favorite things, I invite you to give this a try and get inspired to add whole cloves to more of your cooking. When taping an episode of my farm-to-table show, *How'd That Get on My Plate?*, I took a trip to Gilroy, California, home of the nation's biggest garlic festival. I saw piles of bulbs more than four times my height and just as wide at the base. I stood there in awe, thinking how fast could I cook my way through those bulbs! I par-roast them here, then gently mix them into the seasoned loaf so it hums with the sweet scent of garlic. It's packed with herbs, chewy potato bread for moisture, and a spicy kick from sriracha, but the best part is slicing this meatloaf and hoping for a whole clove in your serving. It reminds me of the baby in a New Orleans king cake!

SERVES 6 TO 8

spicy garlic-studded meatloaf

FOR THE GARLIC

12 garlic cloves

1 tablespoon unsalted butter

Kosher salt

FOR THE SPICY KETCHUP

1½ cups ketchup

1½ teaspoons apple cider vinegar

2 tablespoons sriracha hot chili sauce

FOR THE MEATLOAF

1 egg

2 teaspoons kosher salt

½ teaspoon freshly ground black pepper

1 teaspoon sweet paprika

2 tablespoons Worcestershire sauce

8 to 10 sprigs fresh thyme, leaves stripped and chopped

1 **Prepare the garlic.** Trim a thin sliver off each end of the garlic cloves and discard. In a small pan over medium heat, melt the butter with a pinch of salt. Add the garlic and cook on one side until golden, then flip to cook the other side. (You get extra points if you do the curved side!) Each side should take about 3 minutes. The goal is not to cook them through, just give them color. Remove from heat. Preheat the oven to 375°F.

2 **Prepare the ketchup sauce.** In a medium bowl, stir together the ketchup, vinegar, and sriracha. Set aside.

3 **Blend the meatloaf seasoning.** Whisk the egg in a large bowl, then whisk in the salt, pepper, and paprika until smooth. Add the Worcestershire, thyme, onion, scallion, and ½ cup of the ketchup sauce. Stir to combine.

4 **Mix the meatloaf.** With your fingers, gently crumble both the chuck and turkey. Add half the crumbled chuck to the large bowl, then some bread, then half the turkey, some more bread, and repeat until done. Adding this way will make mixing easier and lighter for a juicier loaf. Add the reserved garlic and, with one hand acting like a pitchfork, gently mix the meatloaf, bringing the egg mixture from the bottom to the top while turning the bowl with the other hand until everything is gently combined. Transfer the meat to a 9 × 5-inch loaf pan and flatten the top. Pour the remaining spicy ketchup sauce on top and spread evenly.

5 Cook the meatloaf. Bake the meatloaf uncovered for 50 minutes. Remove and rest for 10 minutes. Over the sink, tilt the loaf pan slowly to one corner to drain the excess fat and juices. Don't worry, the meatloaf will still be juicy because you let it rest! Slice 1-inch-thick portions and hope for a double-clove slice!

½ cup chopped Vidalia or sweet onion

1 scallion, minced (white and green parts)

1 pound ground beef chuck (80% meat, 20% fat)

1 pound ground dark meat turkey

3 slices potato bread, lightly toasted and cut into ¼-inch cubes

tip! Crumble leftovers and reheat with cooked pasta, stock, and a sprinkle of cheese for a fun remix.

Skip the caprese salad and go straight for the steak! It's just as simple to put together and requires all of the star ingredients to function at their highest level. So pick some fragrant basil, find a pretty marbled steak, and look for smoked mozzarella; it's there just waiting to be a star in your kitchen. I call it the smarter mozzarella, because it's gooey as expected, but smoky too. Any ingredient that brings more than one flavor to the table gets top billing in my kitchen. A layer of it melted over a properly spiced and rubbed steak balances the sweet and tart flavors of quick-roasted Roma tomato slices. Sound easy? It is. Flavor doesn't always equal work in my kitchen. **SERVES 4**

caprese steak

FOR THE RUB

- 1 tablespoon kosher salt
- 2 teaspoons oregano powder
- 2 teaspoons sweet paprika
- 1 teaspoon garlic powder
- ½ teaspoon freshly ground black pepper
- 1 tablespoon liquid smoke
- ¼ cup olive oil

FOR THE STEAKS

- 4 1-pound top loin steaks (prime, 1½ inches thick)
- ¼ cup olive oil
- 12 fresh basil leaves, cut into ribbons
- 6 ounces smoked mozzarella (6 ¼-inch slices)

FOR THE TOMATOES

- 4 Roma tomatoes, sliced ¼ inch thick
- 2 tablespoons olive oil
  Kosher salt and freshly ground black pepper

1 Rub and rest the steaks. In a small bowl, combine the salt, oregano, paprika, garlic powder, pepper, liquid smoke, and oil. Divide the rub equally and rub on all sides of each steak. Allow the steaks to rest at room temperature for 1 hour.

2 Roast the tomato slices. Preheat the oven to 400°F. Line a baking sheet with parchment paper or foil and set a wire rack on top. Place the tomato slices in a medium bowl, drizzle with olive oil, and sprinkle with a pinch of salt and a few grinds of pepper. Toss, then place in one layer on the wire rack. Place the baking sheet in the oven and roast until the edges are shriveled and caramelized, but the center is still moist, about 25 minutes. Remove and allow the tomato slices to cool, then gently chop. Set aside. Remove the wire rack from the baking sheet. Discard the parchment or foil and place the baking sheet back in the oven to await the steaks. Reduce the heat to 375°F.

3 Sear and cook the steaks. Heat 2 tablespoons of the olive oil in a large cast-iron pan over medium-high heat. Just as it begins to swirl but before it smokes, add 2 steaks and sear on one side until the steaks release from the pan to reveal a deep golden brown crust. Transfer to a plate with the uncooked side up. Repeat for the other 2 steaks. Place each steak on the preheated baking sheet with the uncooked side facing down. Cook until about 5°F. from the desired internal temperature (about 10 minutes for rare, 15 minutes for medium rare, and you don't want it well done, do you? Okay, 20 minutes for well done).

4 **Top and broil the steaks.** When the steaks are 5°F. from their desired internal temperature (see page 19), quickly remove the baking sheet from the oven and turn on the broiler. If you don't have a broiler setting, raise the heat to 500°F. Working quickly, top each steak with tomato and basil. Then layer on the mozzarella slices and quickly place the steaks back in the oven under the broiler on the center rack. When the cheese begins to bubble and brown, 5 to 8 minutes, remove from the oven. Cover loosely with aluminum foil. Let rest for 5 minutes before serving.

tip! Chop up leftovers, add tons of spinach or chopped hearts of romaine, and make a wrap.

eating with your hands is fun and relaxes everyone involved. These beef wraps are a quick fix for lunch with friends or a great app for a dinner party. In my old neighborhood of Gravesend, Brooklyn, I lived a block away from a Vietnamese place that made several versions of this wrap. I'd pair my order with some mango bubble tea and sip in bliss after each bite. The heart of this dish is hoisin sauce, a powerful Asian barbecue sauce with a heavy lean on ginger and other seasonings. Not much else is needed to make these lettuce wraps taste delicious, so I keep it simple and only add a few things to punch it up. **SERVES 4 TO 6**

easy beef and ginger lettuce wraps

2 teaspoons vegetable or olive oil

1 pound ground beef chuck (80% meat, 20% fat)

2-inch piece of fresh ginger, peeled and finely grated

2 scallions, chopped (white and green parts)

2 garlic cloves, grated on a rasp or finely minced

2 tablespoons soy sauce

1 teaspoon crushed red pepper flakes

¼ cup hoisin sauce

Kosher salt and freshly ground black pepper

1 head Boston, Bibb, or other butterhead lettuce, leaves separated, cleaned, and dried

¼ cup chopped salted peanuts

1 **Cook the beef.** Heat the oil in a large skillet over medium-high heat, add the beef, and cook until browned, about 10 minutes. Stir in the ginger, scallions, garlic, soy sauce, red pepper flakes, and hoisin sauce. Cook to heat all the ingredients, about 4 minutes, then taste and season with a pinch of salt, if needed, and a few grinds of black pepper. Remove the pan from the heat.

2 **Assemble the wraps and garnish.** Prepare several sets of double-layered lettuce leaves. Scoop a heaping spoonful of filling into the recessed center of each double-ply lettuce cup. Sprinkle with peanuts and eat by folding in half like a taco or wrapping loosely like a burrito. Serve warm.

onton wrappers aren't just for Asian food; the circles or squares are a great shortcut to homemade ravioli. Fill one and fold it over or use two wrappers to sandwich the filling, then simply boil them a few minutes and create a sauce. Like iced coffee, vodka sauce is something I can't remember ever having or hearing of until I moved to New York, but it's on pretty much every Italian menu here. It's a cross between a tomato and cream sauce with a hint of vodka flavor. The alcohol cooks out, so it's kid-friendly, but the flavors are still intoxicating. You'll be surprised how a wonton can make you love Italian food.

SERVES 4 TO 6

easy cheesy beefy ravioli
WITH CHUNKY VODKA SAUCE

FOR THE RAVIOLI

- 1 pound ground beef chuck (80% meat, 20% fat)
- 8 ounces shredded Parmesan cheese
- 1 garlic clove, grated on a rasp or finely minced
- ½ cup Vidalia or sweet onion pulp, grated on the large side of a box grater
- 1 teaspoon dried oregano
- 1 teaspoon kosher salt
- 24 to 30 wonton wrappers, room temperature

1 Mix the filling. In a medium bowl combine the beef, cheese, garlic, onion pulp, oregano, and salt. Using both hands, mix and squeeze the beef and seasonings together.

2 Fill the wonton wrappers. Place a small glass of water next to your working area. Lay a few wonton wrappers, flour side up, on a flat surface. Scoop a spoonful of the filling into the center of each. Dip a finger in the water and lightly trace the border of each wonton. Close by folding it in half and pressing the air out to the edges to seal.

3 Cook the ravioli. Bring a large pot of salted water to a boil. Gently drop in the ravioli, one at a time. Cook until they begin to float and a test ravioli cut in half shows it is cooked through, about 6 minutes. Transfer to a plate with a slotted spoon.

4 **Make the vodka sauce.** In a large saucepan over medium heat, combine the tomatoes, tomato sauce, onion, and vodka. Bring to a simmer and cook uncovered until reduced by half, about 15 minutes. Reduce the heat and stir in the heavy cream and cheese. Bring to a simmer again and cook until thickened, about 5 more minutes. Taste and season with a pinch of salt and a few grinds of black pepper. Add the cooked ravioli to the sauce for just a minute more to reheat them. Or simply place 4 to 5 ravioli on each plate and scoop sauce on each serving.

FOR THE VODKA SAUCE

- 4 Roma tomatoes, seeded and chopped
- 8 ounces canned tomato sauce
- ½ cup chopped Vidalia or sweet onion
- 1 cup your favorite vodka
- 1 cup heavy cream, room temperature
- 8 ounces shredded Parmesan cheese

  Kosher salt and freshly ground black pepper

tips! Freeze the pasta on a parchment-lined plate or baking sheet for 2 hours with a dusting of flour, then place in a resealable freezer bag. Drop them into boiling water straight from the freezer for a fast meal, no thawing needed. ■ These taste great fried as well—just fill a large straight-sided pan with ½ inch oil and fry when the oil begins to swirl, flipping once.

Oxtails should be filed under the "good things come to those who wait" category of cooking. It's a two-day process, but well worth it and pretty easy even given the length of preparation. If you like the idea of fall-off-the-bone beef in a dark, rich stew of onions, garlic, and creamy lima beans, this is a must try. Like gumbo, it works best over a scoop of plain white rice, but egg noodles are fun, too. **SERVES 4 TO 6**

oxtail stew and rice

12 ounces dry lima beans

4 pounds oxtails

3 cups chopped Vidalia or sweet onions

3 scallions, chopped (white and green parts)

4 garlic cloves, smashed

1 bunch (about 25 sprigs) of fresh thyme

2 tablespoons crushed red pepper flakes

1 tablespoon plus 1 teaspoon Hungarian or hot paprika

2 bay leaves

2 tablespoons hot sauce (I like Frank's Red Hot)

1 tablespoon plus 1 teaspoon tomato paste

2 tablespoons kosher salt

¼ cup gravy enhancer (I like Gravy Master)

1 cup red wine (I like merlot or cabernet)

6 cups low-sodium beef broth

4 cups white rice, prepared according to package directions

1 **Soak the beans.** Put the lima beans in a large bowl with 2 quarts water. Drape a dishtowel over the top and soak for 8 hours on the counter.

2 **Marinate the oxtails.** In a large stockpot with a lid, combine the oxtails, onions, scallions, garlic, thyme, red pepper flakes, paprika, bay leaves, hot sauce, tomato paste, salt, gravy enhancer, and wine. Stir to coat the oxtails, cover, and marinate 8 hours or overnight in the refrigerator, stirring occasionally.

3 **Cook the oxtails.** Remove the oxtails from the fridge. Add enough water to cover them by ½ inch. Bring to a boil over medium-high heat, then reduce to a simmer, cover, and cook for 2 hours. When you're 30 minutes into the cooking time, add 2 cups of the beef broth, stir, and cover. Continue this process in 30-minute intervals, with the last 2 cups of broth added 30 minutes before the 2-hour mark. After 2 hours, drain the lima beans and add them to the pot. If the liquid level is below the level of the solids, add enough water to cover by 2 inches. Bring to a boil, then reduce the heat and simmer uncovered for 2 more hours, skimming the fat off the top and stirring occasionally. In the last half hour of cooking, remove any visible thyme stems and the bay leaves. Taste and season with salt if needed. Serve hot with white rice.

tip! If you can't find oxtails, use beef cubes sold for stew, but a quick conversation with your grocer's butcher could help; they often save these good parts for themselves.

Kenner Shrimp and Andouille Boil (PAGE 149)

SEA FOOD

Seafood changed my life; it's the reason I beg you to try and retry flavors you think you don't like. I grew up hating seafood. Though oddly, I did like oysters. Raw, baked, fried—it didn't matter what was done to them, I loved them. Everything else was my kryptonite.

Years later, the Air Force sent me to New Orleans on a news story and that all changed. A guy I liked there took me to dinner with some of his friends. He ordered for the table and everything had seafood in it. I didn't want to look picky, so I plowed through everything that came my way. Then it happened. I caught myself loving gumbo, jambalaya, and étouffée, all studded with seafood that was once on my off-limits list. How many lost years had there been without this joy because the child in me said I wouldn't like it?! I tell this story often, hoping to inspire. Our taste buds grow with us, try things again.

What a nice full-circle moment when my first commissioned recipe, the one that started my catering company years later in New York, was for an all-seafood gumbo. Thank you to New Orleans, that guy ordering for the table, and N.O.R.E. for your no-pork demands (see N.O.R.E.'s Seafood Slumbo, page 161).

Lomi Salmon (PAGE 148)

on't be afraid to make this at home, because what might look complicated is actually easy. This is just like rubbing down a steak, wrapping it, and resting it. I picked up this recipe after a trip to Hawaii. Among the Polynesian spread of poi, poke, and laulau was a bowl of bright salmon with flecks of cilantro. It looked simple, but when I tasted it, the flavors were all over the place in a really good way. This is a salty, sweet, tangy, and tender way to enjoy salmon and it has just the right amount of fresh cilantro to cut through it all. This is a winner on crackers or with white rice tossed with scallions and chopped fresh cilantro. **SERVES 4**

lomi salmon

1 pound wild Alaskan salmon fillet, skin removed

1 cup kosher salt

½ cup sugar

1 bunch fresh cilantro, plus ¼ cup chopped

1 Roma tomato, seeded and chopped

2 scallions, thinly sliced (white and green parts)

2 teaspoons fresh lime juice

1 Wrap and refrigerate the salmon. Rinse the salmon in cold water and pat it dry. In a small bowl, mix the salt and sugar. Lay 2 long pieces of plastic wrap on top of each other to form a cross. Layer half the unchopped bunch of cilantro in the middle of the plastic wrap, add half the salt-sugar mixture, and press the salmon into it, covering the bottom well. Top the salmon with the remaining salt-sugar mixture, rubbing it in well. Then place the remaining unchopped cilantro on top. Wrap the salmon tightly in the wrap and refrigerate for 24 hours.

2 Rinse and prepare the salmon. Unwrap the salmon, rinse off in cold water, and pat dry. Cut into ¼- to ⅓-inch cubes and place in a medium bowl. Add the chopped cilantro, tomato, scallions, and lime juice and toss. Serve chilled or at room temperature.

tips! You can substitute fresh parsley or basil for the cilantro for an equally rewarding infusion of flavor. ■ If you like gravlax with cream cheese on bagels, use this same technique, but substitute a bunch of dill for the cilantro and add an extra ½ cup salt.

his is a quick and easy way to visit the bayou in your kitchen. I talk plenty about New Orleans, but actually lived in Kenner, Louisiana, two towns over on Lake Pontchartrain. If I got a good grade at Loyola, I'd stop at the fish market in Metairie on the way home and stock up for a shrimp boil. I never had anyone over for these boils, as would usually be expected; it was just me and my newfound love of seafood. There are plenty of working parts here, but it's truly as simple as tossing things in a pot and letting it rip. Easy is as easy does. **SERVES 4 TO 6**

kenner shrimp and andouille boil

¼ cup (½ stick) unsalted butter

2 pounds Andouille sausage, cut into 2-inch sections

1 pound pearl onions

1 cup chopped celery

1 green bell pepper, seeded and chopped

4 garlic cloves, thinly sliced

2 tablespoons Old Bay seasoning

1 pound Red Bliss potatoes

1 tablespoon fresh lemon juice

2 tablespoons hot sauce (I like Frank's Red Hot)

2 quarts seafood stock

4 ears of corn, halved, thawed if frozen

2 pounds shrimp, deveined, shell and tail on, thawed if frozen

1 **Brown the sausage.** Put the butter and sausage in a stockpot over medium-high heat. Cook the sausage until it blisters on one side, then flip it and cook until the other side blisters as well, about 10 minutes.

2 **Build the flavor and serve.** Add the onions, celery, bell pepper, garlic, and Old Bay to the pot. Cook, stirring, until everything is tender but not browned, about 8 minutes. Add the potatoes, lemon juice, hot sauce, and stock. If needed, add enough water to cover by 1 inch. Bring to a boil, then reduce to a simmer and cook until the potatoes are fork tender, about 20 minutes. Add the corn and shrimp. Stir and cook until the shrimp become opaque and curl up, 2 to 4 minutes. Serve warm in a bowl or remove with a slotted spoon and serve family style on a platter.

or the record, nothing here is scorched, except maybe your tongue if you can't handle the heat of the Bahamian hot sauce. Just don't tell that to the Tarpum Bay, Eleuthera, fisherman who sold snapper to me once when I was on vacation. He asked me if I knew how to "scorch it" when I cook it—it took me a second to realize he meant "score it," as in cutting lines along the fish before frying. My friend and I giggled and told him yes; we both cook for a living and immediately found it funny. Since then, I've lovingly "scorched" all my whole fried fish, thinking of my favorite tiny island and the concerned fisherman. Listen to your fishmongers; they know best how to prepare your fish. **SERVES 4**

scorched red snapper
WITH BAHAMIAN HOT SAUCE

FOR THE HOT SAUCE

- 10 red, yellow, or orange habanero peppers (a mixture of colors is recommended)
- 1 red bell pepper, seeded and cut into chunks
- Kosher salt
- 5 whole black peppercorns
- ½ cup chopped Vidalia or sweet onion
- 2 garlic cloves, smashed
- ½ cup apple cider vinegar
- ¼ to 1 teaspoon sugar, if needed

1 **Make the hot sauce.** In a medium pot with a lid, combine the habanero peppers, bell pepper, a pinch of salt, the peppercorns, onion, garlic, vinegar, and enough water to cover the contents by half an inch. Bring to a boil, then reduce to a simmer and cook, covered, until everything is tender, about 20 minutes. Remove all the solids with a slotted spoon and put them in a blender or food processor, reserving the liquid from the pot. Blend until everything is broken down, then add a bit of the reserved water until the sauce is a pourable consistency. Taste and add a sprinkle of sugar if needed to mellow out the flavors. Too-hot hot sauce is no fun. Pour the sauce into a sealable container and refrigerate until cold.

2 **"Scorch" (score) the snapper.** Use a sharp knife to make 6 to 8 slits along the length of both sides of each snapper, going down to the bone. Season both sides with salt and black pepper, making sure they get into each slit. In a shallow bowl, combine the flour, cayenne pepper, garlic powder, onion powder, a pinch of salt, and a grind or two of black pepper. Toss with a fork to combine. Coat each snapper on all sides with the flour mixture, making sure to again get into the crevices of the scored (ahem, scorched!) sections. Rest both fish in the flour until ready to fry.

3 **Fry the snapper.** Fill a cast-iron pan with an inch of oil. Turn the heat to medium and when a bit of flour sprinkled in begins to sizzle, but not immediately brown, add the fish. Do this in batches, using two pans or your big mama cast iron frying pan to do it all at once. Whatever you do, don't overcrowd the pan because you want to fry the fish, not steam them. Fry on one side until a peek beneath reveals a golden-brown crust and a bend of the fish reveals cooked white flesh between the slits, 8 to 10 minutes, depending on the size of your snapper. Gently use tongs to grab the tail, then flip and cook on the other side for 8 to 10 more minutes. Transfer to a paper towel–lined plate and allow to rest just a few minutes. Serve family-style on a platter with the Bahamian hot sauce.

FOR THE SNAPPER

- 2 whole red snappers, scales cleaned, top and bottom fins trimmed, tail left on
- Kosher salt and freshly ground black pepper
- 1 cup all-purpose flour
- ½ teaspoon cayenne pepper
- 1 teaspoon garlic powder
- 1 teaspoon onion powder
- Peanut or vegetable oil

tip! Other fish I like to scorch and fry whole are catfish, tilapia, bass, cod, and branzini.

I'm pretty sure I could eat this once a week and never tire of it, which says plenty because I love variety in my kitchen. Using farm-raised mussels cuts down the once-lengthy cleaning process. Be sure to make this recipe with mussels bought that day; store them in the refrigerator covered with a moist paper towel until ready to prepare. A quick brush and a toss in a loaded wine sauce and this is on the table fast. A golden, cheesy piece of garlic bread is required and equally as simple as the mussels. **SERVES 4**

pizza mussels WITH CHEESY GARLIC BREAD

2 pounds farm-raised mussels

3 tablespoons olive oil

3 tablespoons unsalted butter

½ pound pepperoni, chopped

1 green bell pepper, chopped

¼ cup sliced kalamata olives

½ cup chopped Vidalia or sweet onion

Kosher salt and freshly ground black pepper

8 garlic cloves, chopped

1½ cups white wine

¼ cup heavy cream

¼ cup grated Parmesan cheese

1 tablespoon chopped fresh oregano

2 tablespoons thinly sliced fresh basil

Cheesy Garlic Bread (recipe follows)

1 **Prep the mussels.** Rinse and brush the mussels to clean them, removing any beards. Discard any mussels with cracked shells. Refrigerate the mussels in a bowl covered by a damp cloth until ready to cook.

2 **Cook the pepperoni and veggies.** In a large straight-sided pan with a lid, combine the olive oil, butter, and pepperoni. Cook uncovered over medium heat until the pepperoni renders some of its fat and becomes slightly crisp, 6 to 8 minutes. Transfer to a plate with a slotted spoon and set aside, keeping the fat in the pan. Add the bell pepper, olives, onion, a pinch of salt, and a few grinds of pepper to the pan. Cook over medium heat until the onion becomes lightly caramelized, about 15 minutes. Add the garlic and cook until fragrant and tender, about 5 minutes.

3 **Steam the mussels.** Pick through the mussels. If any are opened, give it a good tap on the edge of the bowl. If it slowly closes, keep it; if it doesn't close, discard it. Raise the heat to medium-high and add the mussels and wine, then immediately cover the pan to trap the steam. Shake the pan to make sure everything tosses together and cook for 3 to 4 minutes. Give a peek—if most or all of the mussels are

continues

opened, they are done. If not, cover and cook 1 minute or so more, removing from the heat when done. Add the heavy cream and cooked pepperoni. Pour into serving bowls and sprinkle with the Parmesan, oregano, and basil. Serve with cheesy garlic bread.

tip! Use any leftover broth from steeping the mussels to boil potatoes. Or, toss in a few chunks of fish the next day for a quick fish soup.

cheesy garlic bread SERVES 4

¼ cup (½ stick) unsalted butter

¼ cup olive oil

1 ranch-flavored dip or salad dressing seasoning packet

4 garlic cloves, grated on a rasp or finely minced

8 slices Texas toast or thick-cut white bread

1 cup shredded Parmesan cheese

1 cup shredded mozzarella cheese

1 Make the garlic butter. Preheat the oven to 350°F. In a small pot over medium heat, melt the butter, then add the olive oil, seasoning packet, and garlic. Stir and cook until the garlic is fragrant, about 4 minutes.

2 Top and bake the bread. Brush one side of each piece of bread with the seasoned butter and place on a baking sheet, brushed side up. Repeat for all slices and bake until the edges are golden brown and the center slightly bubbles, about 12 minutes. Turn the oven to broil or the highest temperature possible. Remove the bread and evenly top each slice with Parmesan and mozzarella. Return to the oven and bake until the cheese melts, about 2 minutes. Serve warm.

ever had it? Try it, trust me. Had it? Try *this* one, trust me. **SERVES 6 TO 8**

tuna noodle casserole

FOR THE NOODLES

2 tablespoons unsalted butter

Kosher salt

4 cups egg noodles

16 ounces canned yellowfin or albacore tuna in oil, drained and flaked

10 ounces frozen peas, thawed and rinsed

4 ounces sharp Cheddar cheese, shredded

4 ounces Irish Cheddar cheese, shredded

FOR THE SAUCE

2 tablespoons unsalted butter

1 tablespoon olive oil

½ teaspoon dried thyme

½ cup chopped onion

Kosher salt and freshly ground black pepper

8 ounces baby bella mushrooms, sliced

4 teaspoons Worcestershire sauce

1 tablespoon horseradish

2 tablespoons all-purpose flour

1½ cups chicken stock

2 cups heavy cream

FOR THE TOPPING

3 cups panko

3 to 4 tablespoons olive oil

Kosher salt and freshly ground black pepper

1 **Prepare the noodles.** Butter a 13 × 9-inch baking dish. Preheat the oven to 350°F. Bring a large pot of salted water to a boil and cook the egg noodles until al dente according to package directions. Drain and immediately place the noodles in a colander submerged in a large bowl of ice water. Once cooled, drain and pour the pasta into a large bowl with the tuna, peas, and both cheeses. Mix thoroughly.

2 **Make the sauce.** In a large straight-sided pan over medium-high heat, combine the butter, olive oil, thyme, onion, a pinch of salt, and a few grinds of pepper. Cook until the onion is tender. Then add the mushrooms and cook until tender and darkened, 10 minutes total. Add the Worcestershire sauce, horseradish, and sprinkle the flour over the pan. Stir and cook 1 minute more. Raise the heat and add the stock. Cook until it thickens, then stir in the heavy cream. Simmer about 4 minutes more. Taste and season with salt, if needed. Stir into the prepared noodles and pour into the prepared dish.

3 **Prepare the topping and bake.** In a small bowl, combine the panko, 3 tablespoons olive oil, a pinch of salt, and a few grinds of pepper. Stir until the crumbs evenly soak up the oil, adding more oil if needed (but don't saturate). Sprinkle evenly over the top of the dish and bake uncovered until the top is golden brown, about 35 minutes.

turn the classic Southern side of beans, corn, and vegetables into a one-pot meal by adding chunks of lump crabmeat. Anytime I find a new way to make fish dishes or one-pot meals I'm happy, so to bring them together is a dream. The ingredients are a bit high-low, like wearing diamonds and cubic zirconia together, but what you save in the freezer section, you can spend on some good crab. Always gently pick through whatever kind you buy to make sure there are no shells left. **SERVES 4**

creamy crab succotash

4 strips thick-cut bacon, chopped

1 green bell pepper, chopped

1 garlic clove, minced
Kosher salt and freshly ground black pepper

16 ounces (about 3⅓ cups) sweet corn kernels, drained if canned, thawed if frozen

16 ounces (about 3⅓ cups) lima beans, drained if canned, thawed if frozen

2 cups pearl onions, thawed if frozen

1 teaspoon hot sauce (I like Frank's Red Hot)

⅓ cup heavy cream

1 cup lump crabmeat, picked through, debris and shell bits removed

1 Cook the bacon. In a large skillet over medium heat, fry the bacon until crispy, then transfer to a paper towel–lined plate, reserving the fat in pan.

2 Cook the vegetables. Add the bell pepper, garlic, a pinch of salt, and a few grinds of black pepper to the pan. Cook until softened slightly, about 5 minutes. Add the corn, lima beans, pearl onions, hot sauce, and cream. Bring to a simmer and cook until the vegetables are tender, 15 to 20 minutes.

3 Finish and serve. Stir in the crab and cook just 1 minute more, then add the reserved bacon. Taste and season with a pinch of salt, if needed.

tip! Canned or jarred tuna works great here in place of the crab. The types of beans and vegetables are also interchangeable.

meaty tilapia holds up to the hopped-up flavors in my easy beer-batter recipe. Other meaty fish work well, but farm-raised tilapia is easy to find year-round and the fishy level is low, so it pleases people. If cooking just for yourself, use what you like, but don't leave out the fries—this is the standard pairing with fried fish across the pond. Mine are fluffy and light due to the soaking-then-frying method. Sprinkle on some heat after frying and enjoy a perfect combination. **SERVES 4**

beer-battered tilapia WITH CAJUN FRITES

FOR THE TILAPIA

- 4 tilapia fillets (6 to 8 ounces each), cut in half lengthwise along the seam
- 1 tablespoon fresh lemon juice
- Kosher salt and freshly ground black pepper

FOR THE BEER BATTER

- 1 cup all-purpose flour
- ½ to ¾ cup of your favorite beer
- Grated zest of 1 lemon
- ½ teaspoon garlic powder
- Kosher salt

- Peanut or vegetable oil, for deep frying
- All-purpose flour, for dredging
- Cajun Frites (recipe follows)

1 **Season the tilapia.** Brush both sides of the tilapia with lemon juice. Season both sides with a pinch of salt and a few grinds of pepper.

2 **Make the beer batter.** In a large bowl, combine the flour, beer, lemon zest, garlic powder, and a pinch of salt. Whisk together. The texture should be a bit thicker than pancake batter.

3 **Dredge and fry the tilapia.** In a Dutch oven, large pot, or fryer, pour enough oil to deep-fry and heat it to 360°F. When you add the fish, the temperature will settle at 350°F.; try to keep it there by adjusting the heat. Line up your dredging station right next to the pot—put a bit of flour in a large bowl next to the batter. When the oil is ready, first coat the fish with flour and shake off the excess, then dunk it in the beer batter and immediately into the oil. Repeat, working in batches to keep the temperature at 350°F. Remove the fish when golden and cooked through. Time will vary per piece, but each batch will take 6 to 8 minutes. Transfer the fish to a paper towel–lined plate. Serve with cajun frites.

continues

cajun frites SERVES 4

1 **Prep the potatoes.** Put the potato planks in a resealable plastic bag or large bowl and cover with water. Rest at least 2 hours.

2 **Fry the potatoes.** Remove the potatoes from the water and rinse, then dry them with a clean kitchen towel or paper towels. Set a wire rack inside a rimmed baking sheet. In a Dutch oven, large pot, or fryer, add the garlic cloves and pour enough oil to deep-fry and heat it to 260°F. When you add the potatoes, the temperature will settle at 250°F.; try to keep it there by adjusting the heat. Add the potatoes in batches and fry until limber and light golden, about 10 minutes. Transfer to the wire rack to cool. When all the potatoes are done, remove the garlic cloves and raise the oil temperature to 365°F. The temperature should rest at 350°F. during the second frying. In batches, fry the potato planks again until golden brown and crisp, 10 to 12 minutes, then transfer to a paper towel–lined plate. Immediately sprinkle with Old Bay and a pinch of sea salt and serve with mayonnaise dressing, for dipping.

- 3 pounds russet potatoes (about 4 average), peeled and cut lengthwise into thick planks
- 4 garlic cloves, smashed
  Peanut or vegetable oil
- 1 teaspoon Old Bay seasoning
  Flaky sea salt
- ½ cup zesty mayonnaise-based dressing, for dipping

tips! Don't have beer? Use seltzer water instead. ■ Other great fish to fry are cod, haddock, or any meaty fish.

When I began working at HOT 97 in New York, N.O.R.E. was one of the first people I met. He was nice, welcoming, and one of the more fun rappers to interview. Throughout my four years at that radio station, he was a constant, performing at station events or inviting me to hear new music in his studio. I always showed up with food, then one day, he requested a gumbo with no pork or okra, and he had a list of specific ingredients. This was my first-ever recipe request. So here it is. A gumbo with lump crabmeat, jumbo shrimp, and oysters. Serve this with plain white rice and a glass of pinot grigio, just like N.O.R.E. **SERVES 4 TO 6**

n.o.r.e.'s seafood slumbo

5 tablespoons unsalted butter

2 tablespoons olive oil

1 large Vidalia onion, diced

3 celery stalks, diced

1 green bell pepper, diced

2 garlic cloves, minced

Kosher salt and freshly ground black pepper

1 tablespoon filé powder, plus extra for garnish

1 bay leaf

1½ teaspoons cayenne

1½ teaspoons paprika

½ teaspoon dried thyme

1 teaspoon dried Mexican oregano

1 4.5-ounce can tomato paste

5 cups seafood stock

1 pound haddock, cut into 1½-inch pieces

1 pound jumbo shrimp, shells removed, deveined

12 oysters, shucked

1½ cups lump crabmeat, picked over

2 tablespoons hot sauce

4 cups cooked white rice

1 Build the flavor. Heat the butter and oil in a large stockpot over medium-high heat. When the butter is melted, add the onion, celery, bell pepper, garlic, a pinch of salt, and few grinds of pepper. Cook, stirring, until the veggies are softened and slightly caramelized, about 8 minutes. Add the filé powder, bay leaf, cayenne, paprika, thyme, and oregano and cook until combined and fragrant, about 5 minutes. Add the tomato paste and cook until it turns a deeper red color, about 5 minutes. Add the seafood stock and taste; add more salt if needed. Bring to a boil, reduce the heat, and simmer for 30 minutes.

2 Add the fish and seafood. Ten minutes before serving, add the haddock and simmer for 5 minutes, then add the shrimp, oysters, and crabmeat. Cook until the shrimp and oysters become opaque, another 5 to 8 minutes. Remove the bay leaf. Finish with a few shakes of hot sauce and serve over rice with a sprinkle of filé powder.

I've made this dish as a whole side of salmon, wrapping the entire side in puff pastry, but I love the individual pockets. I'm often in search of ways to make classics a bit different, and if I'm already doing the puff, why beef it up when I can have salmon instead? I make a quick duxelles, or mushroom mixture, kept earthy with fresh thyme and garlic, then finish with a light note of sour cream. This is a knockoff you can be proud of. **SERVES 4**

salmon wellington

FOR THE SALMON

4 center-cut salmon fillets, 3 ounces each, skin removed

1 teaspoon lemon juice

Kosher salt and freshly ground black pepper

FOR THE SPINACH

2 tablespoons olive oil

½ cup chopped Vidalia or sweet onion

1 garlic clove, grated on a rasp or finely minced

2 cups loosely packed fresh baby spinach

Grated zest of 1 lemon

1 teaspoon fresh lemon juice

FOR THE MUSHROOMS

2 tablespoons olive oil

½ cup finely chopped mushrooms

½ cup chopped Vidalia or sweet onion

1 garlic clove, grated on a rasp or finely minced

6 to 8 sprigs fresh thyme, leaves stripped and chopped

1 Prepare the salmon. Brush both sides of the salmon fillets with lemon juice and season both sides with salt and pepper. Set aside.

2 Cook the spinach. Warm the olive oil in a large skillet over medium-high heat. Add the onion and garlic and cook, stirring, until tender, 5 minutes. Add the spinach, lemon zest, and lemon juice, tossing and cooking until the spinach is wilted. Transfer to a medium bowl and set aside.

3 Cook the mushrooms. In the same pan over medium heat combine the olive oil, mushrooms, onion, garlic, thyme, a pinch of salt, and a few grinds of pepper. Cook until the mushrooms are reduced and tender, about 8 minutes. Turn off the heat and stir in the sour cream. Set aside.

4 Assemble and bake. Preheat the oven to 400°F. Line a baking sheet with parchment. Unroll the pastry sheets on a lightly floured surface. Pass a rolling pin lightly over the pastry 2 or 3 times to seal the seams. With 3 swipes of a knife or pizza cutter, cut each pastry sheet into 4 equal rectangles along the width. Working with 4 of the strips, lightly prick the bottoms with a fork. Place 1 heaping spoonful of the mushroom mixture in the center of each rectangle, top with one of the salmon fillets, then layer with a heaping spoonful of the spinach mixture. Wet the edges of the pastry with water and top the rectangles with the 4 remaining pastry pieces. Using a fork, press the tines into the dough to crimp the edges. Transfer to the lined baking sheet. Brush with the heavy cream. Cut three 1-inch diagonal slits in each pastry to allow steam to escape. Bake 25 to 30 minutes, until golden. Garnish with parsley.

Kosher salt and freshly ground black pepper

¾ cup sour cream

FOR THE PASTRY AND GARNISH

All-purpose flour

2 puff pastry sheets, thawed

2 tablespoons heavy cream or whole milk

2 tablespoons chopped fresh flat-leaf or curly parsley

tip! To prepare these in advance for guests, assemble the pastries and freeze them uncooked on a parchment-lined baking sheet for 2 hours, then place in a resealable freezer bag for up to 1 month. Throw them in the refrigerator overnight, then rest them at room temperature for 2 hours before baking.

I love shrimp because it takes just seconds to cook if you buy It already deveined, shelled, and tailed. Check the freezer section for a big bag or kindly ask your fishmonger to do the deed for you. This simple dinner is so fast that from infusing the oil to cooking the pasta and sautéing the shrimp takes twenty minutes flat! The secrets are simple ingredients and steps that allow you to prep and go. You don't need to put on the Ritz to have a classy dinner. **SERVES 4**

shrimp and garlic fusilli

FOR THE INFUSED OIL

1 cup olive oil

Kosher salt

2 tablespoons freshly ground black pepper

FOR THE SHRIMP AND PASTA

1 pound long fusilli

4 garlic cloves, grated on a rasp or finely minced

1 pound shrimp, peeled, deveined, tails removed

¼ cup grated Parmesan cheese

Grated zest of 2 lemons

2 tablespoons fresh lemon juice

2 scallions, finely chopped

1 Infuse the oil and cook the pasta. In a small pot over low heat, combine the oil, a pinch of salt, and the pepper. Steep over medium-low heat until the oil is fragrant with the pungency of the pepper and a quick taste reveals a peppery flavor, 15 to 20 minutes. Set aside. Meanwhile, as the oil is infusing, cook the pasta until al dente as instructed on the package.

2 Make the shrimp. In a large straight-sided pan, combine ¼ cup of the infused oil and the garlic. Cook over medium heat until the garlic is fragrant but not browned, about 4 minutes. Add the cooked pasta and raise the heat to medium-high, tossing and stirring to coat, then add the shrimp and toss. Remove from the heat when the shrimp begin to turn pink and opaque. Continue tossing and the ambient heat will cook it the rest of the way.

3 Garnish and serve. Add the Parmesan cheese, lemon zest, lemon juice, and scallions and toss. Serve warm.

tips! If you prefer a bit of a sauce here, reserve some of the water used to boil the pasta and add it to the pan along with some wine or heavy cream. ■ Use remaining infused oil to fry eggs, make a vinaigrette, or drizzle over hummus.

his dish reminds me of when my mom would plunk an entire head of cauliflower in a pot with just cream, stock, and seasonings until it was tender. Seafood and vegetables together are seldom described as comforting, but please allow me to be the first to claim so with this recipe. The cream sauce and casserole dish ensure you'll get all warm and fuzzy with each scoop.

SERVES 4 TO 6

creamy lobster and cauliflower gratin

FOR THE LOBSTER

- 2 2-pound lobsters, cut in half from head to tail
- 2 tablespoons Old Bay seasoning

FOR THE CAULIFLOWER

- Florets from 1 large head of cauliflower
- 2 teaspoons Old Bay seasoning
- 1 tablespoon olive oil
- 2 tablespoons fresh lemon juice

FOR THE SAUCE

- 2 tablespoons unsalted butter
- ½ cup chopped onion
- Kosher salt
- 2 tablespoons all-purpose flour
- 1¾ cups fish or vegetable stock
- 1¼ cups heavy cream

1 Cook the lobster. Fill a large stockpot with a tight lid with 4 inches of water. Place a metal colander or a steaming basket upside down in the pot, so the curved side sticks up. Cover and bring to a boil, then add the lobsters and quickly cover to keep in the steam. Cook until the shells are bright red and the flesh opaque, 10 to 14 minutes. Remove from the pot and, once cooled, remove the meat from the tail and claws, then roughly chop.

2 Roast the cauliflower. Preheat the oven to 425°F. In a large bowl, combine the cauliflower, Old Bay, olive oil, and lemon juice. Toss to coat and spread the florets onto a baking sheet. Roast until a light golden brown and tender enough to bite, but not soft, about 25 minutes. Remove the florets to a paper towel–lined plate.

3 Make the sauce. In a large straight-sided pan, combine the butter, onion, and a pinch of salt. Cook over medium heat until the onion is tender, about 5 minutes. Add the flour and stir until it disappears and coats the onion. Cook, stirring, for just 1 minute more. Add the stock and continue to stir as it bubbles and thickens. Add the heavy cream and reduce the heat to a low simmer, still stirring. Once the cream thickens some, turn off the heat, add the brie and mozzarella, and stir until both are melted. Taste and season with a pinch of salt, if needed.

4 **Assemble and bake.** Remove the cauliflower from the oven. Lower the oven temperature to 375°F. Butter the bottom and sides of a 13 × 9-inch baking dish. Combine the lobster, cauliflower, and cheese sauce in a large bowl. Stir and pour into the prepared dish. Top with the fried onions and bake until the top is bubbly and the onions are a deeper golden color, about 20 minutes.

½ **pound triple-cream brie (I prefer St. André)**

½ **pound smoked mozzarella, shredded**

2 **cups French-fried onions, crushed, for topping**

Sticky Onion Crunch Wings
(PAGE 195)

Sweet and Sour
Wings (PAGE 196)

CHICKEN

Spicy PB&J Wings (PAGE 194)

One of my first paid jobs was as a hand on a chicken farm in Pennsylvania. I was a preteen member of Future Farmers of America. I was likely just trying to fit in at yet another new school, but I actually don't remember how I got involved. What I do remember is working all day for maybe twenty dollars and losing my love of eating chicken, because there I was, sending them to their end. The great benefit of vocational clubs or training is that they allow you to find a possible career path, including what isn't the right fit! Chicken farming wasn't for me. I transferred to an art and steelwork class and within a month I was back to my old self enjoying chicken and making triangle dinner bells for my dad to ring..

I don't have a favorite part of the bird. I truly love each part in various ways, even the giblets. It makes me feel I am getting a great value. Chicken is such a useful and versatile bird—and inexpensive. It's one of the best things to serve a multitude of guests. Here I share a few of my favorites and tricks. Serve it fast (Easy Grilled Chicken with Apple-Orange Sauce, page 174), serve to impress (Sweet Glazed Butterflied Chicken, page 177), or use less to feed more (Chicken and Wild Rice Casserole, page 184).

This is a perfect "come home from work and get it done" meal. This recipe is as bare as I go with chicken, besides just pushing some tenders on a stick and grilling them with salt, pepper, and olive oil. I really love a quick marinade, a split breast for fast grilling, and some fresh fruit for a sweet-citrus sauce that comes together while the chicken cooks. That even leaves time to set the table—or set up a table in front of the couch. **SERVES 4**

easy grilled chicken
WITH APPLE-ORANGE SAUCE

2 oranges

2 tablespoons sugar, plus more if needed

2 tablespoons honey

1 Fuji or Granny Smith apple, cored and chopped

¼ cup dried cranberries

¼ cup olive oil, plus more to season the grill

1 teaspoon kosher salt

Freshly ground black pepper

4 boneless chicken breasts, butterflied and split

¼ cup chopped pecans, toasted

1 Prepare the oranges. Juice 1 orange into a medium bowl. Slice off the top and bottom of the second orange to create a flat surface on each end. With the orange resting on one cut side, use a knife to cut between the flesh and white pith of the peel, angling the knife to expose the flesh from top to bottom. Make sure to trim off all the pithy white parts. Then, holding the orange in one hand, release the segments by using the knife to slice on either side of each segment's membrane. Save these segments in a separate medium bowl. Squeeze the remaining flesh from the orange that you sectioned to release the remaining juice into the first bowl with just the juice. So now you have orange segments in one bowl and fresh-squeezed orange juice in another bowl. Add the sugar and honey to the orange juice. Whisk to combine, then taste. If needed, adjust with more sugar to sweeten. Add the apple and cranberries to the bowl with the orange segments.

2 Marinate the chicken. Pour half the sweetened juice into a large resealable plastic bag and add the ¼ cup oil, salt, and a few grinds of black pepper. Add the chicken, seal the bag, and toss it a bit before resting on the counter for 25 to 30 minutes. Any longer and the acid in the juice will "cook" the chicken and ruin it.

3 **Cook the sauce.** In a medium pan over medium heat, combine the fruit mixture and the remaining half of the sweetened orange juice. Bring to a simmer and cook until the liquid is reduced and slightly thickened.

4 **Grill the chicken.** Heat a grill or grill pan to medium-high and brush lightly with oil. Remove the chicken from the plastic bag and shake off any excess marinade. Place the smooth side down on the grill and cook for 2 to 3 minutes, then flip and cook 2 minutes more. Transfer to a serving plate, pour sauce over the top, and sprinkle with pecans.

This butterflied chicken is so good, there's hardly a side dish I can think of that doesn't go with it. Try it and you'll know what I mean. I make this a lot. It has a sweet and sticky heat with curb appeal, perfect for a first date at home or the in-laws. **SERVES 4**

sweet glazed butterflied chicken

FOR THE CHICKEN

1 roaster chicken, 5 to 7 pounds, butterflied (see page 178)

Kosher salt and freshly ground black pepper

¼ cup olive oil

FOR THE GLAZE

3 tablespoons unsalted butter

2 tablespoons grated onion (use the smallest side on a box grater or a rasp)

⅛ teaspoon allspice

Kosher salt and freshly ground black pepper

2 garlic cloves, grated on a rasp or finely minced

¼ cup packed light brown sugar

1 tablespoon stone-ground mustard

¼ teaspoon hot sauce (I like Frank's Red Hot here)

2 teaspoons apple cider vinegar

1 **Prepare the chicken.** Season the chicken with salt and pepper. Rest on the counter for 2 hours to come to room temperature. Preheat the oven to 375°F.

2 **Roast the chicken.** Pour the olive oil into a large ovenproof pan over high heat. As the oil begins to smoke, add the chicken, skin side down. Press gently, especially the legs, and allow to sear until a peek beneath reveals golden brown skin, about 10 minutes. Using tongs, flip over so the skin is on top and place the pan in the oven. Roast until the internal temperature is around 140°F., 40 to 45 minutes.

3 **Make the glaze.** In a small pot over medium heat, melt the butter. Add the onion and allspice and a pinch of salt and a few grinds of pepper. Cook until the onion is tender, then add the garlic and cook until tender but not browned. Add the brown sugar, mustard, hot sauce, and vinegar. Reduce, about 5 minutes, then remove from the heat.

4 **Glaze the chicken.** Remove the chicken from the oven and brush on the glaze. Return the chicken to the oven and continue to cook until the internal temperature reaches 165°F., about 20 minutes more.

5 **Serve.** Cover the chicken loosely with foil and let rest for 15 minutes to allow the juices to redistribute. Then cut into sections and serve.

HOW TO DO THE BUTTERFLY

A STEP-BY-STEP GUIDE

This isn't a cheesy '90 s dance, it's a classy way to serve a bird. Butterflying a chicken is a showstopper technique that is seldom done at home, but it's easy. It's also smart because it cuts down the cooking time and maximizes the skin. When you roast a chicken whole, the skin on the bottom is a complete rubbery loss. The solution is an easy butterfly cut, then a good sear before the ride in the oven to roast. Here's the easy way to butterfly your bird.

1. Find the backbone.

2. With kitchen scissors or a sharp knife, cut from the neck to the tail along one side of the back bone.

3. Repeat the cut on the other side.

4. Lay the chicken, skin side down, on the cutting board and place a knife right in the back center of the breast plate (sternum).

5. Gently crack the breast plate by carefully hitting your knife with the heel of your palm. Some like to remove the ribcage bones, but I don't. Bones equal flavor.

6. Done!

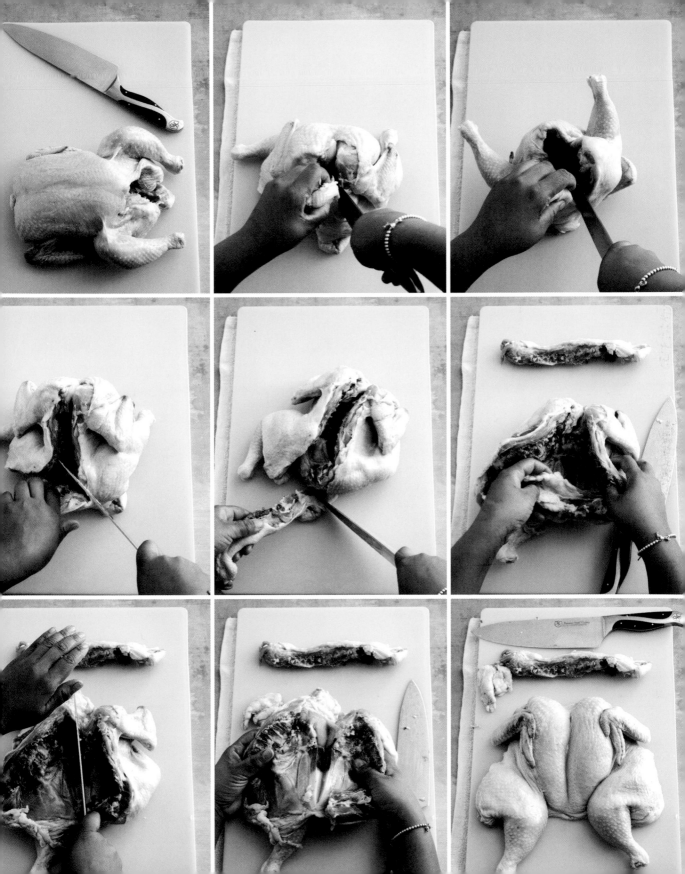

Cordon bleu is a French dish, but I know for sure the first time I had it was in Germany. Back then it was thin chicken breasts, stuffed and rolled up, then cooked. I loved slicing it to reveal stringy cheese and even more meat inside, usually deli ham. My updated version tastes the same; I just use shortcuts. I actually think the changes make the recipe better. Getting cheese to melt inside a stuffed breast can sometimes dry it out. With my easy layering technique I still get all the flavors and textures I love from one of my childhood favorites. Get ready for juicy, crispy chicken, thinly sliced salty ham, and creamy melted Swiss cheese, which always makes me smile. I never met a cheese I didn't like, no matter how stinky. **SERVES 4 TO 6**

easy chicken cordon bleu

1 cup all-purpose flour

Kosher salt and freshly ground black pepper

2 eggs, beaten

2 tablespoons whole-grain mustard

1 teaspoon sweet paprika

3 cups panko

4 boneless, skinless chicken breasts, halved and flattened

Peanut or vegetable oil

16 thin slices deli ham

16 slices Swiss cheese

tip! Turn these into small bites for guests by cutting the chicken into bite-sized cubes before frying, then topping the cooked chicken with cut squares of ham and cheese. Insert a toothpick in each and enjoy a fun finger food with cocktails.

1 Dredge the chicken. In a medium shallow bowl, combine the flour, a pinch of salt, and a few grinds of black pepper. Put the eggs, mustard, paprika, a pinch of salt, and a few grinds of pepper in a second medium shallow bowl and whisk to combine. Put the panko in a third medium shallow bowl. Run each piece of chicken through these bowls in that order: flour, egg, then panko.

2 Fry the chicken. In a large straight-sided pan pour enough oil to just cover the bottom by about a quarter inch. Heat on medium-high and when the oil begins to swirl, add the chicken in batches, angling each piece away from you so there is less splatter. Fry the chicken on one side until golden, about 4 minutes, then flip and fry on the other side just a few minutes more. Add more oil between batches if needed. Transfer the chicken to a baking sheet.

3 Finish the chicken. Turn on the broiler or heat the oven to the highest temperature possible. Top each piece of chicken with 2 slices of ham and 2 slices of cheese. Place in the oven on the center rack and cook until the cheese is melted, 2 to 3 minutes. Remove and serve.

this recipe came to me in a dream. I keep a notebook by my bed and woke up the next morning to scribbles about "maniladas." It's just a dish laden with things that comfort me—stuffed manicotti, cream sauce, and a nod to enchiladas verde (with green sauce). I'm always experimenting with casseroles because I really feel they are the perfect present for a potluck dinner or an at-home solution for a day or two of great leftovers. I know potluck sounds old-school, so if it makes you feel better, we can call it an NBA Finals party or Super Bowl bash . . . same thing. A casserole always trumps a bottle of wine! **SERVES 8 TO 10**

maniladas

18-ounce package
manicotti shells

Kosher salt

FOR THE FILLING

2 tablespoons olive oil

1 Vidalia onion, chopped

2 garlic cloves, minced

1 rotisserie chicken,
shredded

4 Roma tomatoes, seeded
and diced

3 tablespoons chopped
fresh cilantro leaves

½ cup sour cream

FOR THE TOMATILLO SAUCE

1 pound tomatillos, husked,
cleaned, and quartered

1 small red onion,
quartered

1 jalapeño pepper, halved

2 garlic cloves

2 tablespoons olive oil

Kosher salt and freshly
ground black pepper

1 **Prepare the pasta.** Boil the manicotti shells in salted water according to package instructions until al dente. Drain, reserving ½ cup pasta water. Pour the pasta on a tray or baking sheet to cool, so the shells don't stick to each other while you prep the filling. Preheat the oven to 400°F.

2 **Make the filling.** Heat the oil in a large pan over medium heat. When it begins to swirl, add the onion and cook, stirring, until tender, about 3 minutes. Add the garlic and sauté 1 minute more. Remove the pan from the heat and mix in the chicken, tomatoes, cilantro, and sour cream. Set aside.

3 **Make the tomatillo sauce.** Place the tomatillos, onion, jalapeño, and garlic in a small baking dish. Toss with the oil and season with salt and pepper. Roast until the edges of the tomatillos caramelize and the flesh becomes soft, about 45 minutes. Remove from the oven and scrape everything in the dish, including the drippings, into a blender. Blend until smooth. Use just enough reserved pasta water to thin the sauce to a pouring consistency. Taste the sauce and season with salt and pepper, if needed.

4 **Make the cheese sauce.** In a small saucepan, melt the butter over medium-high heat without browning. Add the nutmeg and flour and cook, stirring with a wooden spoon, for 2 minutes. Whisk in the heavy cream and bring to a simmer. Add the cheese and stir until melted. Taste the sauce and season with salt.

5 **Assemble the casserole.** Reduce the heat to 350°F. Stuff the manicotti tubes with the chicken mixture and assemble in a 9 × 13-inch baking dish with the open sides facing up. Pour the cheese sauce over the top. Bake for 30 minutes, or until the cheese is bubbling and a few bubbles are golden brown.

6 **Make your plate!** Drizzle tomatillo sauce on the maniladas before serving.

FOR THE CHEESE SAUCE

3 tablespoons unsalted butter

¼ teaspoon grated nutmeg

3 tablespoons all-purpose flour

2 cups heavy cream, room temperature

2 cups shredded Fontina cheese

Kosher salt

Casseroles usually make a debut in my kitchen at the start of what I know will be a busy week. I can count on the leftovers and if I stumble on a great casserole combo, I jot it down and keep it in mind for special occasions. Because the real purpose of a casserole is to share it—the size implies it. I simply love the warm, woodsy notes from the cinnamon and rosemary; together with the cranberry topping, it all smells like it would warm up a cold night in a forest cabin. The chicken stays moist from the poach, and feeding an entire family with just two chicken breasts is magic. Guests will love it. **SERVES 6 TO 8**

chicken and wild rice casserole

FOR THE CHICKEN

Unsalted butter, for greasing the dish

1 **sprig fresh thyme**

1 **bay leaf**

2 **tablespoons kosher salt**

2 **boneless, skinless chicken breasts**

FOR THE RICE FILLING

1⅓ **cups wild rice**

2 **tablespoons unsalted butter**

5 **ounces button mushrooms, quartered (about 2 cups)**

1 **small onion, chopped**

Kosher salt and freshly ground black pepper

2½ **cups heavy cream**

½ **teaspoon cinnamon**

2 **cups shredded Gruyère cheese**

1 **Prepare the chicken.** Butter the bottom and sides of a 9 × 13-inch casserole dish and set aside. In a large saucepan, combine 5 cups of water with the thyme, bay leaf, salt, and chicken. Bring to a boil over medium heat, then immediately reduce to a simmer and cook until the juices run clear or the internal temperature reaches 160°F., about 15 minutes, depending on the thickness of the chicken. Transfer the chicken to a cutting board and allow to rest for at least 10 minutes. Reserve the poaching liquid in the pot. When cool enough to handle, dice the chicken into ½-inch cubes and set aside.

2 **Cook the rice.** Return the poaching water to a boil, add the wild rice, and cover. Cook over medium heat until the rice grains split, 40 to 45 minutes. Drain the excess water, transfer the rice to a bowl, and set aside.

3 **Make the topping.** In a small pot over medium heat, melt the butter and add the brown sugar, cranberries, rosemary, bread crumbs, and a pinch of salt. Cook, stirring to mash the cranberries, until the sugar is dissolved and the mixture is uniform, about 5 minutes. Transfer to a bowl and set aside. Preheat the oven to 375°F.

4 **Make the filling.** In a large straight-sided pan over medium-high heat, melt the butter and add the mushrooms, onion, a pinch of salt, and a few grinds of pepper. Sauté until the mushrooms are browned, about 6 to 8 minutes. Add the heavy cream and the cinnamon, bring to a boil, then reduce the heat and simmer about 2 minutes to thicken slightly. Add the Gruyère and mix to incorporate. Add the rice and chicken to the pot and stir to combine. Taste and season with salt and pepper, if needed.

5 **Bake the casserole.** Transfer the filling to the prepared casserole dish. Spread the cranberry mixture evenly over the top of the casserole and bake until golden and bubbling, 15 to 20 minutes. Serve hot.

FOR THE TOPPING

2 tablespoons unsalted butter

6 tablespoons packed dark brown sugar

1 cup cranberries, fresh, or frozen and thawed

2 tablespoons chopped fresh rosemary leaves

¼ cup bread crumbs

Kosher salt

tip! The chunks of juicy poached chicken are divine here, but in a pinch you can shred half a rotisserie chicken to speed up preparation. Just use chicken stock to cook the rice.

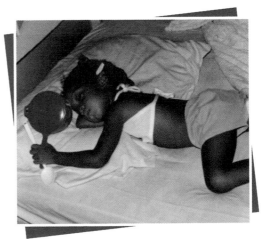

This is foreshadowing how as an adult I would treat my pots, pans, and cooking utensils. I've always guarded them, even in my sleep.

Sure, I'll wait for the slow 'n' low of real BBQ, but sometimes the heart wants what the heart wants, fast. This recipe is perfect when you see that pack of chicken legs or thighs on sale. It will turn a dark meat hater into a devotee. All you have to do is slow-roast, shred, and douse the juicy legs and thighs in one of my go-to sauces, and no one will miss the breasts. Team it with the fastest slaw ever and you can have the feel of summertime BBQ year-round in your kitchen, smoker or hot weather need not apply. **SERVES 6 TO 8**

shredded bbq chicken and fast slaw

FOR THE SLAW

- 1 savoy cabbage, finely shredded
- 1 carrot, finely shredded
- 1 tablespoon sugar
- 1 teaspoon apple cider vinegar
- Kosher salt and freshly ground black pepper
- ¼ cup dill relish
- ½ cup sour cream
- ½ cup mayonnaise
- ½ cup raisins

FOR THE ROASTING PAN

- 4 garlic cloves, smashed
- 1 pint cherry tomatoes
- 3 scallions, chopped (white and green parts)
- 2 tablespoons honey

1 Make the slaw. In a large bowl combine the cabbage, carrot, sugar, vinegar, a pinch of salt, and a few grinds of pepper. Massage the cabbage with your hands until it is tender and wilted, about 5 minutes. Add the relish, sour cream, mayonnaise, and raisins. Toss to combine, then taste and season with more salt, if needed. Serve immediately or refrigerate before serving.

2 Prepare the roasting pan. Preheat the oven to 225°F. Put the garlic, tomatoes, scallions, and honey in a roasting pan.

3 Make the rub. In a small bowl, combine the allspice, cayenne pepper, red pepper flakes, thyme, garlic powder, paprika, onion powder, salt, and a few grinds of pepper. Stir to mix well.

4 Cook the chicken. Coat each chicken thigh all over with the rub. Arrange the chicken over the tomato mixture, covering it as much as possible. Some tomatoes are going to peek out and that's fine; let those bad boys get caramelized later on! Shake any excess rub over the top. In a small bowl, whisk together the honey and apple cider vinegar. Drizzle over the chicken, cover tightly with aluminum foil, and roast for 1½ hours. Remove the foil, then roast for 30 more minutes.

5 **Shred the chicken.** Remove the chicken from the oven to a cutting board, gently shaking off the pan juices before the transfer. Remove the meat from the bones using a fork, tongs, knives, fingers, whatever works! Shred the meat with 2 forks and set aside.

6 **Make the pan BBQ sauce.** Place the roasting pan on the stovetop over medium heat and add the honey, brown sugar, and ketchup. Using a potato masher, smash the tomatoes still in the pan, then stir everything, allowing it to simmer and reduce until slightly thickened, about 5 minutes. Add the shredded chicken back to the pan and stir to coat. Serve with the slaw on bread.

FOR THE CHICKEN

½ teaspoon allspice

½ teaspoon cayenne pepper

1 tablespoon crushed red pepper flakes

1 tablespoon dried whole-leaf thyme

2 tablespoons garlic powder

2 tablespoons sweet paprika

3 tablespoons onion powder

3 tablespoons kosher salt

Freshly ground black pepper

12 skinless chicken thighs, patted dry with a paper towel

2 tablespoons honey

1 tablespoon apple cider vinegar

FOR THE PAN BBQ SAUCE

2 tablespoons honey

¼ cup packed light brown sugar

¼ cup ketchup

12 to 16 slices of white bread or 6 to 8 hamburger buns

tip! This chicken is great on a homemade pizza with shredded cheese, onions, and barbecue sauce in lieu of pizza sauce, or on top of grits for a Southern breakfast.

tip! Try sweetened lemonade or a 50/50 combination of lemonade and tea for the brine as well as the syrup for a different twist on infusing and drizzling flavor.

If you're frying chicken without brining, you're missing a chance to get it flavorful down to the bone. I'm all for crispy and delicious skin being the star, but there are many more bites beneath it, so brining is necessary. It's like the bit of salt in a good chocolate chip cookie. Sure you'll eat one without it, but to have that extra touch is to love it. Brining also keeps it juicy. Why not soak a Southern dish in a Southern drink before frying it the Southern way? It makes sense to me and my taste buds. **SERVES 4**

fried sweet-tea chicken
WITH SWEET-TEA SYRUP

FOR THE BRINED CHICKEN

4 cups sweetened tea

½ cup kosher salt

1 lemon, halved

1 chicken, 4½ to 5 pounds, cut into 10 pieces

FOR THE SYRUP

2 cups sweetened tea

½ cup sugar

Grated zest of 2 lemons

½ cup fresh lemon juice

Kosher salt

3 or 4 sprigs fresh thyme, leaves stripped and gently chopped

FOR THE COATING

Peanut or vegetable oil

2 eggs

2 teaspoons cayenne pepper

Kosher salt and freshly ground black pepper

1 cup all-purpose flour

¼ cup cornstarch

1 Make the brine. In a large bowl, whisk together 2 cups water, the tea, and salt until the salt dissolves. Squeeze the lemon halves into the pot, add the halves and the chicken pieces, submerge, and soak for 2 hours at room temperature.

2 Make the syrup. In a medium pan over medium heat, combine the tea, sugar, lemon zest, and lemon juice. Simmer until reduced and thickened like syrup. Taste and add a pinch of salt. Stir in the thyme.

3 Prepare to fry. In a large pot, heat 6 inches of oil until a deep-fry thermometer reaches 325°F. In a large bowl, whisk together the eggs, cayenne, a pinch of salt, and a few grinds of black pepper. In a paper bag, shake together the flour, cornstarch, a pinch of salt, and a few grinds of pepper. Drain the chicken from the brine and pat dry. Dust the chicken in the flour and shake off excess. Dip each piece in the egg, then back in the flour to coat. Set on a wire rack to let the coating sink in for 15 minutes.

4 Fry the chicken. In batches, fry the chicken until golden brown on both sides and cooked through, 15 to 20 minutes, depending on the size of the piece. Remove from the oil and set on a paper towel–lined plate to drain. Drizzle with the sweet-tea syrup.

just like an overbearing mother, smothering food sounds bad, but it has the best intentions. This is fried and tender, drenched with gravy. It's simple, but filled with comforting possibilities. My dish is a cross between Caribbean stewed chicken and a fish dish I became familiar with in New Orleans called trout almondine. It has a spicy, savory, and nutty flavor and crunchy texture that holds its ground under the gravy. I've simplified it so I can get it out of the kitchen and onto my plate fast. **SERVES 4**

smothered chicken almondine

FOR THE CHICKEN

4 boneless, skinless chicken breasts

Kosher salt and freshly ground black pepper

Peanut or vegetable oil

FOR THE DREDGE

3 cups all-purpose flour

Kosher salt and freshly ground black pepper

2 eggs

2 tablespoons dried thyme

1 tablespoon onion powder

1 tablespoon garlic powder

1 teaspoon cayenne pepper

1 teaspoon chili powder

1 **Season the chicken.** Season both sides of the chicken with a pinch of salt and a few grinds of pepper. Rest on the counter until room temperature, up to 2 hours.

2 **Set up the dredging station.** Set up 3 medium shallow bowls next to the stove. In the first bowl, put 1 cup of the flour and season with a pinch of salt and a few grinds of pepper. In the second bowl combine the eggs and half each of the thyme, onion powder, garlic powder, cayenne pepper, and chili powder. Add a splash of water, a pinch of salt, and a few grinds of pepper, and whisk to combine. In the third bowl, put the remaining flour, thyme, onion powder, garlic powder, cayenne pepper, and chili powder. Stir with a fork to combine.

3 **Fry the chicken.** Pour an inch of oil into a large straight-sided pan. Turn the heat to medium-high and when the oil begins to swirl, start dredging and frying. Dip the chicken in the first flour bowl and shake off the excess, then dunk it in the egg wash, and finally in the seasoned flour. Shake off the excess flour and place the chicken in the oil, laying it down away from you so nothing splatters. Fry for 6 to 8 minutes total, flipping once. Transfer to a paper towel–lined plate and tent loosely with foil or keep warm in a low oven.

4 **Make the gravy.** In a large pan over medium heat, melt the butter with the olive oil. Add the onion pulp and cayenne pepper. Stir in the flour, cooking until the flour is soaked into everything, about 2 minutes. Add the wine and reduce, stirring occasionally, until it has almost evaporated. Add the chicken stock and simmer until the mixture is reduced by one-third and has the consistency of gravy, 6 to 8 minutes. Add the almonds, then simmer about 5 more minutes. Serve warm poured over the chicken with a sprinkle of parsley on top as garnish.

FOR THE GRAVY

5 tablespoons unsalted butter

1 tablespoon olive oil

½ cup Vidalia or sweet onion pulp, grated on a box grater

¼ teaspoon cayenne pepper

2 tablespoons all-purpose flour

1 cup white wine

1½ cups chicken stock

1 cup almond slivers, toasted

¼ cup chopped fresh flat-leaf or curly parsley

tips! This is perfect with rice, mashed potatoes, or roasted Red Bliss potatoes. ■ Don't wait for a family pack of breasts to go on sale! Chicken tenders and boneless thighs cut into chunks are also a great bargain and perfect for this dish.

Sticky Onion Crunch Wings
(PAGE 195)

Sweet and Sour Wings
(PAGE 196)

WINGS

I think it's time to admit that wings are the wind beneath my, well, wings. Truly, without the first wing recipe I share with you, I more than likely wouldn't have this cookbook. My first appearance on the Food Network was preparing my Spicy Original Wings with Emeril Lagasse on *Emeril Live* in 2005. Next thing you know, I'm chasing a dream to share more recipes on my own show. I could do wings in so many different ways, but the simplest is the one that made the cut when Emeril reviewed all my submitted recipes, and I agree, it's truly great because it's a classic. I'll start there, but it gets really crazy after that. Crazy delicious.

Spicy PB&J Wings (PAGE 194)

spicy original wings

These are my babies, the original recipe I made for Emeril. They're so simple and quick to throw together. **SERVES 4 TO 6**

FOR THE CHICKEN

4 eggs

¼ cup heavy cream

2 tablespoons cayenne pepper

Kosher salt and freshly ground black pepper

2 cups all-purpose flour

1 cup cornstarch

Peanut or vegetable oil

3 pounds chicken wings, whole or separated as you like

FOR THE SPICY BUTTER SAUCE

1 cup hot sauce (I like Frank's Red Hot)

1 cup (2 sticks) unsalted butter

3 tablespoons fresh lemon juice

4 sprigs fresh oregano or thyme

1 Prepare the chicken. In a large bowl, whisk together the eggs, cream, cayenne, a pinch of salt, and a few grinds of black pepper. In a large paper bag, shake together the flour, cornstarch, a nice pinch of salt, and a few grinds of black pepper. Place a few pieces of chicken in the paper bag and shake to coat. Shake off as much excess flour as possible, then dunk in the egg mixture. Shake off excess egg wash and put the chicken pieces back in the paper bag. Toss well to coat. Repeat with the remaining wings. Place the dredged pieces on a wire rack to let the coating set, 20 minutes. Line a sheet pan with a wire rack.

2 Make the sauce. In a small saucepan with a lid, combine the hot sauce, butter, lemon juice, and oregano. Bring to a simmer, then remove from the heat and cover the pot to steep for at least 15 minutes. Remove the herb sprigs or leaves.

3 Fry the wings. In a Dutch oven, large pot, or fryer, pour enough oil to deep-fry, about 6 inches, and heat to 360°F. Add the chicken in batches and keep the temperature at 350°F. while frying. Fry the chicken while nudging occasionally until cooked through and crispy, about 13 minutes per batch. Remove with a spider or large slotted spoon and place on the wire rack. Immediately season the chicken with salt.

4 Sauce and garnish the wings. Place some of the sauce in a large bowl and toss the wings in batches, adding more sauce to thoroughly coat. Serve warm.

spicy pb&j wings

Trust me on this. A sweet peanut butter and jelly glaze on the lighter side of spicy is just enough to make you want more and forget about two slices of bread.

SERVES 4 TO 6

FOR THE WINGS

3 pounds chicken wings, whole or separated as you like

Kosher salt and freshly ground black pepper

2 cups all-purpose flour

Peanut or vegetable oil

½ cup peanuts, toasted and roughly chopped, for garnish

FOR THE SAUCE

1 cup smooth peanut butter

1 tablespoon plus 1 teaspoon sriracha hot chili sauce

¼ cup soy sauce

1 cup grape jelly

¾ cup coconut cream

¼ cup hot water

Kosher salt and freshly ground black pepper

1 **Prep the wings.** Place the wings on a baking sheet and season both sides with salt and pepper. Pour the flour in a paper bag or large bowl and toss the wings in batches, then place on a wire rack set inside a baking sheet or on the counter. Rest for at least 30 minutes to get to room temperature, and up to 2 hours.

2 **Make the sauce.** In a small pot over medium heat combine the peanut butter, sriracha, soy sauce, jelly, and coconut cream. Slowly whisk in the hot water to loosen the mixture. Bring the sauce to a simmer, then whisk as it thickens, about 5 minutes. Taste and season with a pinch of salt, if needed, and a few grinds of black pepper.

3 **Fry the wings.** In a Dutch oven, large pot, or fryer, pour enough oil to deep-fry, about 6 inches, and heat to 360°F. When you add your wings, the temperature will settle at 350°F. Try to keep it there by adjusting the heat. Fry the wings in batches until golden brown, 12 to 14 minutes. Drain on paper towels.

4 **Sauce and garnish the wings.** Place some of the sauce in a large bowl and toss the wings in batches, adding more sauce to thoroughly coat. Then place the wings on a serving tray and sprinkle with chopped peanuts. Serve warm.

sticky onion crunch wings

This is my new favorite—dunked in a punched-up hoisin sauce, then rolled in the crunchy onion topping usually kept for the string bean casserole around the holidays.

SERVES 4 TO 6

FOR THE WINGS

3 pounds chicken wings, whole or separated as you like

Kosher salt and freshly ground black pepper

Peanut or vegetable oil

½ cup French-fried onions, crushed (I like French's)

FOR THE SAUCE

1 cup hoisin sauce

½ cup pomegranate juice

¼ cup packed dark brown sugar

2 garlic cloves, grated on a rasp or finely minced

1 tablespoon prepared horseradish

4 scallions, finely chopped (white and green parts)

Kosher salt and freshly ground black pepper

1 Prep the wings. Place the wings on a baking sheet and season both sides with salt and pepper. Rest for at least 30 minutes to get to room temperature, and up to 2 hours.

2 Make the sauce. In a small pot, combine the hoisin, pomegranate juice, sugar, garlic, horseradish, scallions, and a few grinds of black pepper. Cook, stirring, over medium-high heat. When the sauce begins to boil, reduce the heat immediately to a simmer and cook until thickened, about 20 minutes. Taste and season with a pinch of salt.

3 Fry the wings. In a Dutch oven, large pot, or fryer, pour enough oil to deep-fry, about 6 inches, and heat to 360°F. When you add your wings, the temperature will settle at 350°F. Try to keep it there by adjusting the heat. Fry the wings in batches until golden brown, 12 to 14 minutes. Drain on paper towels.

4 Finish the wings. Put some of the sauce in a large bowl and toss the wings in batches, adding more sauce to thoroughly coat. Then place the crushed fried onions in a large bowl and toss the wings in batches to thoroughly coat. Serve warm.

sweet and sour wings

These have the perfect balance of each flavor, and the spritz of lime at the end seals the deal. **SERVES 4 TO 6**

FOR THE WINGS

- 3 pounds chicken wings, whole or separated as you like
- Kosher salt and freshly ground black pepper
- Peanut or vegetable oil

FOR THE SAUCE

- 3 cups apricot jam
- ¾ cup packed light brown sugar
- ½ cup chopped Vidalia or sweet onion
- 1 jalapeño pepper, seeded and finely chopped
- 1 cup orange juice
- 2 tablespoons liquid smoke
- 1½ teaspoons sweet paprika
- 3 garlic cloves, grated on a rasp or finely minced
- Grated zest of 2 limes
- Kosher salt and freshly ground black pepper

FOR THE GARNISH

- 2 tablespoons white sesame seeds
- 3 tablespoons fresh lime juice
- 2 scallions (white and green parts), thinly sliced at an angle

1 **Prep the wings.** Place the wings on a baking sheet and season both sides with salt and pepper. Rest for at least 30 minutes to get to room temperature, and up to 2 hours.

2 **Make the sauce.** In a small pot, combine the jam, brown sugar, onion, jalapeño, orange juice, liquid smoke, paprika, garlic, lime zest, and a few grinds of black pepper. Cook, stirring, over medium-high heat. When the sauce begins to boil, reduce the heat immediately to a simmer and cook until thickened, about 20 minutes. Taste and season with a pinch of salt.

3 **Fry the wings.** In a Dutch oven, large pot, or fryer, pour enough oil to deep-fry, about 6 inches, and heat to 360°F. When you add your wings, the temperature will settle at 350°F. Try to keep it there by adjusting the heat. Fry the wings in batches until golden brown, 12 to 14 minutes. Drain on paper towels.

4 **Sauce and garnish the wings.** In a small, dry pan over medium heat, toast the sesame seeds, tossing while they heat. They will begin to clump, then shine; remove them from the heat and set on a plate or paper towel to cool. Put some of the sauce in a large bowl and toss the wings in batches, adding more sauce to thoroughly coat. Then place the wings on a serving tray and spritz with lime juice. Finish with a sprinkle of sesame seeds and scallions. Serve warm.

honey mustard wings

These are a nod to my favorite dip for nuggets at fast-food places. The sauce is quick to make, and the wings disappear just as fast. **SERVES 4 TO 6**

FOR THE WINGS

3 pounds chicken wings, whole or separated as you like

Kosher salt and freshly ground black pepper

Peanut or vegetable oil

FOR THE SAUCE

1 cup honey

¼ cup packed light brown sugar

¼ cup whole-grain mustard

Kosher salt

1 **Prep the wings.** Place the wings on a baking sheet and season both sides with salt and pepper. Rest for at least 30 minutes to get to room temperature, and up to 2 hours.

2 **Make the sauce.** In a small pot, combine the honey, brown sugar, mustard, and 1 cup water. Bring to a simmer and cook until reduced and thickened, about 15 minutes. Give a taste and season with a pinch of salt.

3 **Fry the wings.** In a Dutch oven, large pot, or fryer, pour enough oil to deep-fry, about 6 inches, and heat to 360°F. When you add your wings, the temperature will settle at 350°F. Try to keep it there by adjusting the heat. Fry the wings in batches until golden brown, 12 to 14 minutes. Drain on paper towels.

4 **Sauce and garnish the wings.** Place some of the sauce in a large bowl and toss the wings in batches, adding more sauce to thoroughly coat. Serve warm.

maple bacon wings

These are sweet and savory wings, soaked in a maple-flavored marinade, fried, and tossed in bacon sugar. Yes, bacon sugar. **SERVES 4 TO 6**

FOR THE MARINADE

3 cups buttermilk

2 cups maple syrup

2 tablespoons dried sage

¼ cup hot sauce
(I like Frank's Red Hot)

3 tablespoons kosher salt

FOR THE WINGS

3 pounds chicken wings, whole or separated as you like

2 cups all-purpose flour

Kosher salt and black pepper

Peanut or vegetable oil

FOR THE GARNISH

1½ cups sugar

12 strips bacon, cooked until crisp and patted dry, free of visible oil

Kosher salt

1 **Marinate the wings.** In a large bowl, combine the buttermilk, maple syrup, sage, hot sauce, and salt. Whisk until the salt dissolves. Divide among large resealable plastic bags and fill with the chicken. Close and rest at room temperature for 1½ hours.

2 **Prep the wings.** In a large paper bag, combine the flour, a pinch of salt, and a few grinds of pepper. Remove the wings from the marinade, shaking off any excess. In batches, toss the chicken wings in the paper bag until fully coated with flour. Place the coated wings on a wire rack and let sit at room temperature until the flour appears to be invisible or soaked into the skin, about 30 minutes.

3 **Make the garnish.** Put the sugar, bacon, and a pinch of salt in a food processor and pulse until granulated. Set aside.

4 **Fry and coat the wings.** In a Dutch oven, large pot, or fryer, pour enough oil to deep-fry, about 6 inches, and heat to 360°F. When you add your wings, the temperature will settle at 350°F. Try to keep it there by adjusting the heat. Fry the wings in batches until golden brown, 12 to 14 minutes. Place some of the sugared bacon in a large bowl or paper bag and toss the wings in batches, adding more sugared bacon as needed. Serve warm.

sweet sriracha whisky wings

I've paired the sweet heat of sriracha with whisky and a chaser of brown sugar. I don't know what I did before I discovered sriracha. Look for it in a tall plastic squirt bottle with a green spout, near the ketchup. **SERVES 4 TO 6**

FOR THE WINGS

3 pounds chicken wings, whole or separated as you like

Kosher salt and freshly ground black pepper

Peanut or vegetable oil

FOR THE SAUCE

1 cup sriracha hot chili sauce

½ cup ketchup

¼ cup packed light brown sugar

¼ cup honey

½ cup whisky (pick your favorite)

Kosher salt and freshly ground black pepper

1 **Prep the wings.** Place the wings on a baking sheet and season both sides with salt and pepper. Rest for at least 30 minutes to get to room temperature, and up to 2 hours.

2 **Make the sauce.** In a small pot, combine the sriracha, ketchup, brown sugar, honey, and whisky. Bring to a simmer and cook until reduced and thickened, about 15 minutes. Taste and season with a pinch of salt and a few grinds of black pepper.

3 **Fry the wings.** In a Dutch oven, large pot, or fryer, pour enough oil to deep-fry, about 6 inches, and heat to 360°F. When you add your wings, the temperature will settle at 350°F. Try to keep it there by adjusting the heat. Fry the wings in batches until golden brown, 12 to 14 minutes. Drain on paper towels.

4 **Sauce the wings.** Place some of the sauce in a large bowl and toss the wings in batches, adding more sauce to thoroughly coat. Serve warm.

pesto wings

Stop wasting pesto on just pasta. Pesto is cleared for take-off on these earthy, crunchy wings. **SERVES 4 TO 6**

FOR THE WINGS

3 pounds chicken wings, whole or separated as you like

Kosher salt and freshly ground black pepper

Peanut or vegetable oil

FOR THE PESTO

4 cups tightly packed fresh basil

3 garlic cloves

½ cup red onion

½ cup pine nuts, toasted

6 ounces Parmesan cheese, cut into chunks or shredded

Grated zest of 2 lemons

2 tablespoons fresh lemon juice

Olive oil

Kosher salt and freshly ground black pepper

1 **Prep the wings.** Place the wings on a baking sheet and season both sides with salt and pepper. Rest for at least 30 minutes to get to room temperature, and up to 2 hours.

2 **Make the pesto.** Put the basil, garlic, onion, pine nuts, Parmesan, lemon zest, and lemon juice in a food processor. Pulse while pouring a stream of olive oil through the top until it comes together and is the texture of a chunky mayonnaise, not loose. Taste and season with a pinch of salt and a few grinds of black pepper.

3 **Fry the wings.** In a Dutch oven, large pot, or fryer, pour enough peanut or vegetable oil to deep-fry, about 6 inches, and heat to 360°F. When you add your wings, the temperature will settle at 350°F. Try to keep it there by adjusting the heat. Fry the wings in batches until golden brown, 12 to 14 minutes. Drain on paper towels.

4 **Sauce the wings.** Place some of the pesto in a large bowl and toss the wings in batches, adding more sauce to thoroughly coat. Serve warm.

bbq chip wings

If a piece of fried chicken fell into the dust at the bottom of your favorite bag of BBQ chips, this would be the smoky sweet result! That's how I came up with this recipe—inspiration struck while turning an empty bag of chips inside out to lick the lining. Don't judge me! **SERVES 4 TO 6**

FOR THE WINGS

- 1 cup all-purpose flour
- Kosher salt and freshly ground black pepper
- 3 pounds chicken wings, whole or separated as you like
- Peanut or vegetable oil

FOR THE COATING

- ¼ cup sweet paprika
- 2 tablespoons onion powder
- 2 tablespoons garlic powder
- ½ teaspoon kosher salt
- ¼ cup plus 1 tablespoon sugar

1 **Prep the wings.** In a large paper bag, combine the flour, a pinch of salt, and a few grinds of pepper. In batches, toss the chicken wings in the bag until fully coated with flour. Place the coated wings on a wire rack and rest at room temperature until the flour appears to be invisible or soaked into the skin, about 30 minutes.

2 **Make the coating.** Put the paprika, onion powder, and garlic powder in a sauté pan over medium-low heat. Toast the spices, tossing constantly to avoid burning, until fragrant, about 5 minutes. Remove from the heat and allow to cool completely. Once cooled, add the salt and sugar. Place in a large bowl or large paper bag for tossing.

3 **Fry the wings.** In a Dutch oven, large pot, or fryer, pour enough oil to deep-fry, about 6 inches, and heat to 360°F. When you add your wings, the temperature will settle at 350°F. Try to keep it there by adjusting the heat. Fry the wings in batches until golden brown, 12 to 14 minutes.

4 **Coat the wings.** Remove the wings from the oil and immediately add them to the bowl or bag with the coating. Toss to coat. Serve warm.

spicy herb baked wings

The rub for these wings is built for a ride in the oven. The warmth allows the flavors of the herbs and spices a chance to intensify. **SERVES 4 TO 6**

FOR THE HERB RUB

Olive oil

3 sprigs fresh rosemary, 4 to 6 inches long

12 fresh sage leaves

1 tablespoon cumin seed

1 tablespoon crushed red pepper flakes

½ tablespoon whole black peppercorns

1 tablespoon garlic powder

1 tablespoon kosher salt

3 pounds chicken wings, whole or separated as you like

1 Prep the rub. Pour an inch of olive oil into a small pan over medium heat. When the oil begins to swirl, add the rosemary and cook, turning the sprigs, until the leaves darken and become crispy, about 2 minutes. Transfer to a paper towel–lined plate. Add the sage to the same pan and cook until the leaves darken, slightly curl, and stop sizzling, just 30 seconds to 1 minute. Transfer to a paper towel–lined plate. In a medium dry pan over low heat, combine the cumin, red pepper flakes, peppercorns, and garlic powder. Toast the spices, tossing constantly to avoid burning, until fragrant, about 5 minutes. Remove from the heat and allow to cool completely. Put the herbs and spices in a spice grinder and pulse until combined. Remove and add salt.

2 Prep the wings. Massage the wings with the herb rub and place on a wire rack set inside a baking sheet to let the rub set, 30 minutes. While the wings rest, preheat the oven to 400°F.

3 Bake the wings. Transfer the baking sheet with the rack and wings to the oven and bake until crispy, flipping halfway through, about 40 minutes total. Serve warm.

ith my basic roasted chicken I go one step further than olive oil, salt, and pepper by adding cumin. It still keeps things simple, just a little Tex-Mex. The aroma of cumin is one of my favorite kitchen scents. Here, I bake the chicken and drizzle a simple sauce for a no-frills dinner that feels special. Anytime I'm trying to cut down on fat, but not flavor, I start here. Besides, the allure of a discounted family pack of chicken breasts, perfect for leftovers, is hard to resist. **SERVES 4**

cumin baked chicken
WITH SWEET HONEY-LIME SAUCE

FOR THE BRINED CHICKEN

2 tablespoons kosher salt

1 tablespoon sugar

1 teaspoon fresh lime juice

4 boneless, skinless chicken breasts, patted dry

FOR THE RUB

1 teaspoon ground cumin

¼ teaspoon cayenne pepper

Grated zest of 1 lime

1 teaspoon kosher salt

Freshly ground black pepper

3 tablespoons olive oil

FOR THE SAUCE

2 teaspoons honey

1 teaspoon confectioners' sugar

1 teaspoon hot sauce (I like Frank's Red Hot)

½ cup olive oil

¼ cup fresh lime juice

3 tablespoons whole-grain mustard

1 **Brine the chicken.** In a large resealable plastic bag, combine 2 cups water with the salt, sugar, and lime juice. Seal and agitate until the salt and sugar dissolve. Add the chicken and reseal, squeezing out all the air so the chicken is completely covered in the brine. Rest on the counter for 1 hour.

2 **Make the rub.** In a small bowl, mix the cumin, cayenne, lime zest, salt, a few grinds of pepper, and olive oil. Stir to combine.

3 **Bake the chicken.** Preheat the oven to 350°F. Remove the chicken from the brine and rinse under tap water. Pat the chicken dry, then massage each piece evenly with the rub. Place the chicken in a baking dish and cover tightly with aluminum foil. Bake until juices run clear or the internal temperature reaches 165°F., about 30 minutes.

4 **Make the sauce.** In a medium bowl, combine the honey, sugar, hot sauce, olive oil, lime juice, and mustard. Vigorously whisk until well mixed.

5 **Serve the chicken.** Cover the chicken loosely with aluminum foil and let rest for 10 minutes. Slice 1-inch-thick pieces along the length and against the direction of the muscle of each breast. Drizzle with the sauce and serve.

The smell of chicken pot pie baking is to me the savory equivalent of baking chocolate chip cookies. I had the frozen single-serve version of chicken pot pie growing up and still cook one from time to time for nostalgia. I make many versions of chicken pot pie and they all start with homemade crust; it's worth it. My Southwestern version is a great balance of flaky crust, creamy chicken and vegetable filling, cumin, Sazon, and what I sometimes call my competition: the grocery store freezer section. **SERVES 4 TO 6**

southwestern chicken pot pie

FOR THE DOUGH

¼ cup ice water

1 teaspoon Sazon seasoning

1¼ cups all-purpose flour, plus more to roll the dough

Kosher salt

½ cup (1 stick) unsalted butter, cut into pieces and frozen

FOR THE CHICKEN

1 pound chicken thighs and legs

4 to 6 sprigs fresh thyme

2 garlic cloves, smashed

Kosher salt

1 **Make the dough.** Stir the ice water and Sazon in a cup until dissolved and set aside. Pulse the flour and a pinch of salt in a food processor. Add the butter and pulse until it's in small pebbles throughout the flour. Slowly add the water and Sazon mixture in a stream, pulsing until the dough comes together. You may not use all the water mixture. Remove the dough, form into a ball, and flatten it into a thick disc. Wrap in plastic and refrigerate.

2 **Poach the chicken.** In a large pot, combine the chicken, thyme, and garlic with water to cover by 1 inch. Sprinkle with a pinch of salt and bring to a boil, then reduce to a simmer. Cook until the chicken reaches an internal temperature of 165°F. or the juices run clear when the flesh is punctured, 20 to 25 minutes. Remove the chicken parts and rest on a plate. Reserve ¼ cup of the poaching liquid. Remove the skin from the poached chicken, pull the meat from the bones, and shred or chop, then set aside.

3 **Make the filling.** In a large sauté pan, combine the butter, oil, serrano pepper, thyme, cumin, and Sazon, and season with a pinch of salt and a few grinds of pepper. Sauté, stirring, until the pan is fragrant, 3 to 4 minutes. Add the frozen vegetable blend, garlic, and the reserved poaching liquid. Raise the heat to create steam and continue stirring until the vegetable blend is cooked, 6 to 8 minutes. Add the flour in sprinkles and stir to combine, then add the milk. Allow to simmer and thicken for about 5 minutes. Remove from the heat and stir in the crema and reserved chicken.

4 Roll out the dough. Preheat the oven to 375°F. Remove the dough from the refrigerator and sprinkle a flat surface with flour. Flour a rolling pin and roll the dough into a circle about ⅛ inch thick. Using a knife or pizza wheel, trim the edges. Center the dough in an 8- or 9-inch pie dish, allowing the excess dough to drape over the edges.

5 Fill the dough and bake. Pour the filling into the dough. Fold the edges over the top of the pie, making sure not to overlap too much dough where it pleats. This amount of dough leaves a hole in the center to vent. In a small bowl, whisk the egg with 1 tablespoon water. Brush the egg wash gently on top of the dough. Bake until the crust is golden brown and the inside is bubbling, 25 to 30 minutes.

FOR THE FILLING

- 2 tablespoons unsalted butter
- 2 tablespoons olive oil
- 1 serrano pepper, seeded and chopped
- 4 to 6 sprigs fresh thyme
- ½ teaspoon ground cumin
- 1 teaspoon Sazon seasoning

  Kosher salt and freshly ground black pepper
- 1½ cups frozen Latin vegetable blend (peas, corn, onion, red pepper, and black beans)
- 2 garlic cloves, thinly sliced
- 2 tablespoons all-purpose flour
- 1½ cups whole milk
- 1 cup Mexican crema

- 1 egg

Grandma's Chopped BBQ
with Two Family Sauces (PAGE 210)

PORK & LAMB

Grandma's Chopped BBQ
  with Two Family Sauces

Curry-Lime Pork Kabobs

Chorizo, Quinoa, and Zucchini Hash

Pork Laulau

Ginger-Braised Pork Belly

Grilled Pineapple Pork

Chicken-Fried Pork Chops

North Carolina Slow 'n' Low House Ribs

Curry-Braised Lamb Shanks with Potatoes

Steak-Grilled Lamb Chops
  with Mango Mint Chutney

I have a love affair with pork and lamb.

I was around six or seven years old when I first looked forward to visiting both sets of my grandparents in the Carolinas. Pork was a big part of each visit. As a kid I didn't eat much at my grandparents' house in South Carolina because Granddaddy Anderson had pigs, and I loved them. I realized that what I didn't eat at the table got put in a slop bucket to feed the pigs, and I really wanted to feed them with him. He was such a dedicated farmer and I looked up to him. I don't even think I understood that the pigs I was feeding were the animals that became bacon and my beloved hot dogs. Visiting my grandparents in North Carolina, however, was less about feeding the pigs and more about eating them. It was my granddaddy Williams' pride and joy to fuss over the spit all day, tending to the roasting pig with his metal bowl of basting juices. It was a sight to see and a time to treasure. We'd wait all day to eat, and it was worth it.

I have included a couple of lamb recipes here as well. I think lamb is the exact opposite of pork when it comes to flavor. Pork needs added seasonings because alone, it's bland, but lamb comes with its own signature flavor that requires balance. So really, they both need the same thing in the kitchen—powerful ingredients that stand out. None of these recipes is shy on flavor.

Curry-Braised Lamb Shanks with Potatoes (PAGE 223)

say I have the "cake gene" and that I got it from my grandma, skipping a generation (sorry, Mommy). As for BBQ, we all got that gene. Seems like everyone in my family has an ability to coax the best out of a slow and low cooking process. My granddaddy was the best, and I wish he could see what I've done with the knowledge he gave me. From the rooter to the tooter (or snout to tail), as we'd say in the Carolinas, nothing is going to break the budget, and it all tastes great. This is for him and Grandma Williams. **SERVES 8 TO 10**

grandma's chopped bbq
WITH TWO FAMILY SAUCES

FOR THE PORK ROAST

1 9-pound boneless pork shoulder, skin trimmed

8 garlic cloves, smashed

2 to 3 cups vegetable stock

FOR THE RUB

½ cup Old Bay seasoning

1 tablespoon onion powder

1 tablespoon garlic powder

1 tablespoon sweet paprika

3 tablespoons olive oil

Carolina Pork Sauce or Apricot BBQ Sauce (recipes follow), for serving

1 **Prepare the pork.** With the tip of a knife, make eight 2-inch-deep pockets all around the pork and insert a smashed garlic clove in each.

2 **Make the rub.** Put the Old Bay, onion powder, garlic powder, sweet paprika, and olive oil in a small bowl. Stir to combine, then rub the seasoning all over the pork. Rest at room temperature for 2 hours.

3 **Slow-roast the pork.** Preheat the oven to 250°F. Fill a roasting pan with vegetable stock 1 inch deep. Add the pork and cover with several layers of aluminum foil. Getting the seal tight is key because this locks in the steam, which helps break down the pork so it's pull-worthy. Roast in the oven for 2 hours covered, then pull back the foil a bit and prick the pork with a fork. If tender and jiggly, remove the foil and roast for 1 more hour. If not, re-cover and cook for at least 30 minutes, but up to 1 hour more, adding more stock if needed. Once you remove the foil, the liquid can evaporate a bit.

4 **Rest and serve.** Remove the roast from the oven, cover loosely with foil, and rest so the juices redistribute. Chop into small chunks. Divide in half and toss with each of the following sauces, or leave dry and ladle a sauce over top.

carolina pork sauce MAKES 4 CUPS

1 Cook the vegetables. Melt the butter in a medium pot over medium-low heat. Add the onion and garlic and season with a pinch of salt and a few grinds of black pepper. Cook until both are tender but not browned.

2 Finish the sauce. Add the ketchup, vinegar, orange juice, and sriracha. Bring to a boil, then add the brown sugar and stir until dissolved, about 2 more minutes. This should be a loose sauce. Refrigerate if not using right away.

- 2 tablespoons unsalted butter
- 1 cup chopped Vidalia or sweet onions
- 2 garlic cloves, grated on a rasp or finely minced
- Kosher salt and freshly ground black pepper
- 2 cups ketchup
- 1 cup apple cider vinegar
- ½ cup orange juice
- ¼ cup sriracha hot chili sauce
- 3 tablespoons packed light brown sugar

apricot bbq sauce MAKES 4 CUPS

1 Sauté the vegetables. Melt the butter with the oil in a large sauté pan over medium heat. Add the onions and season with salt and pepper. Cook until tender, stirring occasionally to ensure the onions do not brown. Add the paprika and garlic, cooking until the garlic is tender, but not browned, reducing the heat if needed.

2 Finish the sauce. In this order, add the brown sugar, apricot jam, ketchup, and sriracha, stirring to combine between additions. Once combined, bring to a simmer and add the vinegar. Taste the sauce and season with a pinch of salt, if needed, and a few grinds of pepper.

- 2 tablespoons unsalted butter
- 2 tablespoons olive oil
- 4 onions, chopped
- Kosher salt and freshly ground black pepper
- 1 teaspoon Hungarian or hot paprika
- 8 garlic cloves, minced
- ½ cup packed dark brown sugar
- 1 cup apricot jam
- 1 cup ketchup
- 2 teaspoons sriracha hot chili sauce
- 2 teaspoons apple cider vinegar

Some dishes sound a bit crazy—you just have to try them to judge for yourself. If someone at the little Cuban restaurant in France had told me that I was ordering fried curried sweet lime-flavored pork, I think I would have passed. But being hungry and fearless—as well as ordering blindly from a foreign menu—got me to an unbelievably happy place without even trying. This is a unique flavor, but a must-try dish. I always get compliments when I make it, and each time I divulge the simple ingredients, I get an astounded look. I like that look, so I'm passing on the flavors in case you'd like that same reaction when feeding your friends and family. **SERVES 4 TO 6**

curry-lime pork kabobs

2 tablespoons mild yellow curry powder

1 tablespoon garlic powder

Grated zest of 2 limes

1 teaspoon kosher salt

Freshly ground black pepper

1 pound pork loin, cubed

1 pound pearl onions

Vegetable or olive oil, for brushing

1 tablespoon fresh lime juice (2 to 3 limes)

1 tablespoon sugar

1 scallion, finely chopped

1 **Season and rest the pork.** Put the curry powder, garlic powder, lime zest, salt, and a few grinds of pepper in a medium bowl. Stir to combine, then add the pork and onions. Toss to coat all the pieces. Let rest at room temperature for 1 to 2 hours.

2 **Grill the pork.** Turn a grill or grill pan to medium heat and brush with oil. If using wood skewers, soak them in water for 1 hour before using. Load the skewers with a piece of pork and then an onion, alternating and piercing each piece from end to end. Place the skewers on the grill and cook fully on one side before rotating. Grill until the onions are tender and the pork is cooked through, 10 to 12 minutes.

3 **Garnish the pork.** Transfer the kabobs to a plate and immediately sprinkle with lime juice, then sugar, and then scallions. Cover loosely with foil and let rest for 5 minutes, then serve warm.

fresh Mexican chorizo, quinoa, and zucchini can be in the same sentence—why not? When I'm in my kitchen working on other recipes, sometimes my meal becomes the sum of parts and pieces of other dishes. I made this after I had some trimmed zucchini ends left over from stuffing various types of squash. I chopped them down and pulled out some other bits from my fridge for a make-shift meal that turned into a first-run delight. Each bite is a textural joy—I really love a hearty meal with character in each bite. **SERVES 4 TO 6**

chorizo, quinoa, and zucchini hash

FOR THE QUINOA

1½ cups quinoa

2½ cups beef stock

¼ cup fresh lime juice

¼ cup chopped fresh cilantro

FOR THE CHORIZO

1 pound Mexican chorizo, casings removed

2 tablespoons olive oil

FOR THE VEGGIES

1 tablespoon unsalted butter

½ cup chopped Vidalia or sweet onion

2 zucchinis, cut into ¼-inch cubes

6 to 8 sprigs fresh thyme, leaves stripped and chopped

2 garlic cloves, grated on a rasp or finely minced

1 red bell pepper, seeded and chopped

1 3- to 4-inch cinnamon stick

1 **Make the quinoa.** In a medium pot, combine the quinoa, beef stock, and lime juice. Bring to a boil, then reduce to a simmer and cover. Cook until the stock is absorbed and the quinoa is al dente, 12 to 14 minutes. Stir in the cilantro and set aside.

2 **Cook the chorizo.** Combine the chorizo and olive oil in a large pan over medium heat. Using a wooden spoon, break up the chorizo until it resembles ground beef and is cooked through, about 10 minutes. Use a slotted spoon to transfer the chorizo to a plate. Leave the chorizo's signature orange-colored fat in the pan.

3 **Cook the vegetables.** To the same pan over medium heat, add the butter, onion, zucchini, thyme, garlic, bell pepper, cinnamon stick, a pinch of salt, and a few grinds of pepper. Cook, stirring occasionally, until the onion and zucchini are tender, about 10 minutes. Add the tomato paste and stir to coat, cooking until it becomes a deeper red, about 5 minutes. Add the beef stock and stir to combine, then reduce the heat and cook 5 minutes more.

4 **Make the hash.** Combine the butter, garlic, and a pinch of salt in a small nonstick pan over medium heat. Add the stuffing cubes and toast while tossing until light golden, about 5 minutes. Set aside. Add the chorizo and quinoa to the pan with the vegetables and toss to combine, then sprinkle with the warm toasted stuffing crumbs. Remove the cinnamon stick and serve warm or at room temperature.

tip! To maintain the crunch, reserve the toasted stuffing crumbs in an airtight container and sprinkle them over the top when you're ready to serve the hash.

Kosher salt and freshly ground black pepper

1 tablespoon tomato paste

¼ cup beef stock

FOR THE HASH

2 tablespoons unsalted butter

1 garlic clove, grated on a rasp or finely minced

Kosher salt

1 cup packaged stuffing cubes, crushed to rice-sized pieces

hawaii's popular main dish of salted pork wrapped in taro leaves needs a little change for people not lucky enough to live there, and the trick is in your produce department. Pick up some collard greens and you can take a trip to the islands. Hawaiians dine on a unique blend of ethnic flavors, and this unctuous seasoned tender pork wrapped in bitter green pockets is totally my speed. I spice it up a bit and though I don't go as salty as an authentic laulau, I get equally tasty results. Get the best gift wrapper in the house to help with the assembly, or just take your time. This is easy. **SERVES 6**

pork laulau

FOR THE COLLARDS

Kosher salt

3 bunches collard greens, long stems trimmed

FOR THE PORK

1 tablespoon plus 2 teaspoons kosher salt

1 tablespoon plus 2 teaspoons ground cumin

1 tablespoon crushed red pepper flakes

1 tablespoon plus 2 teaspoons onion powder

1 tablespoon garlic powder

1 tablespoon dried Mexican oregano

½ teaspoon grated nutmeg

3 pounds boneless pork shoulder, cut into ½-pound portions

1 to 2 cups chicken stock

1 Blanch the collards. Bring a large pot of salted water to a boil. Cook the collards for 3 to 4 minutes, until soft and pliable. Drain and set aside.

2 Prepare the rub. In a large bowl, mix together the salt, cumin, chili flakes, onion powder, garlic powder, oregano, and nutmeg. One by one, place each piece of pork in the rub and toss to coat. Massage the rub into the pork and place on a plate to rest while completing the others.

3 Wrap the pork. Wrap each piece of pork in a blanched collard leaf, folding and tucking the collards around the meat. Use another leaf to wrap over the first one and repeat, using 3 or 4 collards to completely wrap each one. Make little packages this way and place each, seam side down, in an 8 × 8-inch baking dish. This should be a tight fit.

4 Cook the pork. Preheat the oven to 225°F. Add enough stock to reach halfway up the stuffed greens. Cover tightly with heavy-duty aluminum foil and bake until the pork is cooked through and fork tender, 2 to 3 hours.

braising pork belly brings it to its knees. It becomes tender and juicy with the flavors of the braising liquid. In this case, I do a play on sweet and sour with a tiny spot of heat. The key is to keep the braise simple—no need to go too crazy with the flavors. Cook the belly in a moist environment and just let the unctuous pork do the talking. **SERVES 4**

ginger-braised pork belly

1½ pounds pork belly, cut into 4 equal pieces about 3 inches long

2 tablespoons whole-grain mustard

¾ cup sugar

3 tablespoons honey

2 cups soy sauce

2 scallions, chopped (white and green parts)

2-inch piece of fresh ginger, peeled and thinly sliced

1 **Prep the pork belly.** Rub all sides of the pork belly with mustard. Rest at room temperature for 1 hour.

2 **Braise the pork belly.** In a large cast-iron or non-stick pan over medium heat, melt the sugar, stirring constantly. Just when it melts, add the honey and the pork belly, skin side down. Let the skin get crispy, 5 to 8 minutes. Add the soy sauce, scallions, ginger, and 2 to 4 cups water, enough to come 1 inch up the sides of the pork belly. Bring to a boil, then reduce to a simmer and cook the pork belly for 10 minutes per side. Remove and serve.

Pork roast can take forever, so I often cut it down to medallions — that way it marinates faster and fits into my cooking schedule. If I find pork already cut down to size, even better. I usually let the meat and produce sections dictate what's for dinner, seldom having a real grocery list when I go shopping. A list can sometimes narrow my view, and I want to be open to everything in the store. This is a lean cut, so the sauce really does its job, adding flavor and moisture. This is a way to make a roast a bit more everyday, but still special with its very own sauce.

SERVES 4

grilled pineapple pork

4 boneless pork loin chops, center cut, 1 inch thick

Kosher salt and freshly ground black pepper

2 tablespoons Dijon mustard

¼ cup honey

1 cup canned crushed pineapple

2 tablespoons vegetable, canola, or peanut oil

1 **Marinate the pork.** Season the pork with salt and pepper on all sides. In a small bowl, whisk together the mustard, honey, and pineapple. Reserve ½ cup for brushing. Pour the rest into a resealable plastic bag and add the seasoned pork. Toss to coat on all sides, then seal and rest for 2 hours at room temperature.

2 **Grill the pork.** Heat a grill or grill pan to medium-high and brush with the oil. Remove the pork medallions from the bag and shake off the excess marinade. Discard the marinade. Place the pork on the grill and cook 4 minutes per side or until the desired doneness, brushing with the reserved sauce and flipping just once. Transfer the pork to a plate, cover loosely with foil, and let it rest for 10 minutes before serving.

tips! If you don't have a grill, you can sear the pork in a pan, then roast in a 375°F. oven with a few pineapple rings on top until it reaches the desired temperature. (See internal temperatures, page 19.) ■ Cut leftover pork into smaller chunks and add to rice, soups, or mac and cheese. ■ Canned or fresh peaches are great here as well.

I confess, my favorite part of a fried pork chop is the rim of golden, crispy fat along the side. I usually pick the chops with the most fat, knowing some will melt away as it cooks and the rest will melt in my mouth. My seasoning blend is pretty simple, with garlic powder, fresh thyme, and just enough heat from cayenne pepper to make you take another bite. These chops usually end up in my hands for a full-on gnaw session. Like chicken, eat these fresh from the fry, or cold like they do at my local bar, Feeney's, when I stop in for a beer and share my second-day jewels. **SERVES 4**

chicken-fried pork chops

FOR THE CHOPS

- 8 bone-in pork chops, ½ to ¾ inch thick
- 1 tablespoon garlic powder
- Kosher salt and freshly ground black pepper
- Peanut or vegetable oil

FOR THE DREDGE

- 1½ cups all-purpose flour
- ½ cup cornstarch
- Kosher salt and freshly ground black pepper
- 2 eggs
- 8 to 10 sprigs fresh thyme, leaves stripped and chopped
- ¼ teaspoon cayenne pepper

1 **Prep the chops.** Season the pork chops with the garlic powder, then salt and pepper on both sides. Wrap tightly in plastic and rest at room temperature for 2 hours.

2 **Set up the dredging station.** In a large paper bag, mix the flour, cornstarch, a nice pinch of salt, and a few grinds of black pepper. In a shallow bowl, beat the eggs with 1 tablespoon water. Add the thyme, cayenne pepper, a pinch of salt, and a few grinds of black pepper.

3 **Fry the chops.** Fill a large straight-sided frying pan with an inch of oil and heat. Dredge the chops by first dropping them into the flour. Shake off the excess flour, then dunk in the egg mixture, shaking off the excess. Transfer the chops back to the paper bag and shake, tossing until coated. Remove the chops and gently shake off excess flour. When the oil begins to swirl, fry the pork chops in batches until golden, 4 to 5 minutes per side. Transfer to a paper towel–lined plate to drain. Serve hot.

tip! Reheat these and many other fried meats by resting them at room temperature for 2 hours, then placing them in a 200°F. to 250°F. oven on a baking sheet lined with a wire rack or crumpled aluminum foil.

for North Carolina's version of barbecue flavor, there's plenty of vinegar. I balance it with sugar and my granddad's secret ingredient, beer. Sometimes I get a bit emotional making these because the scent reminds me of him. Pick your favorite hoppy beverage and make sure there is extra left for you to enjoy with the ribs. **SERVES 4**

north carolina slow 'n' low house ribs

FOR THE RIBS

½ cup kosher salt

3 pounds baby back pork ribs

1 cup of your favorite beer, room temperature

1 tablespoon liquid smoke

FOR THE BASTING AND DIPPING SAUCE

2 cups apple cider vinegar

¼ cup sugar

1 tablespoon hot sauce (I like Frank's Red Hot)

1 tablespoon crushed red pepper flakes

2 teaspoons liquid smoke

1 teaspoon Worcestershire sauce

Kosher salt and black pepper

1 **Make the brine.** In a large saucepan over medium-high heat, combine the salt and 2 quarts water. Stir until the salt dissolves. Remove the brine from the heat and let cool to room temperature.

2 **Prep and brine the ribs.** Cut ½-inch slits between the bones on the underside of the rib racks. Place the ribs in a large resealable plastic bag. Pour in the brine, seal the bag, and refrigerate for 8 hours.

3 **Make the basting and dipping sauce.** In a small saucepan, combine the vinegar, sugar, hot sauce, red pepper flakes, liquid smoke, Worcestershire sauce, and salt and pepper to taste. Bring to a boil. Whisk until combined, then remove from the heat. Reserve 1 cup of the mixture as a dipping sauce and refrigerate, covered, until ready to serve. Reserve the rest to baste the ribs as they cook.

4 **Cook the ribs.** Preheat the oven to 275°F. Remove the ribs from the refrigerator and discard the brine. Pat the ribs dry and transfer to a rimmed baking sheet lined with a wire rack. In a small bowl, combine the beer with the liquid smoke and pour into the bottom of the baking sheet. Brush the pork with the basting sauce on both sides. Cook, brushing every 20 minutes or so, for about 3 hours, or until the meat is knife-tender. Transfer to a serving platter and serve with the reserved dipping sauce.

This is Dutch oven worthy. If you don't have one, fire up a slow cooker or get your best large, heavy pot to chaperone these shanks on a culinary adventure. This takes a bit of time, but at the end of the ride is a pot of golden potatoes soaked with curry flavor and yellow-tinted shanks that pull like pork (pictured on page 209), but have a taste all their own. I serve this with rice just like the dish that inspired it: curry goat. **SERVES 4 TO 6**

curry-braised lamb shanks
WITH POTATOES

4 lamb shanks (about 6 pounds total)

Kosher salt and freshly ground black pepper

2 tablespoons olive oil

2 tablespoons unsalted butter

1 tablespoon yellow curry powder

1 teaspoon allspice

½ teaspoon paprika

12 ounces pearl onions (about 3 cups), thawed if frozen

1 red bell pepper, seeded and chopped

3 garlic cloves, smashed

8 to 10 sprigs fresh thyme, bundled with kitchen twine or leaves stripped and chopped

1 habanero pepper, pierced with a knife

1 quart chicken stock

1 pound Red Bliss or new potatoes, cut in half

1 **Prep the shanks.** Season the lamb with salt and pepper. Heat the olive oil in a Dutch oven over medium-high heat. When the oil begins to swirl, add the shanks and sear until a deep and golden color on all sides. Transfer the shanks to a plate.

2 **Build the flavor.** Lower the heat to medium and add the butter, curry powder, allspice, and paprika to the Dutch oven. Stir with a wooden spoon until the spices darken and become fragrant, about 2 minutes. Add the onions, bell pepper, garlic, thyme, habanero, a pinch of salt, and a few grinds of pepper. Cook until the vegetables become tender and golden with the spices, about 8 minutes.

3 **Cook the shanks.** Return the shanks to the pot over medium-high heat and add the chicken stock. Cover and bring to a low simmer; cook, stirring occasionally, until the lamb is fork tender, about 2 hours. Taste and season with more salt, if needed.

4 **Add the potatoes and skim.** Remove the habanero pepper and discard. Add the potatoes and simmer until fork tender, about 30 minutes more. If making the shanks the day before, refrigerate and remove the film of fat from the top before reheating. If not, use a spoon to skim and discard the shallow layer of fat from the surface before serving.

Steak sauce on lamb chops just seems lazy and wrong, but to me it's turned out to be a shortcut to success. I made this at the request of a friend and found that with a bit of finesse, it can be a quick and easy way to prepare chops without being fussy. Pick your favorite steak sauce and add my kitchen tricks to make lamb chops tasty. Then lighten up the steak flavor with a quick fruit chutney, and you look like a genius. By the way, eating these with your hands is allowed.

SERVES 4; MAKES 1 CUP CHUTNEY

steak-grilled lamb chops
WITH MANGO MINT CHUTNEY

FOR THE CHUTNEY

- 2 tablespoons olive oil
- ½ onion, chopped
- 1 teaspoon crushed red pepper flakes
- ¼ teaspoon cinnamon
- 1 teaspoon grated nutmeg
- Kosher salt
- 1-inch piece of fresh ginger, peeled and minced
- 2 tablespoons golden raisins
- 2 tablespoons dark raisins
- ¼ cup packed light brown sugar
- 1 tablespoon granulated sugar
- 1 mango, peeled and diced
- 1 Granny Smith apple, cored and diced
- 2 teaspoons apple cider vinegar
- ½ cup orange juice
- 8 to 10 fresh mint leaves, cut into thin ribbons

1 **Make the chutney.** In a medium straight-sided pan, heat the olive oil over medium-high heat. Once the oil begins to swirl, add the onion, red pepper flakes, cinnamon, nutmeg, and a pinch of salt. Cook until the onion is tender but not browned and the spices are fragrant, 8 to 10 minutes. Add the ginger, raisins, brown sugar, granulated sugar, mango, apple, vinegar, and orange juice. Gently bring to a simmer and cook, stirring occasionally, until the mango and apple are tender, about 15 minutes. Taste and season with salt, if needed. Remove from the heat and stir in the mint. Refrigerate (it's best when served chilled or room temperature).

2 **Prepare the marinade.** In a medium bowl, combine the steak sauce, honey, oregano, mint, garlic, a pinch of salt, and a few grinds of pepper. Whisk together and pour half the sauce into a large resealable plastic bag. Refrigerate the other half. Add the lamb chops to the plastic bag, seal, and mix by squishing the bag to fully coat the chops. Let rest in the refrigerator for at least 2 hours. Before grilling, remove both the reserved sauce and the plastic bag from the refrigerator and rest on the counter until room temperature, no longer than 2 hours.

3 Grill the lamb. Heat a grill or grill pan to medium-high. Remove the lamb from the bag and shake off any excess marinade. Discard the marinade. Grill the chops, brushing with the reserved sauce, to the desired doneness, about 4 minutes per side for medium rare. Flip only once. Transfer to a plate and cover loosely with aluminum foil. Let rest for at least 10 minutes before serving. Top with the chutney.

FOR THE LAMB CHOPS

- 2 cups steak sauce
- 1 cup honey
- 8 sprigs fresh oregano leaves
- ½ cup lightly packed fresh mint leaves, cut into ribbons
- 8 garlic cloves, sliced
  Kosher salt and freshly ground black pepper
- 4 double-rib lamb chops

STARCHY SIDES

Bahamian Peas and Rice

Roasted Sweet Potato Mash

Sausage Spooner

Rosemary and Thyme Potato Chips

Garlic Hasselback Potatoes

Yuca and Plantains in Garlic Sauce
   with Caramelized Onions

German Baked Potatoes
   with Sweet Bacon and Scallion Dressing

Lemon-Thyme Spaetzle

Creamy Collard Pesto with Pasta
   and Mushrooms

Spicy Macaroni and Cheese

Creamy Stovetop Mac and Cheese

Roasted Tomato and Herb Couscous

I was, and still am, a macaroni and cheese kid.
In my opinion it belongs in the entrée category, but I
know there are people who think I'm wrong. So this
group of recipes starts a list of my favorite ways to fill
out a plate with dishes I could also call the main event.
Whether it's pasta, rice, potatoes, or any other starch,
I'm a sucker for them, and they are my downfall! As we
say in our family, once on the lips, forever on the hips.
I giggle when I think about that saying because it's so
true. I'm not saying these recipes will give you curves,
but if you eat them as an entrée instead of a side,
don't blame me if they do. If served in a casserole dish
they are travel-ready for parties away from home. And
meatless Mondays don't miss a beat with my creamy
collard pesto (page 243). My idea of a great side dish is
one that should be able to stand on its own, too, so go
ahead—just don't do it every day. All in moderation,
right?

This is a recipe I adapted from my friends in Tarpum Bay, Eleuthera, a tiny town on a small island in the Bahamas. I visit often and rent a car from Columbus and his wife, Dauphine. One day they invited me over for Sunday supper; I had truly thought they'd never ask. I asked if I could show up early and watch them cook. It was such a fun time, filled with sipping a mixture of red wine and cranberry juice while taking notes on how to make some of the best peas and rice I've ever had. This is perfect with my Scorched Red Snapper (page 150).

SERVES 6 TO 8

bahamian peas and rice

⅓ cup olive oil

6 strips bacon, chopped

1 cup chopped Vidalia or sweet onion

1 green bell pepper, seeded and chopped

1 celery stalk, finely chopped

5 or 6 sprigs fresh thyme

Kosher salt and freshly ground black pepper

2 garlic cloves, grated on a rasp or finely minced

2 cups rice, rinsed in a sieve until the water runs clear

1 15-ounce can black-eyed peas, drained and rinsed

4 Roma tomatoes, chopped

1 8-ounce can tomato sauce

1 tablespoon Worcestershire sauce

1 habanero pepper, pierced with the tip of a knife

1 **Cook the bacon and vegetables.** In a large pot over medium-high heat, combine the oil, bacon, onion, bell pepper, celery, thyme, a pinch of salt, and a few grinds of pepper. Cook, stirring, until the bacon is crisped and the onion is tender and fragrant, about 10 minutes.

2 **Toast the rice.** Add the garlic and rice and toast the rice until it has a nutty or popcorn-like scent, about 10 minutes more.

3 **Add the peas and liquid.** Stir in the peas, tomatoes, tomato sauce, Worcestershire, habanero pepper, and 3 cups water. Bring the pot to a boil, then reduce to a low simmer and cover. Cook until the rice absorbs the moisture, 35 to 40 minutes. Try to avoid lifting the lid until the 30-minute mark, as the steam helps cook the rice.

This is a healthier way to get sweet potatoes on the table around the holidays. Sure, there's butter, but just a bit. I'm used to my family's way, which is thick potato slices in a syrup of brown sugar, plenty of butter, and spices, with toasted marshmallows on top. I still make it that way sometimes, but in the summer months I break this out, usually with a roasted bird. **SERVES 4 TO 6**

roasted sweet potato mash

4 pounds sweet potatoes, peeled and cut lengthwise into quarters

2 large Vidalia or sweet onions, peeled and quartered

Olive oil

Kosher salt and freshly ground black pepper

¼ cup (½ stick) unsalted butter

1 Prep and roast the potatoes and onions. Preheat the oven to 375°F. Place the potato and onion wedges on a rimmed baking sheet. Drizzle with olive oil to coat, then rub it all over each piece with your hands. Season with a sprinkle of salt and a few grinds of black pepper. Roast until the potatoes and onions are tender and golden, 30 to 40 minutes.

2 Blend to serve. Remove the baking sheet from the oven and scrape everything, including the juices, into a food processor. Add the butter and blend until smooth. Taste and season with more salt, if needed.

tips! If you like white or yellow turnips, substitute them here or do a combination of turnips and sweet potatoes. ■ Sometimes I add cinnamon, cumin, herbs, or other spices to the final blend, depending on what I'm serving with the potatoes. The next day, I toast some bread and spread the mash like mayo for a quick chicken or turkey sandwich.

I was too happy with myself here. A kitchen Christmas, complete with an oven, a stand mixer, and a blender. **(Charleston, SC, 1982)**

Spoon bread is a bit of a Southern throwback, but to some it's a new discovery. This is like a cornbread pudding that is softer than traditional cornbread, but thicker than proper polenta, and you serve it with a spoon—hence the name. It's easy to fill with flavor and here I stud it with some of my favorites: chiles, scallions, cheese, and spicy sausage. The ideas are endless. **SERVES 8 TO 10**

sausage spooner

FOR THE CHORIZO

2 tablespoons unsalted butter

7 ounces Mexican chorizo, casing removed

½ cup chopped Vidalia or sweet onion

1 garlic clove, grated on a rasp or finely minced

FOR THE CORNMEAL

¾ cup cornmeal

2 cups whole milk

1 cup buttermilk

3 eggs

FOR THE FILLING

1 4.5-ounce can chopped green chiles

1 cup shredded Cheddar cheese

1 cup shredded mozzarella cheese

¾ cup sweet corn kernels

2 scallions, finely chopped (white and green parts)

1 tablespoon unsalted butter

1 **Saute the chorizo.** In a medium skillet over medium heat, combine the butter, chorizo, onion, and garlic. Stir to keep the onions from browning, until the chorizo is cooked through and resembles ground meat, about 10 minutes. Pour into a large bowl. Preheat the oven to 400°F.

2 **Prepare the cornmeal.** In a medium pot over medium heat, whisk the cornmeal, milk, and buttermilk to keep the cornmeal from clumping or sticking while simmering. When it begins to thicken, turn off the heat and stir until it has the texture of loose grits or oatmeal.

3 **Temper the eggs.** In a small bowl, whisk the eggs while slowly adding a spoonful of cornmeal mixture. Whisk vigorously to combine. If the bowl isn't warm, add more cornmeal mixture while whisking until the eggs are as warm as the cornmeal mixture. Then slowly pour the eggs into the cornmeal, whisking vigorously.

4 **Bake the spoonbread.** Pour the cornmeal mixture into the chorizo with the chiles, cheeses, corn, and scallions. Stir to combine. Butter the bottom and sides of a 9 × 13-inch dish. Pour in the batter and bake until the edges are golden and the center is set, 25 to 30 minutes. Serve hot.

The inventor of the mandoline has my everlasting devotion and love. The first logical use is paper-thin chips of all kinds. The combination of rosemary and thyme has been in my head since before I started cooking. My mom had a spice and herb cabinet with lists of what worked together and for what type of preparation, and I would sit there and just read it while watching her cook. Somehow it sank in more than staring at multiplication tables. Probably because you can't eat numbers. **SERVES 4**

rosemary and thyme potato chips

1½ pounds fingerling potatoes

1 pound sweet potatoes

4 sprigs fresh rosemary

Vegetable oil

Kosher salt

8 to 10 sprigs fresh thyme, leaves stripped and gently chopped

1 **Slice and soak the potatoes.** Using a mandoline or a sharp knife, thinly slice the fingerling and sweet potatoes. Put the potatoes in a large bowl of ice water and refrigerate for 1 hour.

2 **Prepare the rosemary.** Put the rosemary in a pot large enough to hold the potatoes and pour in oil to come one-third of the way up the sides. Heat the oil to 360°F. When the rosemary turns golden and crispy, transfer it with tongs to a paper towel–lined plate and season with a pinch of salt, leaving the oil in the pot. Once cooled, strip the leaves from the stalks and gently chop.

3 **Dry and fry the potatoes.** Strain the potatoes and thoroughly dry by laying them out on a paper towel–lined surface and patting the tops with paper towels as well. Add the potatoes to the oil in batches, making sure to keep the temperature at 350°F. Fry until golden, about 3 minutes per batch. Transfer the chips to a paper towel–lined bowl and sprinkle immediately with the rosemary, thyme, and salt to taste. Serve warm or let cool.

Years ago I was reading through some of my old cookbooks and a recipe caught my eye. It touted the creamy crunch of potatoes sliced card thin, but kept intact—they weren't sliced all the way through—then oven roasted with olive oil. I decided to give a few potatoes this accordion-top treatment and had the idea to slide garlic slices in some of the divides. A favorite was born. I can't believe something harvested from the dirt with rakes can taste so good.

SERVES 4

garlic hasselback potatoes

1½ pounds red new potatoes (about 20)

5 garlic cloves, thinly sliced

6 tablespoons unsalted butter, melted

3 tablespoons olive oil

Kosher salt and freshly ground black pepper

1 tablespoon finely chopped fresh chives, for garnish

1 Prepare the potatoes. Preheat the oven to 400°F. Using a wooden spoon as a cradle, place each potato in the spoon and make several parallel slits into each potato top, ⅛ inch apart, making sure not to slice through to the bottom completely—stop at the wooden spoon as a guide. Place 3 garlic slices between slits at the crown of each potato. Toss potatoes in a medium bowl with the butter and olive oil.

2 Roast the potatoes. Place the potatoes on a baking sheet and sprinkle with salt and pepper. Bake until the tops are crispy and the potatoes are cooked through, about 1 hour. Top with chives.

"In garlic sauce" has caught me on many occasions when I'm out to eat. If my eyes scan it on a menu, my view gets very narrow and I seldom see what else is available. A garlic sauce is best used when whatever is swimming in it is ready to soak up flavor. Yuca, a tuber also called cassava, and plantains are a perfect starchy match, ready to absorb whatever flavors are thrown at them. Think of them as vanilla ice cream waiting for mix-ins—both are excellent additions to any repertoire and pre-trimmed yuca can now be found in the freezer section. Look for them and try a new way to enjoy garlic sauce. **SERVES 4 TO 6**

yuca and plantains in garlic sauce WITH CARAMELIZED ONIONS

FOR THE YUCA AND PLANTAINS

- 1 24-ounce bag frozen yuca, thawed
- 3 tablespoons unsalted butter
- 8 to 10 sprigs fresh thyme, leaves stripped and chopped
  Kosher salt
- 1 tablespoon apple cider vinegar
- 4 garlic cloves, grated on a rasp or finely minced
- 3 green plantains, cut into 2-inch sections, halved lengthwise, then peeled
- 2 cups chicken stock

FOR THE ONIONS

- 2 tablespoons unsalted butter
- 2 tablespoons olive oil
- 2 cups chopped Vidalia or sweet onions
  Kosher salt and freshly ground black pepper

1 **Cook the yuca and plantains.** Trim the larger yuca pieces into portions the size of an egg. Put the butter and thyme in a large pot over medium heat and season with a hefty pinch of salt. Cook until the thyme is fragrant, about 4 minutes. Add the vinegar and garlic and cook until tender and fragrant, about 4 more minutes. Add the prepared yuca and plantains as level as possible, then add the chicken stock. Add water to reach 1 inch above the yuca; the plantains will float. Cover and bring to a boil, then reduce to a simmer and cook, stirring occasionally, until the yuca and plantains are fork tender, 25 to 30 minutes.

2 **Caramelize the onions.** In a large pan over medium-low heat, combine the butter, oil, onions, a pinch of salt, and a few grinds of pepper. Cook, stirring, until the onions wilt and become deep golden, about 25 minutes. Set aside.

3 **Combine to serve.** With a slotted spoon, transfer the yuca and plantains to a deep serving dish. Pour about 1 cup of the liquid from the pot over the onions, add to the serving dish, and toss gently. Serve warm.

Potato salad in Germany is like BBQ in North Carolina. It's sweet and tangy, with an emphasis on tangy. These boiled-then-baked potatoes are fleshy and perfect for infusing with those flavors. Just poke some holes with a skewer to help them soak up the goodness, then poach them before a quick ride in the oven. A bacon and scallion vinaigrette comes together in minutes for a topping way better than cold sour cream. A must try . . . it's wunderbar! All this potato needs is a steak riding in the passenger side. **SERVES 4**

german baked potatoes
WITH SWEET BACON AND SCALLION DRESSING

FOR THE POTATOES

4 russet potatoes

6 garlic cloves, smashed

½ onion, cut into big chunks

4 strips bacon

1½ cups apple cider vinegar

2 tablespoons liquid smoke

¾ cup sugar

Kosher salt and freshly ground black pepper

1 tablespoon olive oil

FOR THE DRESSING

8 strips bacon, chopped

¼ cup olive oil

Kosher salt and freshly ground black pepper

¼ cup apple cider vinegar

¼ cup sugar

4 scallions, finely chopped (white and green parts)

1 Boil the potatoes. Use a skewer to make 20 to 30 deep holes all around the potatoes. Put the potatoes, garlic, onion, bacon, vinegar, liquid smoke, sugar, 6 cups water, a big pinch of salt, and a few grinds of pepper in a large pot. Bring to a boil, reduce to a simmer, and cook until the potatoes are fork tender all the way through, about 40 minutes. As the potatoes finish cooking, preheat the oven to 400°F.

2 Bake the potatoes. Transfer the potatoes to a baking sheet and brush with olive oil all over. Season the skins with salt and bake for 10 minutes, rolling over halfway through.

3 Make the dressing. Put the bacon, olive oil, and a few grinds of pepper in a medium skillet over medium-high heat. Cook until the bacon is crisped, about 8 minutes. Add the vinegar, sugar, and a pinch of salt. Simmer until the sugar and salt dissolve, about 2 minutes. Remove from the heat and stir in the scallions.

4 Serve the potatoes. Remove the potatoes from the oven and split each down the center with a knife, squeezing the ends to open the center. Flake each a bit with a fork, then fill with an equal amount of dressing and serve.

tips! Make this into a warm German-style potato salad by using 2 pounds of Red Bliss potatoes instead and cooking them the same way, but with fewer pokes before the poach and a shorter poaching time. When you remove them from the oven, instead of splitting them, mash each individually by pressing once with the back of a spoon. Then combine with the dressing in a large bowl, toss, and serve warm. ■ Serve this family style by refrigerating the potatoes after baking; once cooled and firm, cut ½-inch slices and lay them overlapping on a platter. Drizzle the hot dressing over the top.

I turn into a giddy kid when making, eating, or ordering spaetzle. This is Germany's answer to dumplings, and they are a mouthful of chewy and pan-crisped starch. When I lived there as a child, spaetzle was my favorite side, but there was never a flavor, it was all about the texture and scooping some up with the gravy on my plate, usually from jaegerschnitzel (see my BK Jaegerschnitzel on page 131). Now, with my adult palate and the ability to cook spaetzle myself, I play with the flavors and enjoy this combo of lemon zest and fresh thyme. No plate gravy needed. **SERVES 4 TO 6**

lemon-thyme spaetzle

FOR THE BATTER

3 eggs

1 cup whole milk

18 to 20 sprigs fresh thyme, leaves stripped and finely chopped (about 2 tablespoons)

⅛ teaspoon grated nutmeg (5 or 6 scrapes on a rasp)

½ teaspoon dry mustard

¼ teaspoon cayenne pepper

Grated zest of 1 lemon

1½ teaspoons kosher salt, plus more for the pot

½ teaspoon freshly ground black pepper

2 cups all-purpose flour, plus more for texture

FOR THE PAN-FRY

2 strips bacon, chopped

2 tablespoons unsalted butter

1 tablespoon fresh lemon juice

Kosher salt and freshly ground black pepper

1 **Make the batter.** In a large bowl, whisk the eggs, milk, thyme, nutmeg, mustard, cayenne pepper, lemon zest, 1½ teaspoons salt, and black pepper. Gradually whisk in the flour to make a thick, tight batter. Add more flour by the spoonful until it has the proper texture. (It should feel stretchy and thick, like it wouldn't drip through a colander whole, but could be pressed through and remain stringy, not doughy.)

2 **Boil the spaetzle.** Fill a double boiler with a colander, or steamer, insert halfway with water and add a pinch of salt. Bring to a boil and place the colander section over the pot. Add a heaping cup of spaetzle batter at a time to the colander, and with a rubber spatula, press the batter through the holes into the boiling water. Be sure to scrape the bottom of the colander between pressings and stir the spaetzle into the water so the next batch of batter doesn't stick to the one before it. The spaetzle is ready 1 minute after it floats to the top. Remove with a slotted spoon and strain through a fine-mesh sieve to remove as much water as possible (shake it!). Continue to work in batches, adding more spaetzle to the sieve and giving a shake each time to remove excess water.

3 **Pan-fry the spaetzle.** In a large pan over medium-high heat, cook the bacon until crisp. Remove with a slotted spoon and set on a paper towel–lined plate. Add the butter to the bacon fat in the pan and allow it to melt, then add the boiled spaetzle. Water and oil can produce splatters, so be careful! Allow the spaetzle to build a golden crust, then toss and cook until it's mostly golden all over, but still tender, 2 to 4 minutes. This may have to be done in batches depending on your pan size. If cooking in batches, use a slotted spoon to transfer the crisped spaetzle to a plate, leaving the fat in the pan for the next batch. When the last batch is done, add all the spaetzle and the bacon back to the pan and toss. Sprinkle with the lemon juice, and taste and season with salt and pepper if needed. Serve warm.

tips! Try these other flavor combinations for the spaetzle: cumin and cilantro, Hungarian or hot paprika and rosemary, garlic powder and oregano, or black pepper and sage. ■ If you don't have a double boiler, try poking holes in a disposable aluminum pie pan with chopsticks or a pen. Place it over the top of the pot and use it just as you would a double boiler with a steamer.

tip! This pesto is great smeared on bread for a sandwich or on warm crostini as a side to a bowl of soup, tossed with wings, or stirred into fluffed rice.

I'm a sucker for pesto. It's a simple template—something green, some nuts, cheese, and olive oil. I like these loose boundaries in my kitchen because they allow for creativity. If you play with the pesto rules long enough, you'll come up with something you absolutely love. That is how I came up with these hearty collards blitzed with their Southern counterpart of pecans. I've fallen in love with this pesto combo. I also like a pour of heavy cream at the end. I let it cook a bit more to thicken and smooth it out, but the dish is great without it too. **SERVES 4 TO 6**

creamy collard pesto
WITH PASTA AND MUSHROOMS

FOR THE PESTO

Kosher salt and freshly ground black pepper

1 bunch collards, ribs discarded and leaves roughly chopped

¾ cup pecans

3 garlic cloves

6 ounces Parmesan cheese, 1 ounce grated, 5 ounces broken into chunks

½ cup kalamata olives, pitted

Olive oil

FOR THE PASTA

2 tablespoons olive oil

8 ounces wild mushrooms, lightly chopped

Kosher salt

13 ounces perciatelli, bucatini, or linguini pasta, cooked al dente according to package directions

1 **Blanch the collards.** Bring a large pot of salted water to a boil. Blanch the collards until they're bright green, about 1 minute. Remove, shake off excess water, and transfer to a food processor.

2 **Make the pesto.** In a dry skillet, toast the pecans until fragrant. Chop and set aside half. Transfer the other half of the pecans to the food processor with the garlic, the 5 ounces of chunked Parmesan, and all the olives. Pulse to combine and then, with the food processor on, drizzle olive oil in a slow stream until the pesto comes together. Taste and add salt only if needed (the olives and cheese often do the trick). Add a few grinds of black pepper to taste.

3 **Start the sauce.** Heat the olive oil in a large straight-sided pan over medium heat. When it begins to swirl, add the mushrooms and a pinch of salt and cook, stirring, until the mushrooms are wilted, about 8 minutes.

4 **Finish the pasta.** Add the pesto and pasta to the pan and stir to coat. Serve with the reserved chopped pecans as garnish.

This is the dish that got me cooking for people and eventually started my catering company. I'd make it at home and then bring the leftovers to work, usually with some greens and brownies. It got me a crew of great friends who would soon ask me to hang out all the time, and they all expected me to bring the food. I like making people happy, so when the request was more than I could handle with my full-time job, I kept saying yes, but I started charging for the groceries, thinking they would ask less often because now it was costing them. That actually had the opposite effect, and I soon found myself with a catering business. This macaroni and cheese was always on the menu.

SERVES 6 TO 8 AS A MAIN DISH (OR UP TO 14 AS A SIDE)

spicy macaroni and cheese

FOR THE CROUTONS

1 tablespoon unsalted butter

4 slices white bread, cut into ½-inch squares

Kosher salt

FOR THE PASTA

1 tablespoon unsalted butter

8 ounces Cheddar cheese, shredded

8 ounces Colby cheese, shredded

8 ounces pepper Jack cheese, shredded

2 cups elbow pasta, cooked until almost al dente

1 **Make the croutons.** Melt the butter in a skillet over medium heat. Add the bread cubes and toast until light golden, 4 to 6 minutes. Transfer to a paper towel–lined plate and season with a pinch of salt. Set aside.

2 **Prepare the pasta.** Butter the bottom and sides of a 13 × 9-inch casserole dish. Preheat the oven to 350°F. In a medium bowl, toss together the Cheddar, Colby, and Jack cheeses. Put the cooked pasta in a large bowl and add two-thirds of the blended cheese. Set aside.

3 **Make the custard.** Put the following ingredients in another large bowl, whisking between each addition to combine: flour, salt, black pepper, cayenne pepper, mustard, nutmeg, sour cream, egg, onion, heavy cream, and half-and-half. Pour the custard over the pasta and cheese blend. Toss to combine.

4 **Bake the casserole.** Pour the macaroni and cheese mixture into the prepared baking dish. Cover with the remaining shredded cheese blend. Bake uncovered until the cheese is almost set and the top is just beginning to brown, about 35 minutes. Remove from the oven and sprinkle the croutons on top. Return to the oven and bake until golden brown, about 10 minutes more.

FOR THE CUSTARD

- 2 teaspoons all-purpose flour
- ½ teaspoon kosher salt
- ½ teaspoon freshly ground black pepper
- ½ teaspoon cayenne pepper
- ½ teaspoon dry mustard
- ⅛ teaspoon grated nutmeg
- ¼ cup sour cream
- 1 egg, beaten
- ¼ cup grated Vidalia or sweet onion
- 1 cup heavy cream
- 1 cup half-and-half

Put down the various colored boxes of mac and cheese. Leave the micro-wave alone and give this a try. Because, I don't know about you, but I could eat a box of the store-bought stuff all by myself and still not have the satisfying comfort of real homemade macaroni and cheese. I understand the reason for the box—childhood nostalgia and fast prep. So, I developed my own box-killing recipe. This is the real deal and it's just as easy. **SERVES 4 TO 6**

creamy stovetop mac and cheese

2 tablespoons unsalted butter

½ small onion, grated with juices retained

Kosher salt and freshly ground black pepper

1 garlic clove, minced

¼ teaspoon freshly ground white pepper

¼ teaspoon Hungarian or hot paprika

2 cups heavy cream, room temperature

6 ounces Colby Jack cheese, shredded

6 ounces smoked Gouda, shredded

1 pound baby shell pasta, cooked al dente according to package directions

4 strips cooked bacon, crumbled

¼ cup chopped fresh flat-leaf or curly parsley

1 finely chopped scallion (white and green parts)

1 Build the flavor. Melt the butter in a large sauce-pan over medium heat. Add the onion and juices, a pinch of salt, and a few grinds of black pepper. Cook until tender, about 2 minutes. Add the garlic, white pepper, and paprika, and continue to cook for a few minutes to let the flavors and aroma bloom. Slowly stir in the heavy cream. Bring to a simmer, stirring occasionally, and cook until slightly thickened, about 8 minutes. Add the Colby and Gouda cheeses and stir until melted, then remove from the heat.

2 Add the pasta and serve. Stir in the cooked pasta and toss until thoroughly combined. Season with salt and pepper to taste. Transfer to a serving bowl and serve warm, garnished with bacon, parsley, and scallion.

Couscous is a busy cook's best friend. Most store-bought couscous is already presteamed and dried, so all you have to do is take it the final yards to the end zone for a kitchen touchdown. Boiled stock and a five-minute steep does the trick, so imagine adding a few extra touches for a dish that looks beautiful and holds up to the second-day test. There's nothing better than something that tastes great hot as well as cold in my kitchen. Play with the couscous starting here and check the variations below. **SERVES 4**

roasted tomato and herb couscous

FOR THE TOMATOES

3 Roma tomatoes, sliced into ½-inch discs

2 tablespoons olive oil

Kosher salt and freshly ground black pepper

FOR THE COUSCOUS

1 cup couscous

2 tablespoons olive oil

½ cup finely chopped Vidalia or sweet onion

Kosher salt and freshly ground black pepper

3 garlic cloves, roughly chopped

1½ cups chicken stock

¼ cup chopped fresh basil

¼ cup chopped fresh flat-leaf or curly parsley

Grated zest of 1 lemon

tip! Variations for couscous are endless. Try a Greek salad version with sliced olives, chopped cucumber, feta cheese, and a simple olive oil and vinegar dressing. Or toss with pesto for a quick side.

1 **Roast the tomato slices.** Preheat the oven to 400°F. Set a wire rack on a baking sheet lined with parchment paper or aluminum foil. Place the tomato slices in a medium bowl. Drizzle with olive oil and sprinkle with a pinch of salt and a few grinds of pepper. Toss, then place in one layer on the wire rack. Roast until the edges are shriveled and caramelized, but the center is still moist, about 25 minutes. Remove and allow the roasted tomato slices to cool, then gently chop. Set aside.

2 **Make the couscous.** Pour the couscous into a large bowl with a lid or have plastic wrap ready to cover. In a medium pot over medium-low heat, combine the oil, onion, a pinch of salt, and a few grinds of pepper. Cook, stirring, until the onion is tender and fragrant, but not browned, 6 to 8 minutes. Add the garlic and cook until tender and fragrant, another 6 to 8 minutes (the onions may caramelize a bit; that's okay). Add the stock and bring to a boil. Immediately pour the stock into the couscous and stir, then quickly cover. Let rest for 5 minutes. Add the basil, parsley, lemon zest, and reserved tomatoes; fluff with a fork. Taste and season with a pinch of salt, if needed. Serve warm or cold.

VEGE
TABLES

Kale in Coconut Milk

Quick Any-Veggie Fix

Easy Braised Cabbage

Onion Ring Casserole

Green Bean Casserole Mashup

Pan-Fried Tomatillos
    with Sweet and Spicy Cream Sauce

I make vegetable sides to enjoy solo.

And the same goes for these recipes. Yes, they are there to complement the star of the plate, but they shouldn't receive any less attention or thought. I can't remember having any of the usual childhood aversions to eating vegetables, but I do have my favorites and I'm sharing them with you. In a pinch I'll just do my Quick Any-Veggie Fix on page 253, but if given time, I work up dishes to showcase the best of what grows from the earth. I even tried gardening once, but found myself obsessed with the weather and once it came time to harvest, it was hard to actually eat the vegetables that I'd tended; I'd built a bond. I ended up giving away most of my harvest, not able to bring myself to actually cook my hard work. It shows you how dedicated I was to the art of gardening—just not the art of eating the fruits of my labor. I wonder if I'm the only one who feels that way? These days, a farmers' market will do, and I now grow flowers, succulents, and sustainable bamboo.

Kale has such a bitter bite that coconut milk is the perfect match to relax it a bit. Wilted and soaked with the flavor of pancetta, this kale is great alongside baked fish and grilled or braised chicken. I picked up my love for kale when I couldn't find any collard or turnip greens during my time as a Californian. I found the taste to be similar and I really love the texture of the frilly leaves. This is a quick sauté, made even faster when I rinse and clean the kale as soon I get home from shopping. **SERVES 4 TO 6**

kale in coconut milk

1 tablespoon unsalted butter

¼ pound slab bacon (fatback), sliced, then cut into small ½-inch-thick rectangles

½ cup chopped Vidalia onion

1 bunch kale (1½ to 2 pounds), ribs discarded, chopped

Kosher salt and freshly ground black pepper

½ cup coconut milk

1 cup beef broth

1 **Crisp the bacon.** Put the butter and bacon in a large pan and cook over medium heat until the bacon begins to crisp and renders most of its fat. Using a slotted spoon, transfer to a plate (no need to line with a paper towel).

2 **Cook the veggies.** Add the onion to the pan and cook until softened, 5 to 8 minutes. Add the kale and season with a pinch of salt and a few grinds of pepper. Cook, tossing, until it wilts, about 5 minutes.

3 **Finish and serve.** Add the coconut milk and broth and continue to cook until the kale softens, another 10 minutes. Season with salt and pepper to taste. Add the reserved cooked bacon, toss, and serve.

tip! If you can't find kale, any dark, leafy green will work here, but the more bitter the better.

When I say "any veggie," I mean it. This is the quickest way to get vegetables on the table, unless you just go raw. My favorites are leafy greens, frozen veggie packs, mushrooms, corn, and even just an array of onions and peppers. From here you can have fun with lemon zest, toasted nuts, your favorite herb blend—whatever you like. **SERVES 4**

quick any-veggie fix

1 pound fresh or frozen vegetables, 1 kind or a mixture, chopped if necessary (corn, peas, lima beans, carrots, spinach, etc.)

2 tablespoons olive oil

½ cup chopped Vidalia or sweet onion

Kosher salt and freshly ground black pepper

2 garlic cloves, grated on a rasp or finely minced

½ cup chicken stock

½ cup fresh orange juice

1 **Prepare the vegetables.** Peel, trim, or chop fresh vegetables if needed. There's no need to thaw frozen vegetables, except spinach. If using spinach, thaw and remove excess water by wrapping in paper towels or a clean kitchen towel and squeezing.

2 **Cook the veggies.** In a large straight-sided pan with a lid, heat the olive oil over medium-high heat. When the oil begins to swirl, add the onion, a pinch of salt, and a grind or two of pepper. Cook until tender, about 8 minutes. Add the garlic and your chosen vegetables and sauté until just slightly tender. Stir in the stock and orange juice. Bring to a boil, then cover and reduce to a low simmer. Cook until the vegetables are tender and the liquid is reduced and slightly thickened, 10 to 15 minutes.

tips! This is all about vegetables, but don't be afraid to add cooked sausage, bacon, shredded chicken, or even fruits— try dried cranberries, chopped apples, or fresh blueberries. ■ Substitute apple cider or another fresh fruit juice for the orange juice.

This cabbage is both simple and complex—simple because the Ingredients are easy to find, and complex because each ingredient packs such a powerful flavor profile. I enjoy sharing recipes from my kitchen, especially when they are dishes I make again and again. This is one of those recipes. The aroma is wonderful, with a hint of sweet orange and the savory flavors of everything else. This side dish goes with many things in any season. **SERVES 4 TO 6**

easy braised cabbage

¼ pound slab bacon (fatback), sliced, then cut into small ½-inch-thick rectangles

2 tablespoons olive oil

1 cup chopped onions

Kosher salt

½ teaspoon whole black peppercorns

½ teaspoon celery seeds

2 garlic cloves, smashed

1 head of green cabbage, cored and thinly sliced

2 cups chicken stock

2 cups orange juice

2 tablespoons liquid smoke

2 tablespoons apple cider vinegar

1 **Cook the bacon.** Cook the bacon in a large pot until it's crisp and the fat is rendered. Transfer with a slotted spoon to a paper towel–lined plate, reserving the bacon fat in the pan.

2 **Prepare the cabbage.** Add the olive oil and onions to the bacon fat and season with a pinch of salt. Add the peppercorns and celery seeds. Cook, stirring, until the onions are tender and celery seeds fragrant, about 5 minutes. Add the garlic and stir in the cabbage. Toss the cabbage to coat and season with another pinch of salt. Cook, tossing, until wilted, about 5 minutes.

3 **Braise and serve.** Pour in the chicken stock, orange juice, liquid smoke, and vinegar. Bring to a boil, then reduce to a simmer. Cover and cook until the cabbage is tender, about 40 minutes. Serve warm topped with the reserved bacon.

tips! If you cannot find slab bacon, try a smoked ham hock instead, and reduce the liquid smoke to 1 tablespoon. ■ This is a great brunch dish next to a steak or scrambled eggs.

french fries were my favorite fast-food side until I started working at Sonic Drive-In while in high school. Then onion rings took over. Without a Sonic in my backyard, I've whipped up my own onion ring breading to get by. And everything tastes better as a casserole, so I found a way to fit circles into a rectangle.

SERVES 4 TO 6

onion ring casserole

FOR THE SAUCE

2 tablespoons olive oil

½ cup chopped Vidalia or sweet onion

Kosher salt and freshly ground black pepper

1 garlic clove, minced

½ cup plus 2 tablespoons tomato paste

½ cup packed light brown sugar

¼ teaspoon cinnamon

1 28-ounce can crushed tomatoes with basil

½ cup cider vinegar

1 tablespoon unsalted butter

FOR THE ONIONS, DREDGE, AND TOPPING

Vegetable or peanut oil

1 cup all-purpose flour

2 eggs

½ teaspoon sweet paprika

Kosher salt and freshly ground black pepper

2 cups panko

1 **Start the sauce.** Heat 2 tablespoons olive oil in a large pan over medium-high heat. When the oil begins to swirl, add the onion, a pinch of salt, and a few grinds of pepper. Cook until tender, about 5 minutes. Reduce the heat to medium, then add the garlic and stir to incorporate. Add the tomato paste, stirring to mix, and cook until slightly deeper in color, about 5 minutes.

2 **Finish sauce.** Add the brown sugar, cinnamon, crushed tomatoes, and vinegar to the pan, stirring to incorporate between each addition. Taste and season with salt, if needed. Butter a 13 × 9-inch baking dish. Pour the sauce into the dish and set aside.

3 **Dredge and fry the onions.** Heat 1 inch of vegetable or peanut oil in a heavy-bottomed skillet to 350°F. Place the flour on a large plate. In a medium bowl, whisk the eggs, paprika, a pinch of salt, and a few grinds of black pepper. Mix the panko and thyme in a wide bowl. Keeping the onion slices intact, dredge completely with flour, coat with the egg mixture, then dredge only the smaller or tapered side of the onion surface in the panko mixture. Carefully transfer to the oil, panko side down. Fry until golden, about 4 minutes.

4 **Finish the dish.** With a spatula, carefully nestle the onion slices into the baking dish, panko side down, forming a single layer. Discard the flour and egg mixture, but keep the panko portion of the dredge. Add the olive oil to the reserved panko and stir to moisten. Season with salt and pepper, then sprinkle the remaining panko over the baking dish. Bake until the crumbs are golden brown and the onions are tender, 25 to 30 minutes. Serve warm.

10 to 12 sprigs fresh thyme, leaves stripped and gently chopped

2 large Vidalia onions, cut into 1-inch-thick slices, rings intact

2 tablespoons olive oil

This is something I created in my kitchen for the winter holidays. Combining two dishes to make one gives you more space in the oven and one less dish to wash or make room for on the table. This casserole works for me during the holiday rush, but it also makes an appearance at the end of spring/beginning of summer. It's a great way to bridge the seasons with comfort and fresh vegetables.

SERVES 6 TO 8

green bean casserole mashup

FOR THE POTATOES AND GREEN BEANS

- 2 Yukon Gold potatoes, peeled and cut into 1-inch chunks, peels reserved
- 2 garlic cloves, smashed
  Kosher salt
- 1 pound fresh green beans, trimmed and cut into thin strips on an angle

FOR THE MUSHROOM CREAM SAUCE

- 2 tablespoons olive oil
- ½ cup chopped Vidalia or sweet onion
- ½ serrano pepper, seeded and chopped
- 8 to 10 sprigs fresh thyme
- ½ teaspoon Hungarian or hot paprika
  Kosher salt and freshly ground black pepper
- 1 pound baby bella mushrooms, sliced
- 1 tablespoon Worcestershire sauce
- 1 cup heavy cream, room temperature

1 Prepare the potatoes. Cut the reserved potato peels into thin strips, then soak in a large bowl of water for 20 minutes. Fill a large pot with water. Add the garlic and a small handful of salt. Bring to a boil and add the potatoes. Cook until fork tender, 6 to 8 minutes. Remove the potatoes and garlic with a slotted spoon and drain in a sieve. Transfer to a large bowl.

2 Blanch the green beans. Add the green beans to the same water. Bring back to a boil if needed, then simmer until the beans are bright and tender, 6 to 8 minutes. Drain in a colander, then transfer to a large bowl.

3 Prepare the mushroom cream sauce. In a large straight-sided pan over medium heat, combine the olive oil, onion, serrano pepper, thyme, paprika, a pinch of salt, and a few grinds of black pepper. Cook until the onion is tender, then add the mushrooms and Worcestershire sauce and season again with salt and pepper. Cook until the mushrooms wilt and become tender, about 10 minutes. Remove the thyme sprigs and slowly stir in the heavy cream. Bring to a simmer and cook, stirring, until the cream thickens a bit, 6 to 8 minutes. Once thickened, turn off the heat and stir in the crema. Preheat the oven to 375°F.

4 **Prepare the potatoes and green beans.** Add the jalapeños and three-quarters of the mushroom mixture to the potatoes and mash everything until combined. Add three-quarters of the cheese to the potatoes and stir to combine. Add the remaining cheese and mushroom cream sauce to the green beans. Stir to combine.

5 **Make the topping.** Pour the potato strips into a colander and give them a final rinse under running water until it appears to be clear. Pour them onto a clean, dry kitchen towel and pat dry as much as possible; using paper towels works too. In a medium bowl, combine the potato strips, sage, thyme, paprika, olive oil, a pinch of salt, and a few grinds of black pepper. Toss the potato peels in the seasonings to coat.

6 **Assemble the casserole.** Butter the bottom and sides of an 8 × 8-inch baking dish. Spread the potatoes over the bottom of the dish, then layer the green bean mixture over the top. Sprinkle the topping evenly over the beans and press down gently. Bake until the potatoes brown and begin to crisp on the edges, about 30 minutes.

½ cup Mexican crema or sour cream

8 pickled jalapeño slices, finely chopped (about 1 medium pickled jalapeño)

6 ounces white Cheddar cheese, shredded

FOR THE TOPPING

6 fresh sage leaves, finely chopped

6 sprigs fresh thyme, leaves stripped and gently chopped

Pinch of Hungarian or hot paprika

2 teaspoons olive oil

Kosher salt and freshly ground black pepper

1 tablespoon unsalted butter, for greasing the pan

tip! To prepare in advance, build the casserole, but leave off the topping and refrigerate. Refrigerate the potato peel strips in a bowl of water. Before baking, rest the casserole at room temperature for about 1 hour, then make the topping and bake as instructed.

I love fried green tomatoes, but I also love eating food when I want it. Luckily, the season for tomatillos runs longer than that for green tomatoes in Brooklyn, and tomatillos have that tart flavor I enjoy. I get them at a local farmers' market and fry them using this easy recipe. Leaving out the egg in the dredge makes a great crunch and my slightly spicy cream sauce is perfect. **SERVES 4 TO 6**

pan-fried tomatillos
WITH SWEET AND SPICY CREAM SAUCE

FOR THE SAUCE

½ cup sour cream

½ cup whole-milk Greek yogurt

¼ cup honey

2 tablespoons hot sauce (I like Cholula for this)

Kosher salt

FOR THE FRIED TOMATILLOS

6 tomatillos, husked and cleaned, sliced ½ inch thick

Kosher salt

1 cup all-purpose flour

1 cup buttermilk

1 cup plain bread crumbs

1 cup fine-milled cornmeal (such as Indian Head)

8 to 10 sprigs fresh thyme, leaves gently chopped

2 tablespoons garlic powder

2 tablespoons chili powder

Vegetable or peanut oil

1 **Make the sauce.** In a medium bowl, mix the sour cream, yogurt, honey, and hot sauce. Taste and season with a pinch of salt, if needed. Refrigerate while making the tomatillos.

2 **Season and press tomatillos.** Line up the tomatillo slices on a plate and season both sides with a pinch of salt; let rest for 10 minutes. Pat both sides dry with a paper towel.

3 **Dredge the tomatillos.** Put the flour and a pinch of salt in a shallow dish. Pour the buttermilk into a second shallow dish. In a third shallow dish, combine the bread crumbs, cornmeal, thyme, garlic powder, chili powder, and a pinch of salt. Stir with a fork. Coat the tomatillo slices first with the flour and then shake off the excess. Dip in the buttermilk, then press both sides into the bread crumb mixture. Transfer to a plate as you complete the rest.

4 **Fry the tomatillos.** Coat the bottom of a large straight-sided pan with oil. Heat over medium-high heat until the oil begins to swirl. Add the coated tomatillo slices in one layer and fry on one side until a peek beneath reveals a golden crust, then flip and fry the other side, 4 to 6 minutes total. Transfer to a paper towel–lined plate and sprinkle with a pinch of salt. Serve warm with the sauce.

tips! Make a sandwich with the fried tomatillos, pepper Jack or provolone cheese, and mixed baby greens on toasted bread. Use the sauce as a spread. ■ Leftover sauce doubles as a great vegetable dip or a dressing for a cucumber or fruit salad.

Red Velvet Swirl Brownies
(PAGE 287)

SWEET STUFF

Celebration Trifle Cake

Fake Crepes

Fruit Crunch Pie

Mini Espresso Cakes
  with Peanut Butter Frosting

Shake, Rattle, and Scoop Ice Cream

Berry Fool with Amaretti Cookies

Double Chocolate Bread Pudding
  with Bourbon Whipped Cream

Beer-Battered Peach Fritters
  with Lemon-Rosemary Syrup

Choco-Nutty Pie

PB&J Sundae

Red Velvet Swirl Brownies

A proper meal includes dessert. My grandma made me fall in love with sweets—she always had something sweet on the menu when we visited, and even when a meal wasn't on the table, I remember her giving me a handful of change so I could run and get candy at Baldwin's, the neighborhood corner store. The owner would let me dig my hand into the bowl of fun and take whatever I could hold for a handful of nickels and pennies. It wasn't a visit to Grandma's without her squash pie, pound cake, or red velvet cake. I actually thought pound cake was so named because you gained a pound after you ate it! It never stopped me from eating it, and it still doesn't now. Here are a few sweet notes from my kitchen as I continue my grandma's tradition of always leaving room for dessert.

PB&J Sundae (PAGE 284)

This is truly a celebration cake. I've whipped it up in my kitchen for New Year's Eve parties and for friends to celebrate good news, and I even made it once for Vice President Joe Biden, his wife, Dr. Jill Biden, and some very deserving military war veterans in the vice president's kitchen. That was a trip filled with anxiety about what to wear! I knew though how easy this would be to prepare, and what a show stopper it would be. It was truly an honor to serve the veterans. I hope you have many occasions in your life to make this as well. **SERVES 8 TO 10**

celebration trifle cake

FOR THE CAKE

¼ cup sugar

¼ cup fresh lemon juice

¼ teaspoon almond extract

1 store-bought angel food cake (about 1 pound), cut into 1-inch slices

FOR THE CREAM CHEESE SPREAD

⅔ cup sugar

16 ounces cream cheese, room temperature

2 cups heavy cream, room temperature

FOR THE TRIFLE

1 pint blueberries

2 pints strawberries, hulled; 1 cup chopped, the rest quartered lengthwise

1 **Prepare the cake.** In a medium pot, combine the sugar, lemon juice, and ¼ cup water. Heat over medium-high heat, stirring to dissolve the sugar. Remove from the heat and stir in the almond extract. Using a brush, lightly coat both sides of each slice of cake with the mixture. Then cut the cake slices into 1-inch cubes.

2 **Make the cream cheese spread.** In a stand mixer with the whisk attachment, cream the sugar and cream cheese until smooth and light. Add the heavy cream and blend on medium-high speed until smooth and the texture of whipped cream, about 2 minutes.

3 **Assemble the trifle.** Use a 3-quart trifle dish. Divide all ingredients into thirds. Make sure each layer is even all the way to the sides of the dish so the layers are apparent from the outside. The cake is the bottom layer, then dollop the cream cheese mixture and gently spread. Place the quartered strawberries around the rim of the dish and place half the chopped strawberries in the center. Repeat the cake and cream cheese layers, then top with blueberries. Repeat the cake and cream cheese layers. For the final fruit layer, create a design using the remaining chopped strawberries and the blueberries. Refrigerate for 1 hour before serving.

I f you decide to make this past midnight, then you're on the right path. I think most of my desserts are developed in my kitchen in the wee hours of the night. I have an incurable sweet tooth that will wake me up like a nightmare and put me to work until it's satisfied. This layman's version of a crepe is in its own lane because it's tasty, fast, and easy to make when you're sleep-cooking. And it's easy to remember how to make the next day, at a proper time. **SERVES 4**

fake crepes

¾ cup chocolate hazelnut spread

4 8-inch wheat tortillas, room temperature

¼ cup (½ stick) salted butter

1⅓ cups miniature marshmallows

½ cup finely chopped hazelnuts

tip! Stir a heaping spoonful of peanut butter or almond butter into the chocolate hazelnut spread for a fun flavor.

1 **Prepare the tortillas.** Divide the chocolate hazelnut spread among the tortillas and spread evenly on one side.

2 **Cook the crepes.** On a griddle or in a large skillet over medium heat, melt 2 tablespoons of the butter until bubbly. Add 1 or 2 of the tortillas with the chocolate hazelnut spread side facing up. Visualizing an imaginary line down the center of each, put ⅓ cup marshmallows over one half of each tortilla, keeping them in a single layer. Allow the tortillas to slightly bubble in the pan; peek underneath for a golden, toasted color. Quickly fold the uncovered half of the tortilla over the side with the marshmallows, making a half circle, then slightly press down to seal. Flip when the marshmallows are slightly melted and spongy, about 1 minute. Remove after just a few seconds, as this flip is just to reheat the other side of the tortilla, not to melt the marshmallows. Transfer each crepe to a cutting board and cool for just 1 minute. Place the remaining 2 tablespoons butter in the pan and cook the remaining tortillas.

3 **Coat the crepes.** Place the chopped hazelnuts on a plate. Cut the crepes in half, then quickly press the cut side and rounded edges in the nuts to stick. Serve immediately.

I am hard-wired to think every proper dinner deserves a sweet ending. I'm also a sucker for a shortcut. This is a cross between a blueberry and apple pie. Don't worry about making the crust or the granola. Sometimes fast wins out over technique, in a landslide. **SERVES 6 TO 8**

fruit crunch pie

1 premade pie crust

FOR THE FILLING

2 Granny Smith apples, peeled, cored, and thinly sliced

8 ounces blueberries

½ cup golden raisins

½ cup dried cranberries

½ cup granulated sugar

¼ cup packed light brown sugar

1 teaspoon pumpkin pie spice

Grated zest of 1 lemon

2 tablespoons all-purpose flour

Kosher salt

FOR THE TOPPING

1 cup cinnamon-flavored granola mix

1 tablespoon fresh lemon juice

2 tablespoons unsalted butter

¼ cup packed light brown sugar

Kosher salt

1 **Prep the crust.** Unroll 1 pie dough round and press into the bottom of a 9-inch pie pan. Using your pointer finger, press the dough flat and up the sides, letting the excess hang over. Using a fork, press the dough down on the lip of the pie pan all around. Use a knife to remove the excess crust around the edges and discard any scraps. Chill for 30 minutes. Preheat the oven to 400°F.

2 **Make the filling.** In a large bowl, combine the apples, blueberries, raisins, cranberries, granulated sugar, brown sugar, pumpkin pie spice, lemon zest, flour, and a tiny pinch of salt. Stir to coat.

3 **Mix the topping.** Put the granola, lemon juice, butter, brown sugar, and a tiny pinch of salt in a food processor. Pulse just once or twice to break up the granola and combine the ingredients.

4 **Bake the pie.** Fill the prepared crust with the fruit filling. Level with a rubber spatula or the back of a spoon and evenly sprinkle with the topping. Use aluminum foil strips to tent the edges of the crust and prevent overbrowning. Reduce the oven temperature to 375°F. and put the pie in right away. Bake until the filling is bubbling and the granola is golden, 35 to 40 minutes.

I bought a baking tin at a kitchen store because I thought the size and shape of the cups were perfect for mini loaves. I love to give food as gifts, so I thought about what my first mini loaf would be. I settled on espresso cakes because I've long loved the idea of a coffee cake actually tasting like coffee. I now use that baking tin only for this recipe, like my grandma's biscuit-only mixing bowl. These are dense cakes that stay moist and go perfectly with a tall glass of ice-cold milk.

MAKES 12 (4 BY 2-INCH) MINI LOAVES

mini espresso cakes
WITH PEANUT BUTTER FROSTING

FOR THE PAN

- 2 tablespoons unsalted butter
- ¼ cup all-purpose flour

FOR THE BATTER

- 2½ cups all-purpose flour
- ½ heaping teaspoon baking powder
- ½ teaspoon baking soda
- ¼ teaspoon kosher salt
- 1 cup sour cream
- ¼ cup instant espresso powder
- 1 cup (2 sticks) unsalted butter, softened
- 1½ cups granulated sugar
- 2 whole eggs plus 2 yolks
- 1 teaspoon vanilla extract

FOR THE FROSTING

- ½ cup (1 stick) unsalted butter, softened
- ½ cup creamy peanut butter
- 1 cup confectioners' sugar
- Kosher salt

1 Prepare the baking tin. Butter and flour the mini loaf tins, shaking out excess flour. Preheat the oven to 350°F.

2 Mix the batter. In a small bowl, whisk together the flour, baking powder, baking soda, and salt. In another small bowl, mix together the sour cream and espresso powder until the granules dissolve. In a stand mixer fitted with the paddle attachment, cream the butter and granulated sugar on medium speed until light and fluffy. Add the eggs, yolks, and vanilla and mix until combined. On low speed, add half the flour mixture, scraping down the sides with a rubber spatula between additions. Mix until just combined. Add half the sour cream mixture and mix until combined. Repeat with the remaining flour and sour cream.

3 Bake the cakes. Spoon batter into each recess to fill it halfway, then smooth the top with the back of the spoon. Bake for 25 minutes or until a toothpick comes out clean when inserted in the center. Cool in the pans for 10 minutes, then remove from the pans and cool on racks.

4 **Make the frosting.** In a stand mixer, blend the butter and peanut butter on medium-high speed until smooth. Add the confectioners' sugar and mix until smooth. Taste and add a tiny pinch of salt, then blend again to incorporate. Taste again (cook's treats!); there should be a slight hint of salt. Spread or pipe the frosting over the loaves.

tips! If you're giving these cakes as presents, put the frosting in a container and wrap it with a piping bag or a plastic bag with instructions for how to squeeze out the love. ■ If you like the idea of salty and sweet together, find some flaky sea salt and sprinkle it over the frosting.

I always wondered what the statistics were on ice cream shops in the winter, and how much business they do. When a craving for ice cream arrives during a New York winter, leaving the house for it is torture and the wooden crank we had when I was younger took too long. Homemade ice cream has been unnecessarily complicated. I admit, I have an ice cream maker, but I never use it because I don't want to clean it. Save yourself the money and just use a sealed plastic bag and a plastic container. Then all you have to do is shake it a few minutes. It makes a loud rattle, but in a few minutes it's time to scoop. This is pretty simple. Below is my base and a few ideas of where to go with it. **SERVES 4 TO 6**

shake, rattle, and scoop ice cream

FOR THE ICE CREAM BASE

- 1 cup heavy cream
- 1 quart buttermilk
- 14 ounces sweetened condensed milk
- 12 ounces evaporated milk
- 1 teaspoon vanilla extract

FOR THE FILLING (OPTIONAL)

- 2 cups mix-ins of your choice (crumbled candy bars, crumbled cookies, candied nuts, pretzel thins, crisped maple bacon, sliced bananas, strawberries, chocolate chips, strained fruit cocktail, peanut butter, cubes of cake)

Coarse sea salt

1 **Make the base.** In a large bowl, whisk together the heavy cream, buttermilk, sweetened condensed milk, evaporated milk, and vanilla extract. Add the filling (any combination adding up to 2 cups).

2 **Prepare the ice cream.** Put 2 cups ice and ½ cup coarse sea salt in a large plastic storage container with a lid (1 or 2 gallon works well). Pour the base mixture into a heavy-duty 1-gallon resealable plastic bag and seal, squeezing out as much air as possible (double-bag if you like). Place this bag in the plastic storage container and cover with the lid.

3 **Shake and serve.** Shake vigorously for 10 to 15 minutes. Pass it around at the picnic or party and in no time, you'll have homemade ice cream. If the ice completely melts while shaking, add a bit more ice and salt, and continue shaking. When your ice cream has the right texture, take the bag out of the container and rinse it off quickly in cold water to remove the salt. Scoop out the ice cream, or cut a hole in the corner of the bag and squeeze it out. Store in the freezer in the plastic bag with as much air pressed out as possible.

Fresh berries and homemade whipped cream are the basics for this classic dessert, called a fool. No one really knows why it was named a fool in the first place. One thing is for sure, it's foolproof, and you'd be a fool not to give it a try in your kitchen! I love a bit of texture, so I crumble Italian amaretti cookies and sprinkle them over the top. Amaretti are tiny macaroon-sized cookies made with sweet and bitter almonds, but I've used graham crackers, vanilla wafers, and even granola as a topping in a pinch. And ladies, don't let the dainty look of this dessert make you feel like the guys won't like it. I left these in a room of guys watching a game once and came back in five minutes to empty glasses. **SERVES 6 TO 8**

berry fool WITH AMARETTI COOKIES

FOR THE BERRIES

- 1 pint strawberries, hulled and chopped
- 1 pint blueberries
- 1 pint raspberries
- ¼ cup orange juice
- ¾ cup sugar

FOR THE WHIPPED CREAM

- 1 quart heavy cream, very cold or set in an ice bath
- 2 tablespoons honey
- 2 teaspoons sugar
- 1 teaspoon almond extract

16 amaretti cookies, gently crushed

1 **Soak the berries.** In a large bowl, toss together the strawberries, blueberries, raspberries, orange juice, and sugar. Let rest at room temperature for 30 minutes, tossing a few times.

2 **Whip the cream.** In a large bowl, whisk the heavy cream until soft peaks form. Add the honey, sugar, and almond extract. Continue to whisk until stiff peaks form.

3 **Fold the fools.** Remove the berries from the bowl with a slotted spoon and add to the whipped cream. Use a rubber spatula or large spoon to gently fold the berries into the cream. Pour into serving glasses or dishes and serve with amaretti cookies crumbled over the top.

ecipes like this make me crazy in a good way. They materialize from my pantry and stick around in my repertoire for the long haul. It had never occurred to me to use croissants and raisin bread in bread pudding until I desperately wanted some and those were the two breads I had in my kitchen. As if the buttery, flaky, raisin-studded base weren't enough, I decided chocolate syrup and a crunchy topping along with a spiked whipped cream would be even better. Editing when dessert is involved is tough! Eat this with a tall glass of water to balance out the calories, or just throw all caution to the wind and pour a frosty glass of whole milk.

SERVES 12 TO 14

double chocolate bread pudding WITH BOURBON WHIPPED CREAM

FOR THE BAKING DISH

2 tablespoons unsalted butter

FOR THE CUSTARD

6 cups whole milk

1½ cups chocolate syrup

3 tablespoons packed light brown sugar

½ teaspoon cinnamon

½ teaspoon kosher salt

⅛ teaspoon grated nutmeg (5 or 6 scrapes on a rasp)

6 eggs

6 croissants, cut into 1-inch chunks

1 loaf cinnamon-raisin bread, cut into 1-inch squares

1 cup semisweet chocolate chips

FOR THE TOPPING

6 tablespoons cold unsalted butter, cut into small cubes

1 Prepare the baking dish. Grease the bottom and sides of a deep lasagna dish with the butter. Preheat the oven to 350°F.

2 Make the custard and soak the bread. In a large bowl, whisk together the milk, chocolate syrup, brown sugar, cinnamon, salt, nutmeg, and eggs. In another large bowl, combine the croissant and bread chunks and sprinkle the chocolate chips over the top. Pour the chocolate custard over the bread and toss to soak it up. Allow to rest for 10 minutes.

3 Make the topping. In a medium bowl, toss the butter with the flour to coat all sides of the butter. Add the pecans, brown sugar, salt, and cinnamon. Mix together with your hands to blend the butter into all the ingredients.

4 Assemble the bread pudding and bake. Pour the soaked bread into the prepared dish, making sure all the chocolate chips don't settle on the

continues

- 2 tablespoons all-purpose flour
- 1 cup pecans, chopped
- ½ cup packed light brown sugar
- 1 teaspoon Maldon sea salt
- ½ teaspoon cinnamon
- Bourbon Whipped Cream (recipe below)

bottom. Sprinkle the topping evenly over the dish. Bake uncovered until the edges are golden brown and the center springs back a bit when touched, 45 to 50 minutes. Allow to cool and settle for about 30 minutes, then cut into squares, or just dig in right away. Serve with a dollop of Bourbon Whipped Cream.

bourbon whipped cream
MAKES 2 CUPS

- 1 cup heavy cream, cold
- 1 tablespoon bourbon
- 1 tablespoon sugar

Make the whipped cream. In a large bowl, whisk the heavy cream until soft peaks form. Add the bourbon and sugar and continue to whisk until stiff peaks form when the whisk is removed from the bowl. Refrigerate and serve cold.

nother treat from my book of easy sweets is this quick batter of beer and flour filled with fruit. This is great for fresh fruit, but canned works as well—what you use depends on the time of year you want to make this and how much effort you want to put into it. It's actually a high-low dessert, meaning the lemon-rosemary syrup is a bit fancy, but the rest is pretty simple and easy to prepare. This is one of those recipes that sticks with you—in your head and on your hips. Blame me if this happens to you—I'll take it. **MAKES 15 TO 18**

beer-battered peach fritters
WITH LEMON-ROSEMARY SYRUP

FOR THE SYRUP

- ¼ cup fresh lemon juice
- 1 cup sugar
- 1 sprig fresh rosemary, 4 to 6 inches long

FOR THE FRITTERS

- 4 peaches, peeled, cored, and finely chopped
- ¼ cup packed light brown sugar
- 2 tablespoons granulated sugar
- ½ teaspoon pumpkin pie spice
- ¼ teaspoon allspice
- Pinch of grated nutmeg
- Grated zest of 2 lemons
- 1 cup all-purpose flour
- Kosher salt
- 7 ounces beer
- Peanut oil

tip! Replace peaches with 2 peeled, cored, chopped apples; 3 peeled, cored, chopped juicy pears; or 2 ripe mashed bananas.

1 **Make the syrup.** In a small pot over medium-high heat, combine the lemon juice, ½ cup water, and sugar. Stir to dissolve the sugar as much as possible, then add the rosemary. Bring to a simmer and cook until the liquid reduces a bit and has the consistency of pancake syrup, about 10 minutes. Strain through a sieve and discard the rosemary. Refrigerate for at least 1 hour to cool.

2 **Make the fritters.** In a large bowl, stir together the peaches, brown sugar, granulated sugar, pumpkin pie spice, allspice, nutmeg, and lemon zest; set aside. In another large bowl, combine the flour and a pinch of salt. Make a well in the center and whisk in the beer until combined. It should be slightly thicker than pancake batter. Gently fold in the peach mixture and let rest 10 minutes at room temperature.

3 **Fry the fritters.** Pour oil 2 inches deep into a large pot over medium-high heat. Bring the temperature to 360°F. so that after adding the fritters, the temperature rests at 350°F. Once the oil is ready, using a small ice cream scoop or large tablespoon, gently drop dough into the oil in batches. Fry until golden brown on both sides, flipping once, about 4 minutes total. Transfer to a paper towel–lined plate. Serve with chilled syrup.

his pie is the next logical step for a pecan pie lover, adding chocolate and even more nuts. As a child, I remember my grandma making the best pecan pies. Since she was a North Carolina resident, a state perfect for nut crops, she'd always have a big bowl in the living room full of various nuts and a nutcracker beside it, ready for snacking. I'd sit and nudge the Brazil nuts out of the way and pick out all the pecans and walnuts, putting my kid strength to work for my belly. I think I still prefer pecans and walnuts as an adult because they were the easiest to crack as a kid. Plus they're buttery, with such an inviting aroma when cooked. There's nothing better than the natural potpourri a dessert can create in your kitchen. **SERVES 6 TO 8**

choco-nutty pie

FOR THE CRUST

1¼ cups all-purpose flour, plus more for rolling the dough

Kosher salt

½ cup (1 stick) unsalted butter, cut into tiny cubes and frozen

¼ cup ice water

Nonstick cooking spray

FOR THE FILLING

5 tablespoons unsalted butter

1 cup packed light brown sugar

1 cup light corn syrup

Kosher salt

1 cup pecan halves

1 cup walnut halves

2 tablespoons walnut liqueur or any other nut-flavored liqueur

½ cup semisweet chocolate chips

3 eggs, beaten

1 **Make and rest the crust.** In a food processor, combine the flour, a pinch of salt, and the butter. Pulse until the butter and flour are blended and the butter is dispersed throughout. Slowly add the ice water and pulse until everything comes together. Remove the dough and, using a bit of flour so it doesn't stick to your hands, form a disc and wrap it in plastic. Refrigerate for 30 minutes.

2 **Prepare the crust.** Preheat the oven to 400°F. Remove the dough from the refrigerator and, on a lightly floured surface, roll it out ⅛ inch thick. Place in a 9-inch pie pan, allowing the excess to hang over the edge. Using a fork, press the dough down on the lip of the pie pan all around. Use a knife to remove the excess crust around the edges; discard the scraps. Spray the shiny side of a piece of aluminum foil with a bit of nonstick spray and press the sprayed side against the dough. Fill with dry beans or pie weights and bake until the edges are golden and the sides are set, about 15 minutes. Remove the foil and weights and bake another 10 minutes, until cooked through. Remove from the oven and allow to cool at room temperature.

3 **Make the filling.** In a medium pot over medium-high heat, combine the butter, brown sugar, corn syrup, and a tiny pinch of salt. Bring to a boil, then reduce to a simmer and cook until the brown sugar is no longer granulated. Add the pecans, walnuts, and liqueur. Stir to coat, then remove from the heat and add the chocolate chips, stirring to allow them to melt in the heat of the pot. In a small bowl, vigorously whisk the eggs while spooning in a bit of the warm chocolate-nut mixture until the egg mixture is warmed as well. Pour this small batch of warmed egg into the pot and stir until everything is blended.

4 **Bake the pie.** Reduce the oven temperature to 350°F. Pour the filling into the prepared pie crust. Use aluminum foil strips to tent the edges of the crust and prevent overbrowning. Bake until set, about 40 minutes. Let cool before slicing.

The look on my face is of excitement. When Mommy brought out the flour and a baking sheet, she meant business. **(Lawton, OK, 1977)**

there are flavor combos I make in many different ways, and the classic combo of peanut butter and jelly is one of them. From pancakes to wing sauce, I truly adore the whimsical idea of the childhood sandwich elevated to other areas of the menu. This time it's for dessert and not a thing is missing, not even the bread. Use your favorite jelly, jam, or preserves here; chunky or smooth peanut butter is also your choice. I had mostly grape jelly and smooth peanut butter growing up, but find I love the chunks in strawberry jam and peanut butter these days.

SERVES 4

pb&j sundae

FOR THE ICE CREAM

- 1 pint vanilla ice cream, softened
- ¼ cup strawberry jam or grape jelly (or your favorite flavor)

FOR THE CROUTONS

- ¼ cup (½ stick) salted butter
- 2 slices white bread, crusts removed, cut into ½-inch cubes
- 3 tablespoons sugar

FOR THE PEANUT BUTTER SAUCE

- ½ cup heavy cream
- ½ cup packed dark brown sugar
- ½ cup crunchy or smooth peanut butter

1 Prepare the ice cream. Transfer the ice cream to a mixing bowl and add the jam. Using a rubber spatula, fold in the jam so it is streaky and not uniformly mixed. Return to the pint container and freeze until set, about 2 hours.

2 Make the croutons. Melt the butter in a small skillet over medium-high heat. Add the bread cubes and stir to coat on all sides. Continue stirring until the bread is golden brown on all sides. Remove from the heat and transfer to a paper towel–lined plate. Sprinkle with the sugar and toss to coat. Set aside.

3 Make the peanut butter sauce. Combine the heavy cream and brown sugar in a saucepan and bring to a boil. Reduce the heat to a simmer, add the peanut butter, and stir until combined and melted. Make this just before serving.

4 Assemble the sundaes. Scoop the ice cream into serving bowls, drizzle with the peanut butter sauce, and top with croutons. Store any leftover sauce in an airtight container in the refrigerator. (To reheat, add a bit of milk or heavy cream to loosen, then microwave in 8-second intervals until warm, stirring between each zap.)

This is one of those recipes that turns out like a picture in a magazine every time I make it. It's amazing how a simple swirl can add curb appeal to these brownies. With the flavors of chocolate on the bottom and sweetened cream cheese swirled on the top, it's just as tasty as it looks. And really there's no trick—just drag it in a random pattern, bake, and enjoy the view. **MAKES 16 BROWNIES**

red velvet swirl brownies

1 tablespoon unsalted butter

FOR THE RED VELVET LAYER

½ cup (1 stick) unsalted butter

1 cup sugar

1 teaspoon vanilla

¼ cup cocoa powder

Kosher salt

1 tablespoon liquid red food coloring or 2 teaspoons food coloring gel

1 teaspoon vinegar

2 eggs

¾ cup all-purpose flour

½ cup chopped walnuts

FOR THE CREAM CHEESE LAYER

8 ounces cream cheese, softened

¼ cup sugar

1 egg

⅛ teaspoon vanilla extract

1 **Prepare the pan.** Butter an 8 × 8-inch baking pan and set aside. Preheat the oven to 350°F.

2 **Mix the red velvet layer.** Melt the butter in a small saucepan over medium heat. Transfer to a large bowl and mix between each addition of the sugar, vanilla, cocoa powder, salt, food coloring, and vinegar. Whisk the eggs in a small bowl and combine with the warm cocoa mix. Fold the flour into the chocolate batter and combine lightly. Add the walnuts and stir.

3 **Mix the cream cheese layer.** Blend the cream cheese, sugar, egg, and vanilla in a medium bowl.

4 **Assemble the brownies.** Pour the red velvet layer into the bottom of the prepared pan, saving ¼ cup batter for the top. Gently spread the cream cheese layer on top of the red velvet layer. Then randomly dollop the remaining red velvet batter over the cream cheese layer. Using a skewer or the sharp end of a knife, drag the tip through the cream cheese mixture to create a swirl pattern. Bake for 30 minutes. Transfer to a cooling rack and allow to cool completely before cutting into 2 × 2-inch brownies.

DRINKS

Brooklyn Iced Tea

Easy Piña Colada

Irish Iced Coffee

Orange-Mango Mojito

Beer Punch

Cucumber and Watermelon Lemonade

Motor City Hot Toddy

I like to have these drinks to relax, and I never thought I'd say that. Growing up I saw drinks as things that made people excited. They were always served at my parents' parties and when we were in Germany, beer was king (especially during Oktoberfest). So drinking always meant a party, not a relaxing afternoon at home or on vacation. Now, as an adult, I totally get it. When I'm having a party, I use them as a barricade between myself and hungry party guests. People usually show up ready to chow down, but a get-together should be a balance of great food, drink, music, and lots of conversation, so I try to encourage the conversation and patience for the meal with a hello drink. Everything seems better with a good beverage and it doesn't have to be alcoholic, it just has to tempt your taste buds and quench your thirst.

Brooklyn Iced Tea
(PAGE 292)

I'm proud of the New York City borough I've chosen as my home. I've moved so much in my life, mostly not by choice, so the few cities I've picked are everything to me. I thought I'd toast Brooklyn with a drink fit for anyone! My blend is a Long Island challenge, subtracting a few spirits and adding sweetened iced tea. It's smooth so pour it and enjoy the second round. **SERVES 4 TO 6**

brooklyn iced tea

6 ounces limoncello

3 ounces dark rum

3 ounces tequila

24 ounces sweetened iced tea, no lemon flavor added

Crushed ice

Lemon slices, for garnish

1 **Pour and fuhgeddaboudit.** Pour the limoncello, rum, tequila, and iced tea into a pitcher. Stir and refrigerate until chilled.

2 **Serve.** To serve, pour the chilled mixture into ice-filled highball glasses outfitted with a straw and garnished with a lemon slice on the rim or in the glass.

tip! If you want to be ready for a drink on a moment's notice, just keep the liquor in the freezer and make sure the tea is ice cold. Then you can skip the "chilling" part.

There are few drinks I like with an umbrella, and the piña colada makes the cut. Whenever I make it, I feel like I'm on a mini vacation. Freeze the remaining coconut cream and pineapples in an airtight resealable freezer bag with the air squeezed out and flattened, then break off chips to make smaller batches for a stay-cation. **SERVES 4 TO 6**

easy piña colada

8 ounces light rum

8 pineapple rings

½ cup coconut cream

2 teaspoons fresh lime juice

6 cups ice

4 to 6 ounces light rum (optional)

1 **Blend the ingredients.** Put the rum, pineapple, coconut cream, lime juice, and ice in a blender. Blend on high until smooth.

2 **To serve.** Pour evenly into glasses you've chilled in the freezer and top with 1 ounce of rum (as a finishing touch), a straw, and hopefully an umbrella.

there are two coffee seasons in Manhattan. I was very aware of this when I first moved here on the cusp of summer and fall in 2001. One week I could get an iced coffee at the corner stand; the next week, as the weather changed, it was all about hot coffee. I looked silly asking for cold coffee as the wind whipped around the corner, as it only can in a city with tall buildings. I got what I wanted, because it turns out you can get whatever you want in any season in New York. But there's nothing like the first iced coffee of the summer. This is my adult version.

SERVES 6 TO 8

irish iced coffee

2 cups sugar

3 cups French vanilla coffee beans, coarsely ground

3 cups Irish cream liqueur

Ice

1 Make the simple syrup. In a small pot, combine 1 cup water and the sugar. Bring to a boil and stir until the sugar dissolves. Pour into a container with a lid, cover, and refrigerate.

2 Soak the ground coffee. In a plastic container with a lid, combine 8 cups water and the ground coffee. Cover and shake a few times. Rest on the counter for a full 24 hours, stirring every so often when you think about it. (I know, but it's worth it.)

3 Strain the coffee. Layer 2 coffee filters for double-ply strength and press them inside a mesh sieve set over a large bowl. Slowly pour the coffee and water over the sieve and allow the coffee to drip through. Don't be tempted to press out the extra liquid, as it will make the coffee cloudy. And the only thing you want making your drink cloudy is the Irish cream. Besides, you may want some of this with just sugar—it's quite tasty and not at all like brewed coffee. Add another 2 cups water to the coffee.

4 Mix and refrigerate. Pour in the Irish cream and stir. Refrigerate until ice cold, about 2 hours. Fill glasses with ice and pour in the Irish coffee. Add simple syrup, to taste, and stir.

I love drinking mojitos at home. They're simple and you don't even need a muddler or a shaker. Look around your kitchen for substitutes and step up your at-home bar game. The mango makes this pretty—perfect for a garden party or brunch. **SERVES 4**

orange-mango mojito

1 cup tightly packed fresh mint

¼ cup sugar

1 cup orange juice, no pulp

8 ounces mango juice

2 teaspoons fresh lime juice

8 ounces white rum

1 orange, sliced ¼-inch thick

2 cups ice

1 **Muddle the mint.** In each individual glass, add a quarter of both the mint and sugar. Using a muddler or wide handle of a wooden utensil, crush the sugar into the mint to bruise it and make it fragrant.

2 **Add the liquid and serve.** In a pitcher or liquid measure, stir together the orange juice, mango juice, lime juice, rum, orange slices, and ice. Stir very well for about 5 seconds. Pour into each prepared glass and serve.

I remember my parents being into beer in the '80s. I love it now and cook with it often. This punch surprises beer lovers and others who say they don't care for beer, much less beer with fruit. I always say that if you don't like something, you just haven't had it the right way. It's a bit sweet, but has bubbles. It's pretty festive too. And great with bratwurst. **SERVES 6 TO 8**

beer punch

8 strawberries, chopped

½ cup blueberries

⅓ cup sugar

¼ cup grenadine

¼ cup fresh lime juice

4 12-ounce beers (your favorite, pilsner or pale ale)

1 **Macerate the berries.** In a medium bowl, combine the strawberries, blueberries, sugar, grenadine, and lime juice. Stir to coat. Cover and refrigerate for at least 1 hour, stirring a couple times to help create juices.

2 **Combine and serve.** When ready to serve, scoop equal amounts into lowball glasses. Pour 6 ounces of beer into each and give a gentle stir. Drink!

tip! If serving a group and trying to stretch your beverages, add 12 to 24 ounces of lemon-lime soda or tonic water.

This recipe is dedicated to my late great-uncle, Uncle K. He lovingly called me his alcoholic niece, not because it's true, but because it seemed to him that every time he saw me on *Cooking for Real*, I was making a drink or having some wine. That wasn't the case either, but the moniker stuck and my family got a kick out of it. Now when I enjoy a drink, if my mind is in the right place, I think about him ribbing me and I toast his memory. So for him, this is a drink without alcohol, but it would taste great with a shot of vodka. **SERVES 4 TO 6**

cucumber and watermelon lemonade

6 cups watermelon chunks

2 English cucumbers, peeled and cut into chunks

1 cup fresh lemon juice

8 ounces tonic water

Sugar

Ice

Cucumber slices, wedges, or spears

Watermelon slices, wedges, or spears

Lemon slices or wedges

1 **Blend the watermelon and cucumber.** Put the watermelon and cucumber chunks in a blender and puree until liquid. Place a fine-mesh sieve over a large bowl. Pour the liquid into the sieve and allow the juice to slowly drip into the bowl, without forcing through any of the pulp. Discard the solids. This should yield about 3 cups of juice.

2 **Blend and serve.** In a pitcher, combine the sieved juice, lemon juice, and tonic water. Stir, taste, and sweeten with sugar until it's how you want it. Fill highball glasses with ice and pour the lemonade evenly over each glass. Garnish with cucumber, watermelon, and/or lemon slices in each glass.

Yes, watermelon is delicious; ashy knees are not.
(Back porch, Columbus, GA, 1983)

I first learned of the curing qualities of the "hot toddy" when I moved to Detroit for a radio job. The worst winter in years hit in 1998 and I immediately got sick. Everyone's remedy for me was to make a toddy and enjoy the restorative values of alcohol. Not a soul mentioned conventional medicine. It sounded funny then, but I tried it, and years later, I enjoy a good toddy at the first sign of the sniffles.

SERVES 4 TO 6

motor city hot toddy

½ orange, halved

4 whole cloves

3 cups apple cider

2 cinnamon sticks, 3 to 4 inches long

Brandy

1 cup heavy cream, whipped to soft peaks (see Bourbon Whipped Cream, page 280)

1 Prep the orange. Stud the orange pieces with 2 cloves each.

2 Steep the ingredients. In a medium saucepan, bring the cider, cinnamon, and orange pieces to a boil, then reduce to a simmer and cook for 10 minutes.

3 Assemble and serve. In each coffee cup or mug pour 1 shot (or 2) of brandy. Ladle in the hot cider and top with a generous dollop of whipped cream.

tip! Add a 1-inch disc of peeled ginger while steeping for a warming bite.

THANK-YOUS

the friends: Jeff Bromberger, Monique Mackey, Victor N.O.R.E. Santiago, Talib Kweli Green, Christina Tuschen, Charlie Batch, Fiona Byrne, Kesha McLeod, Bushman, Hassan Rasul, Kevin Saunders, Eric Brown, Rosanna Scotto & the Scotto family, Sara Gore, Anthony Freeman & the Freeman family, Derek Pearson & family, RL Altman, Evan "Supalawya" Freifeld, Bruce Seidel, Dupré Kelly & family, John Singleton, Columbus Carey & family, Fiola & staff at Shantzii's.

the bosses: Preston Jones, Chad Starr, Mr. Gerry Procter, Larry Gilliam, Ernest James, Lebron "LBJ" James, Lance Panton "what conflict of interest?", Nate Bell, Tamara Knechtal, Tracy Cloherty, Barry Mayo, Bob Tuschman & Allison Page—thank you for so much, Michael Smith, Brooke Johnson, Beth Burke, Kandy Klutch.

the companies and coworkers: Sonic Drive-in, USAF, KSAT-12, Emmis Broadcasting, Clear Channel Radio, Cox Communications, Radio One, Montgomery Broadcast Company, Salem Broadcasting Company, Al Wissam Clothing, Rancho Cucamonga Library, Sirius/XM, Scripps Networks, *People* magazine, *Clean Eating* magazine, *Hip Hop Weekly* magazine, *Food Network Magazine*, *Rachael Ray Show*, the *Today* show, Rainey Farrell, Bianca, Lish & team, *Good Morning America*, *NY Live*, *The Katie Show*, *The View*, *Anderson Cooper Live*, *Good Day NY*, *Access Hollywood Live*, *Covino & Rich Show*, *Martha Stewart Radio*—Jon Costantino, Steve Gonzales, Lisa Mantineo, Liz Aiello, Neil & the staff at Petite Abeille on Hudson, Suzanne at Chip Shop in Brooklyn, Rawia & family at Tanoreen in Brooklyn, Mother's Restaurant in New Orleans, Stone Park Café in Brooklyn, Feeney's Bar in Brooklyn, Spa Belle's on 23rd in Manhattan, WME Entertainment, Jon Rosen, Jason Hodes, Jeffrey Googel, Strand Conover, Dorian Karchmar, Jenni, Julia, Liz, Suzanne, Ross, Andy McNicol, Beth Dick, Clarkson Potter, Emily Takoudes—my editor ☺, Jessica Freeman-Slade, Jane Treuhaft, Ashley Tucker, Pam Krauss, Donna Passannante, Doris Cooper, John Lee & his photography & styling team, Ray Gomez (George Michael!!), Darren Wylie, Donna Cruz, DJ Fingers, LT. Dre, Angie Martinez, DJ Enuff, DJ Camilo, DJ Greenlantern, Mister Cee, Megatron (R.I.P.), Uptown Angela, Koren Vaughn, DJ Kayslay, Reggie Hawkins, Rodney Morandi, Barbie Anderson, Patrick 9th Wonder Douthit, Jen Darrow & the team at High Noon Entertainment, Al Roker Productions, Craig Anderson & the team at Concentric Productions, Oksana Pidhoreckyj, Hadiiya Barbel & team, Mylah Morales, JJ Makeup Artist & team, Preston Ciriani, TJ Rudy, Lashawn Browning, Venos V-Man Ford, Ryan Scott, Food Network & Cooking Channel—Susie Fogelson, Irika Slavin, Lauren Mueller—LaLa I miss you, Robert Irvine, Kelsey Nixon, Justin Warner, Geoffrey Zakarian, Jeff Mauro, Eden Grinshpan, Gabriele Corcos & Debi Mazar, Simon Majumdar, Guy Fieri—your advice from the start has held true, Bobby Flay, Aaron McCargo Jr., Melissa d'Arabian & your lovely family, the Neelys, Santos Loo aka Santo Lee, Jacob Schiffman & family, Marc Istook, Food Network Kitchens, Marketing, Sales, Programming & Online, Karen Grinthal & the entire sales staff, hardest working in the biz with a smile!, Philip Radiotes—the one man web team!, Lee Schrager, Jevon, Mark & Gordon—the trio of fun & all things good on TV.

the family: Williams and Anderson, Uncle Rodney.

the believers: "Sunny" at FoodNetworkFans.com—thank you for your support from the start & I hope as you watch down on all I do that I make you smile, Rob Love & family, Lisa Ellis, Jadakiss, Sheek Louch, Styles P, Kendall Freeman—for the Jeezy check, Havoc—for the flight & casino, Skip Dillard, Jay Eidt & the entire *Cooking for Real* crew, Cordell Patrick, Tre Black (RIP), Henry Amore, Monica Starr, Jason Cruz, Spike Mendelsohn, Michael Newman (Newman!), Ernest James, David Cummings, Karen Katz, Frankie Darcell, Patty Jackson, Joe Kardel & family, Dr. Ian Smith, Elina Brown, Colby Colb, Patty Jackson, Shelley Wade, Adam Nettler, Lia Aponte, Remy Martin—I'll make you mac 'n' cheese any day, J.C.—thank you for teaching me to DJ, Frau Richter—my German teacher, Ms. Valentine—my English teacher, Rachael Ray—words just ain't right here, you are a shining example and I intend to make you proud, Emily Reiger, Veda, Rebecca Soldinger's team (Bridget and Brittany), RRShowCooks (STANK TURKEY!), Eddie, Sreal, Andrea, Jimmy, Dom & the entire RRShow field team, Janet Annino, Joe Hahn (same time, same place), Sam Oropesa, Lys at CookinginStilettos.com, Jen, Badlands Booker, Dr. Bob & Al Jaffee, your influence is in these pages (see tribute, page 304), the city of Vidalia, GA . . . thank you for allowing me to mispronounce your city's name with love.

All publishers, editors, producers, people I've met throughout the years on my journey of life, if I forgot your name specifically please don't charge it to my heart. I am truly aware life is a series of moments that add up to my present. What a present it is, thanks to you. I appreciate you for being there along the way.

ON THE MOVE

Where I've lived (in order):

Lawton, OK
Charleston, SC
Augusta, GA
Columbus, GA
Norfolk, VA
Bad Kreuznach, Germany
Heidelberg, Germany

Nussloch, Germany
Carlisle, PA
Boiling Springs, PA
San Antonio, TX
Indianapolis, IN
Seoul, South Korea
San Antonio, TX **(again)**

Kenner, LA
Montgomery, AL
Detroit, MI
Jersey City, NJ
Rancho Cucamonga, CA
Brooklyn, NY

Places I've eaten and been inspired:

Austria
Bahamas **(Nassau, Eleuthera)**
Belgium
Denmark
France **(Paris, Strassbourg)**

Grenadines
 (Petit St. Vincent, Union Island
Guam
Honduras
Italy
Jamaica

Japan
Mexico
Netherlands
Panama
Puerto Rico
Switzerland

And I've been to every state except: Maine, Minnesota, North Dakota, South Dakota, Wyoming

INDEX

ICE CREAM & MY DREAM

- Drastic measures like chasing a truck and popping at the seams -
- are things we do 4 ice cream. Gallon, pint, or scoop to spare -
- Swarovski crystals can't compare. Smiles are there as we meet! -